THE
ROAD
BENEATH
MY FEET

FRANK TURNER

THE ROAD BENEATH MY FEET

headline

First published in Great Britain in 2015

Cataloguing in Publication Data is available from the British Library

Hardback ISBN 978 1 4722 22015

Typeset in Bell MT Std by Palimpsest Book Production Limited,
Falkirk, Stirlingshire

Printed and bound in Great Britain by
Clays Ltd, St Ives plc

MIX
Paper from
responsible sources
FSC www.fsc.org   FSC® C104740

Headline's policy is to use papers that are natural, renewable and recyclable
products and made from wood grown in sustainable forests. The logging and
manufacturing processes are expected to conform to the environmental
regulations of the country of origin.

HEADLINE PUBLISHING GROUP
An Hachette UK Company
338 Euston Road
London NW1 3BH

www.headline.co.uk
www.hachette.co.uk

DEDICATION

For Lexie, Josh Burdette and Robb Skipper, and all the others who
ended up heading home.

INTRODUCTION / DISCLAIMER

You hold in your hands a book, a book that I wrote, all by myself. This is an unlikely but pleasantly surprising turn of events for me. For a start, I was always a bookworm as a kid, and I still read incessantly now, so to actually have one that has my name and ugly mug emblazoned across the cover is pretty cool. I will be giving many, many copies to friends and family (and maybe enemies too) next Christmas.

One reason I was not expecting this book to exist is that I'm not generally much keen on autobiography as a genre. There are, of course, notable exceptions to this – Ben Franklin's, for example, or Churchill's – but I feel like you either need to have won a war or be knocking on death's door to justify the exercise. I haven't won any wars and I have no plans to shuffle off this mortal coil just yet, so when the idea of my writing a book was first floated by my friend Dan from Portland, I laughed it off.

After my initial short shrift, the point was raised that I'm a public, vocal fan of Henry Rollins (which I am) and have read many of his published tour diaries and travel memoirs. It was also suggested that the book need not be an autobiography in the strict sense, starting with birth and ending in the nursing home; it could be a specific set of recollections about a certain period of time. I felt my defences weakening.

The next stage of the process was to convince me that anyone, anywhere, would be interested in me rambling on about the minutiae of my experiences at great length. While I obviously spend a fair amount of my professional life engaged in self-promotion, that relates to the music I make, not to what I had for breakfast or where I slept.

I wrote a sample entry or two and sent them off to some close friends for comment. I was expecting the worst, but even my friend Evan, historically my harshest critic (he has to do something to pass the time), came back saying it was an interesting read.

And so it began. The project ebbed and flowed, as these things tend to do. It took a lot longer than I thought it would (I feel like I owe professional writers an apology for underestimating their trade). It took me through troves of old emails, blog entries, flyers, posters, conversations with friends, photos and long late-night sessions of racking my brain, trying desperately to remember what, if anything, might have happened on the date in question.

And now, at last, you have the finished book in your grasp. I remain a little nervous about the whole exercise, but I hope you enjoy it. There are a couple of short disclaimers before you dive in. I'm aware, painfully so, that I'm incredibly fortunate to do what I do for a living; I'm also not under the impression that it's earth-shakingly significant, in the grand scheme of things. Hopefully I don't come off as overly self-pitying or self-important. I'm grateful to all the people who have helped me on my way and if I've left anyone out, I apologize, profusely. In particular I'm grateful to you, dear reader, for being interested enough in what I have to say to justify the whole project and thus letting me get my name on the front of a book.

And finally, this is *my* version of what happened. In fairness, I was pretty pissed for quite a lot of this and long months and years on the road can roll into each other in the cosy haze of hindsight. I've done my best to be fair and accurate, but if you were there and remember it differently, or just generally think I'm talking bollocks, I'll back you up in the argument in the pub.

Right, enough disclaimers, on with the show.

PROLOGUE

MILLION DEAD, SHOW # 247

The Joiners Arms, Southampton, UK,
23 September 2005

I remember noise. Walls of feedback, ringing ears, a sense of defeat.

Million Dead were nearly done.

We'd decided to break up a few weeks before the tour, so everyone knew that this was the end. We'd even announced it as a farewell tour, and as a result the shows had generally been packed out and feverish. Ironically I think these were probably the best shows we ever played. We'd been at the top of our game onstage – fast, visceral, tight, intense. The same cannot be said, alas, for how things were back in the dressing room or in the van.

What to say about Million Dead? It was the defining experience of my late adolescence, my early twenties – it was my formative musical experience. But we were also just another jobbing under-ground hardcore band that made some small ripples and fell apart. By the end of it, relations within the group had broken down completely and we'd essentially retreated into two opposing camps, with Jamie Grime (our stage tech) and Graham Kay (our sound guy) caught as innocent civilians in the middle. The final tour was characterized by moody silences, sharp words and nihil-istic excess, especially on my part. The tour laminates had all the dates listed, and then, on the twenty-fourth (the day after the tour finished), it said 'Get a Job'. Talk about focusing the mind.

The night before, we'd played a show at The Underworld in Camden, London. We filmed the show and looking back now, I still think that together we were fantastic – sharp and aggressive, melodic and anthemic. We played what I consider to be probably our best show to 600 or so people crammed against the stage and then I'd got titanically fucked up (again) afterwards. The final journey south wasn't a fun one.

I grew up in Winchester, which isn't a city on many touring schedules, so Southampton was generally the place to go for shows. In fact, I'd seen my first ever show at The Joiners in 1995 or thereabouts: a band called Snug, who happened to feature a youthful Ed Harcourt on guitar (more on him much, much later). Million Dead had played there many times before, but there was a sense of anticlimax hanging over everything. As well as being a smaller venue than The Underworld, the previous evening we had managed to skirt around the issues because of the fact we had one more show to go. Now that the end was staring us in the face and there was no more road to run, a dark cloud descended. No more pretending.

The problem with Million Dead was pretty unremarkable. We were terrible communicators and fell out of friendship with each other as time went by. We all built up enough resentment against each other to make the whole thing unworkable. That's really all there is to it. Like most youthful, Arcadian ideals, the bald facts of the denouement are mundane rather than monumental.

I remember sound check. It's not generally a romanticized part of the touring experience, and with good reason, but it made me feel very sad that night. Every drummer has their own drum-check ritual and I remember hearing Ben (Dawson) playing that same old beat when Graham called out 'Full kit please!' from the sound desk and thinking it was the last time I'd hear it. When check was over I walked out of the room feeling angry and cheated that it was all coming to an end.

The time for doors rolled around. The show was sold out and our guest list was already creaking under the strain, but still there were a lot of people hanging around outside, trying to get in to see us one more time. Their devotion made me feel humbled but also embarrassed. I had a girl with me who I'd met on tour a few days before who I didn't really know but who I was clinging on to for some kind of stability. I also had a pack of cigarettes; I'd been wrestling with smoking the whole time I was in the band, but basically had it under control. However, I'd promised myself that if the band split I'd smoke a whole damn pack after the last show. I was prepared.

The show began. As it happens, the venue had recently been refurbished. The old stage had essentially been a glorified shelf in one corner of the room and bands often had problems getting the drum kit up there comfortably, let alone putting anything in front of it. The new layout was much better, but as it turned out they were still having teething problems with the air conditioning in the room. When the crowd was packed in there it was stiflingly hot, which started causing problems. I took my shirt off and drank water, but I was sweating incredibly hard and starting to get spots on my vision. The heat wasn't the only thing to blame – after two weeks of being solidly drunk and high while pushing myself as hard as I could during shows, my body was starting to rebel. The atmosphere in the room was weird – negative, not happy. Unlike the previous night, the band wasn't playing so well. It felt like the break between us was actually becoming physically real onstage as the songs went by. Finally we started cutting songs out of the set because we couldn't handle the heat. I started blacking out. I lay on the stage, in the eye of the storm, surrounded by sound and fury, feeling heart-broken – these songs would never be played again.

During the last, desperate rendition of 'The Rise and Fall' – a song we always closed with because we could descend into a kind of free-form noise jam – I dived into the crowd. I'd always been close with Jamie and Graham, our crew, and as the band fell apart I felt closer to them than anyone else. I surfed over the crowd to Graham at the sound desk and held his hand in the air briefly, before heading back to the stage. In the spirit of the music I usually screamed some kind of stream-of-consciousness thing at this stage in the set and that night I remember yelling 'I tried my best' as hard as I could.

It all sounds pretty melodramatic when I write it down, but in truth, once the show was done, it was crushingly banal. I smoked my cigarettes and gave Ben a hug. We'd been playing together since we were eleven and now we were done. He wrote something on the dressing-room wall about it being our last show there. Everyone scattered, I don't really know where the rest of the band went, or when. I went with my new lady friend to some nonevent of a house party, ended up staying up all night and caught the first train of the grey morning home to Winchester alone.

What next?

PART ONE

SHOW # 8

Utopia Cafe, Southend-on-Sea, UK, 6 October 2005

I caught the train out to Southend with Jamie, my guitar and a bag of CD-Rs that I'd burned off at home. We were coming from London, where I'd been hanging out, sofa surfing, drinking too much.

Back in the summer, things with Million Dead had come to a head. Ben and I met up one sunny afternoon in a bar in north London called Nambucca, which was run by friends of ours – a place that will come to feature heavily later. Over a couple of beers we talked the situation through and decided glumly that we were through with the band, at the end of our tether. We went over to the lock-up in Blackhorse Road where we rehearsed and told the others. The rehearsal was over pretty quickly after that. But we decided to fulfil our commitments and do the tour that we already had booked, making it a swansong-type affair.

All of this meant that I had some time to consider what I wanted to do after the band was done. I knew I wanted to keep making music, despite the doubts of my friends and disapproval of my parents. It just felt like I had more to say and I had to at least try. In particular, I wanted to stay on tour – I'd fallen in love with that lifestyle. I'd recently moved out of my flat in London, stored my stuff in the corners of my parents' house in true bourgeois-rebel style and committed myself to the road full time. I was young and fired up enough to be able to eschew creature comforts. Between Million Dead tours I'd been out with my friends Reuben, running their merch stand. I didn't want to put a new band together straight away and as much as I loved Ben, there was too much baggage there for me to jump straight back into playing with him. The internecine politics had worn me out.

The other factor playing on my mind was that I felt like I was pretty much done with (post-) hardcore as a style – not to listen to, but to play. As Million Dead travelled around the UK and Europe, I'd increasingly found myself lying in bus bunks or crammed in van cabs listening to stuff like Josh Rouse, the Johnny Cash American Recordings series and Springsteen's *Nebraska*. I'd also revived my love for Counting Crows, a band my older sister Jo had got me into when we were younger. Perversely, a lot of the classics, especially Neil Young, were new to me; I grew up with punk and metal. After years of self-conscious musical awkwardness and trying to be dark and angular all the time, hearing simple chords and simple words was immensely refreshing and I felt like the music told me deeper truths.

So before the band broke up I'd played a handful of solo shows, with my old acoustic guitar. The sets had been all covers and reworked Million Dead songs at first, but over time I'd started writing my own material. Two songs in particular, 'The Real Damage' and 'Romantic Fatigue', had arrived and I'd played them at Nambucca on open-mic nights. After that fateful band meeting, I'd gone back to the bar to drown my sorrows. Dave Danger, an old friend and drummer for The Holloways, ran the bar. We talked it through over some whisky and I asked him what he thought I should do. Without a second's hesitation, he told me to stick with the acoustic songs I'd been writing. Sensible Jay, Nambucca's other kingpin (also known as Beans On Toast), agreed wholeheartedly. Their conviction made me think I should at least give it a shot.

So I put the word out that once the final tour was done, this is what I was going to be doing, at least for the foreseeable future. I think a lot of people were slightly incredulous and didn't see where I was coming from at the time. To be fair I'm not sure I knew where I was coming from either, but it felt like I was hanging in the breeze and I needed a healthy dose of self-confidence to make whatever it was I was going to do work. I wrote a few more songs (with practice, they started to come more easily; I got used to writing on my own) and started burning off CD-Rs with a few home demos on them to sell at shows.

This show was slightly different, however. It was the first one since the band had officially come to an end, the first one without a safety net. I can't remember now how the show came to be booked, but it was in the upstairs room of a small cafe in Southend. The promoter had booked a heavier, emo-style band as support – something that happened a lot in the early days due to associations with my old band. The PA system consisted of a few battered club speakers, which the support band succeeded in blowing up about halfway through their set. So when my time rolled around, I stood on a chair in the middle of the thirty or so people there and played unamplified. I think I played about half covers and half originals. People were there mainly out of some kind of bemused curiosity, pretty much all Million Dead fans. I got a smattering of applause and sold a few CDs, then Jamie and I ran to the station to get the last train back to the capital.

I remember sitting on the train talking with my old friend and trying to work out if I was doing the right thing or if I was totally out of my mind. In the old band we'd had a motto to keep us going whenever things got tough: 'Think Black Flag'. The old kings of hardcore had had it a thousand times worse, we reasoned, so we should man up and get on with it. But one of the other reasons I love that band is that they were committed to creative freedom and self-belief – they made the records they wanted to, not what people expected of them. And I was in the middle of deciding what kind of music I wanted to make.

I slept on the floor at Jamie's house that night.

SHOW # 18
The Fenton, Leeds, UK, 17 November 2005

The Fenton is a pretty typical venue on the underground UK touring 'toilet' circuit. It's essentially the upstairs room of a pub, reached by a rickety staircase, with just enough space to cram about a hundred people in, but more used to housing fewer than that. The stage is low and the PA leaves much to be desired. The venue staff has that mix of apathy and determination that keeps underground music scenes alive. It smells of piss, stale sweat and duct tape, hope and disappointment.

Most of the gigging I did at this stage consisted of a long string of little shows that I hammered together myself. I did, however, do a short run of shows, which probably qualifies as a tour, with my friend Sam Duckworth, better known as Get Cape. Wear Cape. Fly. I met Sam in his hometown of Southend in the Million Dead days – he'd promoted a bunch of shows for us at a venue called Chinnery's there – and despite being really young at the time he'd done a great job. I think he supported us as Get Cape one time, which is how I knew of his music. Things were brewing for him around this time and he was not far off blowing up in a major way. I think those were pretty much the last underground shows he did and he invited me along.

We rolled around the UK in a van, playing to a hundred or so people a show. In Nottingham some gargantuan drinking efforts resulted in Sam buggering up his ankle (by falling down a flight of stairs, as I recall), so he was hobbling around on crutches after that. We'd got into a game on the tour of seeing who could sound check the fastest. With just acoustic guitars and vocals, and occasionally a laptop for Sam, it wasn't the marathon I was used to from Million Dead, so I seem to remember one of us getting it down below thirty seconds or so. We also developed a collective obsession with pub quiz machines and on more than one occasion we poured the sum of our merch takings from a show into whisky and trivia.

The Leeds show was a special one. We arrived to the frankly bemusing news that the show was sold out. There were quite a few people gathered aimlessly at the bottom of the stairs who couldn't get in, wondering what the hell was going on, much as we were. After some frantic negotiating, we cut a deal whereby Sam and I would play a short extra set out in the car park for the disappointed punters, among them my little sister Gilly, who'd recently started university in Leeds.

The gig inside went well, as far as I can remember. Afterwards we dutifully headed out into the cold. It had recently snowed and it was so cold that playing guitar was a challenge, due to aching fingers and strings as sharp as razor wire. About twenty-five people had stuck around and a few more came from the first show. Sam and I stood side by side against a fence and yelled our hearts out to the faithful. I remember playing stupid covers and at one point beatboxing (badly) for one of Sam's more electro-oriented tunes. After about an hour of shivering, sore throats and shaky tunes, it was over. I'm always more interested in music when it breaks out of the mould and becomes a dialogue, an interaction, rather than just a lecture from 'artist' to 'punter'. The fact of playing with just one acoustic instrument, as I'd just discovered, made it much easier to escape those confines. Afterwards, I trekked back to my sister's student house, feeling like we'd made some-thing interesting happen.

SHOW # 21

Silks Bar, Basingstoke, UK, 24 November 2005

Once I'd found my feet with the first few solo shows, I got into the habit of booking a rolling UK tour quite quickly. I had my guitar, a bag of clothes and a laptop and some CD-Rs to burn off demos. I generally knew where I was going to be about a month ahead of time and would constantly email people about more shows to keep myself on the road. I was asking £50 a show (later I added my train fare on top, once my Young Person's Railcard ran out) and I was travelling on my own. I think I had a Woody Guthrie complex of some kind, although it has to be said that the trains in the UK, with which I became intimately familiar, for better or worse, didn't feel much like the great American box-truck convoys steaming across the prairie.

This show was pretty typical of that time. I didn't know the promoter prior to the show but he was enthusiastic on email and seemed like he had his shit together. The venue didn't have a stage, just one end of the room designated as the performance area, with a shitty vocal PA propped up on some rickety poles. As I remember it, about forty people showed. I played for about an hour, playing more new songs that I was finishing off, including 'This Town Ain't Big Enough for the One of Me', a tirade about small-town mentality that was a little close to home, both figuratively and literally, given that we were just down the road from Winchester. At the end of my designated set, the wall of people across my end of the room wouldn't let me stop playing for a long while. I physically couldn't get away, so I kept going with more old Million Dead songs and random covers, but had to beg for clemency by the time I'd run down to playing Weezer songs album by album and even a Disney cover or two.

After the show I went to the promoter's house, drunk a bunch of whisky, attempted unsuccessfully to chat up a pretty girl and slept on the sofa. The next morning I was up early and off to the station to catch a train to the next show. It wasn't the healthiest way to live but it certainly had its share of romanticism – for a time.

SHOW # 33
New Riga Theatre, Riga, Latvia, 15 January 2006

I'd seen in the New Year with a mock-heroic bout of Bacchanalian debauchery in London and in the haze of hangover and come-down, in the pale morning light of a new year, it felt like the path I was choosing to go down was more certain. As more time passed since the end of the band, I increasingly started to look forwards, which was, I suppose, a positive development. Making a career in music on my own (and indeed on my own terms) was starting to seem realistic, or at least worth a shot. Part of that process was starting to think, even in the most tentative way, of going overseas.

Million Dead had been out to play in Latvia twice. It all started with a hook-up from Kneejerk, the band Ben and I had been in before-hand. Edgars, a promoter from the Baltic states, had been in touch, via Myspace as I recall, to ask about booking Kneejerk for some shows and had been a little put out to hear that we'd broken up several years before. Nevertheless, he put a schedule together for our new band to go out and play and we'd had an amazing, eye-opening time. Not many bands pass through that part of the world (even less so back in 2005) and the youth of the country were still finding their way around rock 'n' roll. All of which meant that they were hugely enthusiastic and grateful to anyone who made the effort to come and play, so the shows were generally packed out and over the top.

I got the impression that Edgars was a little dubious about my foray into solo acoustic music, but I'd sent him one of my many CD-Rs and he'd decided to take a chance on having me over – after all, there was only one of me. In the end I negotiated to take Jamie out as well, to help on the technical side of things and to be a friend and native English speaker to keep me company. I decided that, while I could deal with touring on my own in the UK, doing it so far away from home without a companion might be a step too far.

So Jamie and I arrived in Riga in the freezing-cold January snow. On that first evening in the country, Andzs, a friend from the Million Dead shows, introduced the two of us to Riga Black Balsam – a thick, black, syrupy shot of toxic alcohol that we grimaced and knocked back. After several shots each we discovered that we were supposed to sip it slowly. About half an hour later Jamie was hugging the massive Christmas tree in the city centre, in the snow, with his trousers round his ankles, while I sat next to him laughing my arse off.

We did one show in Riga in a classic European punker-bunker venue called The Depo. After a day off of recovery and solidifying new friendships, we took the bus out to Liepāja, a coastal city that in Soviet times had been a closed military zone. I played at a venue called Fontaine Palace, run by the eponymous Louie Fontaine, who seemed to be a Latvian cross between Elvis and Chris Evans. Another travel day followed and then, on our last day in the country, Edgars had suggested a second Riga show, in the plush and modern surroundings of the New Riga Theatre, announced the day before and publicized mainly by word of mouth.

There was a plentiful, polite, seated crowd in for the show. I played on the floor at the front while the seats sloped up away from me. I remember it being a great show – I played well and in the context of not being in a punk venue or noisy bar, I was able to play some slower, gentler songs I'd been working on. This was also the night where I met Karlis – a formidable, hulking Latvian, bearded and broad of shoulder, who was also an eccentric and raging drunk. During the show he actually came up on stage to offer me a drink – Jack Daniel's and Coke, naturally – but he didn't have a glass to offer, so he suggested pouring the ingredients straight into my mouth, where I could mix them at my own leisure. Being in front of the crowd, I could hardly resist. During the course of the evening, he also told us his favourite king was Charles I and that he liked trampolining very much, but, alarmingly, was minded to shoot gypsies with his 'double-barrelled shooting gun'. Jamie and I were a captive audience.

At the end of the show I finished my set with a cover of Abba's 'Dancing Queen'. I'd learned the song for a night a friend of mine put on at Nambucca with a seventies theme, but had actually come to really appreciate and enjoy the craft of the music and played it with my tongue firmly not in my cheek. I think it was probably Karlis who started it, but by the middle of the song I had the audience on their feet and surrounding me in a series of concentric circles, holding hands and doing some kind of Baltic folk dancing, which involved walking sideways and bending your knees to bob down at apparently random intervals, while singing along. It was a magical moment: drunk, fun, transcendent. Jamie and I headed back to the UK having made firm new friends.

SHOW # 44

Rachel's House, Newcastle, UK, 3 February 2006

Back in the UK, my train tour continued apace. Things were still pretty hand-to-mouth as far as shows were concerned, but at least I was getting better practised at it. It's strange, we did tour a fair amount with Million Dead, but looking back I almost feel like I learned most of what I know about survival on the road in this period of peripatetic solitude. From the small things – like how to make a pillow from your shoes and jacket, through to the more profound things – such as self-reliance and staying sane when you're constantly on the move.

After a short run of shows in Scotland and a trip through the slightly more obscure parts of the north-east (Sunderland and Hartlepool), I headed for Newcastle. I'd tried to get myself a show in a bar or a venue through various old contacts and had drawn a complete blank. So in the end my friend Rachel offered to have me play at her place. I met Rachel when she made a really cool, short fan documentary about Million Dead's farewell tour and we'd stayed in touch since. I rolled into town and pitched up at her small house in the suburbs. About twenty people showed up in dribs and drabs, mostly old Million Dead fans or interested friends.

I was still finding my feet as a solo performer – it's a very different thing from playing with a band, particularly a hardcore one. In that setting, you have the confidence of camaraderie and you have a wall of noise behind you that is both a shot in the arm and a safety net. When it's just you with an acoustic guitar – and in this setting, no PA of any kind – you feel much more exposed, almost naked. Over the years it's something I think I can say I've got pretty good at, but back in February 2006 I was still a novice. So I was nervous at this show, sitting on a chair a few feet away from the people at the show, slightly uncomfortable about the whole thing. When I was growing up I used to sit around with my sisters and our friends and play songs all the time, but in that context everyone was singing and I was merely leading the congregation. It's different when everyone is paying attention, examining you.

In the end I had a fun show and in particular I remember it because I tried out a new song. In my early twenties I had one serious relationship, which took a long time to die out completely. We were that annoying couple that kept breaking up and getting back together all the time, to the chagrin of all our friends. Around this time it'd finally burned out and I wrote one last song about it all called 'Worse Things Happen at Sea'. When I finished it, I wasn't at all sure that it was any good, in fact I nearly scrapped it at one point. But in the context of this show I thought I might as well give it a try and see how it went across. To my surprise everyone loved it, in fact people were saying it was my best work to date. I was surprised but pleased. I guess I'm not always the best judge of my own material. It's funny how these things work out.

SHOW # 52
Steamboat Tavern, Ipswich, UK, 14 February 2006

I've always meant to write a song about this show.

There's a bleak, failed romanticism to the idea of Valentine's Day alone in Ipswich.

I had a particularly long stretch of solo shows around this time and the experience was starting to wear me down. The run had included a series of shows in houses, university halls of residence and squats. When you're on your own and in someone else's home you have to be quite aggressively gregarious if you're to survive – you're on away territory, you need to be friendly and accommodating. But it takes a fair amount out of you being surrounded by strangers all the time and if the shows are small and often quite sparsely attended, it gets a little trying. I had a particular low point after a house show in Wigan. The show itself was OK, but I had a tiny, hard-sided sofa to sleep on which didn't even begin to fit me. On top of that, some weirdo kid who'd clearly done a lot of speed was bouncing up and down on one arm of my useless attempt at a bed and telling me, rapidly and incessantly, that he wasn't a thief. That hardly gave me the confidence to nod off with my bag and guitar in the room – not that I could sleep through his inane chattering. No sleep, no friends, no money – a bad but familiar combination.

Being single at the time, the significance of the date, 14 February, had escaped me when I was booking this show. It was only as the day approached that it occurred to me that this could present a problem. I've never been one for staying at the houses of people I don't know if I can find someone I do know. But during this time I would often end up asking the crowd, just before I played my last song, if anyone would let me sleep on their sofa or floor (if I found someone with a spare bed I was doing well). That night, not really knowing too many people in Ipswich, I'd planned to do the same, but because of the auspicious date, pretty much everyone at the show was coupled up and had plans for a private evening in that were not best added to by some vagrant occupying the front room.

I spent some time before my set asking around to see if I could pin anything down, but it was really starting to seem like everyone was hooked up. A particularly ambitious attempt to chat up the barmaid yielded only the offer of sleeping on the floor in the bar once the show was done if I really couldn't find anywhere else. In the end I think it was one of the guys from Secondsmile, a band on the bill that I'd played with before, who took pity on me and let me throw a spanner in his romantic works by holing up at his house. I was feeling pretty sorry for myself that night, though I think I could see the funny side of it too. Great material for a song – I'll get round to it one day.

SHOW # 61
Quicksilver Mail, Yeovil, UK, 5 March 2006

Reading back through the list of the shows that I've done, one slightly uncomfortable fact starts to leap out at me. It's not just that I have been drinking too much for too long, but also, around this period of my life I got pretty heavily involved in doing drugs. It's a subject that I feel a little awkward writing about, but at the same time it's pretty integral to understanding what I was doing, or trying to do, at this time.

I'd started doing various pills and powders towards the end of my time in Million Dead. At the start it was limited by inexperience and the fact that the others heavily disapproved of that kind of behaviour. But as the band fell apart, my mood darkened and I stopped caring so much what the others thought. By the time of our farewell tour I was getting high most days. In the aftermath of that collapse, I had big drug nights (and days) a couple of times a week – as much as I could afford, really.

I'm not particularly anti-drugs (actually, I happen to believe in the complete legalization of all drugs. I don't really see how it's anybody's business but your own, both the right and the responsibility – but that's an argument for another time). I've also had some awesome experiences when I was fucked out of my mind. But there's a line and around this time I definitely went way over it and often. It's reasonably fair to say that *Sleep Is for the Week* is, in some senses, an album about doing too much cocaine. The story behind 'The Real Damage' was certainly powder-fuelled. As well as being stunningly unhealthy, staying up for days and not eating anything, it also meant I played some pretty bad shows and that in particular is not something I'm proud of.

This show is a case in point. The night before I played in Harlow, a town in Essex that's just outside the north-east of London. Not knowing too many people in that part of the world, and it being a Friday night, I'd headed south after the show, back into the capital's heart of darkness. A lot of my friends, particularly from the Nambucca scene, were running club nights in London at this time, so I headed down to a club in Camden, where I blagged my way in on the guest list and holed myself up in the backstage room. I had about £100 in my pocket from the last few shows and it didn't take me long to hand the whole lot over to a shady character in return for a few small lottery-ticket wraps of powder. Fired up and raging, I snorted and blathered the night away. Soon enough I was at some random afterparty at a stranger's house, drawing what little cash I had from ATMs to buy more supplies. Once you pass about 8 a.m., the logic of the drugs starts to suggest that you should stay awake and burn through to the next evening, but that takes more fuel. It's a pretty dumb decision at the best of times, but when you have a show to play that evening, it's especially unintelligent.

At some point in the afternoon I managed to stumble my way to a train station and get myself heading down towards Yeovil. Everything is pretty blurred in my memory at this point, but I made it to the venue, even managing a sound check, all the while drinking beer and sneaking off for regular bathroom pit stops. I succeeded in playing the show and getting paid, but I cannot imagine for a moment that it was anything less than pitiful as a display of musicianship. Afterwards I even managed to get myself back to the house of a girl I'd just met, before finally passing out, exhausted, pale and sweating, finished.

The next day I woke up feeling disoriented, famished, aching and sorry for myself. I'd managed to lose the cash I'd been paid for the show and forget the name of my semi-clothed host. I had to jump trains towards Brighton for my next show, which also suffered from the after-affects of my self-degradation – all dirty fingernails, raw voice and non sequiturs.

So this, people, is the reality of the sex and drugs part of Ian Dury's unholy trinity, as I experienced it. It's sordid, painful, expensive and embarrassing to recollect and certainly not anything I'm trying to glorify or glamorize. The fact is, however, that in the midst of this rambling, self-extending tour, I spent a lot of time out of my mind. It was a reflection of being pretty unhappy on some deeper level and being angry about what happened with the band. It comes through in a lot of the songs I wrote in this time period. Just listen to *Sleep Is for the Week*. I'm happy to say that, while I'll indulge on the odd special occasion, my days of decadent self-destruction are firmly in the past.

SHOW # 67
Nambucca, London, UK, 19 March 2006

It's time then, to talk about Nambucca. On the one hand it was just another seedy north London pub, a dilapidated dive bar run by indie kids with delusions of grandeur. On the other, it was the epicentre of something special – no matter how small or short-lived – and my second home, perhaps even my first for a while.

I actually used to live on pretty much the same street. The pub stood on a corner on the upper Holloway Road and one of the student hovels I inhabited while I was at university and playing in the old band was further down the street. The pub had been closed up until just around the time I was moving out, early 2003 or so. On the day I finally departed and gave my keys back to the landlord, I ran into my friends Dave and Jay outside. They were passing acquaintances at the time, friends of Ben's from working at Tower Records. I asked what they were up to in my neighbourhood and they told me they'd just moved into the empty flat above the bar and were going to start running the place. We laughed at our poor timing and I went on my way.

Over time the two of them really opened the place up, setting up regular band nights, pub quizzes and so on, moving more and more people into the rooms upstairs as they made them vaguely habitable and over time a real scene developed. Sensible Promotions, their company for running gigs and club nights in the capital, was based there. The Sunday night open-mic affair, Sensible Sundays, became a pretty regular hang-out for various up-and-coming acoustic musicians – Laura Marling, Jamie T, Kid Harpoon and others. Dave's band, The Holloways, formed at the bar and initiated their plans for world domination from the basement.

There were a lot of drugs floating around the scene and I really do mean *a lot*. As the whole British indie guitar scene of that era kicked off, Dave and Jay found themselves at the centre of it, which led to a lot of hangers-on and star-fuckers clogging up the after-parties. I remember seeing Babyshambles stumble through plenty of sets downstairs and seeing queues of starry-eyed, trust-fund kids waiting to get through the back door into the flats upstairs, boldly brandishing dealers' phone numbers as if they were VIP tickets.

Nambucca. I suppose it was much like any other place that

briefly holds the underground spotlight – frantic, wild, deceptive at times, intoxicated and intoxicating, too big for its boots, but – without wishing to overly romanticize the place – it had something intangibly special at its core. I had many of the nights of my life there, most of which didn't involve sleeping, and the friends I made there remain some of my closest. The song 'I Knew Prufrock Before He Got Famous' is essentially about the core people who made it what it was in its heyday.

I played there many, many times, trying out my early solo material at countless Sensible Sundays and, more often than not, if I swung by for a drink I'd end up playing a few numbers on Jay's battered old acoustic, usually followed by him knocking out some of his tunes, which he was writing under the name Beans On Toast. I'm not even sure if all of them count as shows as such, but there was usually a crowd of sorts.

Show #67 was a pretty typical Nambucca occasion, although it was memorable for its own reasons. We'd all been out at one of Dave and Jay's club nights the previous evening. As dawn rolled around and more powders arrived at the party to keep us going, Jay's indefatigable business acumen turned to the new day's agenda. Sensible Sundays usually had a couple of booked name acts among the volunteer hopefuls, but he realized in the grimy half-light that no one was down for that evening. In a predictable development, he decided that he and I would take the bullet on this one. After some brain-addled discussion, a few more conditions were added to the brew. Firstly, Zoniel, one of the girls who lived upstairs and helped out with the clubs, announced imperiously that we all had to wear at least one turquoise item of clothing if we were to take the stage. I had a cardigan, Jay a shirt and Danny (a Nambucca friend, later to get his own song – 'Dan's Song') ended up DJing in a turquoise towel with a hole cut through the middle for his head, wearing it like a poncho (we never did find out whose it was). Kid Harpoon arrived home from a party at some point in the morning and heartily joined in the mayhem.

The second rule was that we had to play each other's songs. I've always been slightly sceptical about the notion of musical 'scenes', but we were a group of peers all writing acoustic songs together and we'd all sing along with our friends' compositions. The challenge now was, could you actually play one yourself, on a stage, leading the chorus rather than accompanying and when we were all totally wasted to boot?

In the event, our mass texts about the impending chaos brought a small audience mostly consisting of people we knew, so the musical shambles that followed was, mercifully, not widely witnessed. But we did manage to hack through a few mutual songs and even in the confusion of it all it seemed to capture something of what was special about the place to me. I remember that Sam Get Cape showed up towards the end of the evening with his new friend Walter Schreifels, of Gorilla Biscuits and Rival Schools fame, and that they were totally bemused by the scene before them. My consciousness was rapidly fading by that point, chemicals notwithstanding, and I finally faded out on a mattress in the corner of Zoniel's room, still wearing my turquoise cardigan.

A short postscript: for some reason, the date of this show stuck in my mind. I have a memory for shows and not much else (hence the contents of this book!). A year to the day later, I was driving through West Texas with musicians Jonah Matranga and Joshua English in a rental car. We passed through Las Cruces, a town I knew from a song by Two Gallants, a band Jay and I both love. I texted him to let him know where we were and that a year had passed since Turquoise Sunday. He replied, through the radio waves, the miles and the time zones, to say we should do it again when I got home. I held him to it.

SHOW # 81

Meesh's House, Newbury, UK, 14 April 2006

In the midst of all the travelling hedonism, I had other things on my mind. My parents lived in Winchester and through this time I had some of my stuff piled up in the corner of a room that also served as my mum's home office. In the few gaps between shows and London adventuring I'd head back there to recover and relax. All was not well with my parents' marriage, however, and around this time things kicked off in a pretty apocalyptic way.

This show was another case of me filling in a spare tour day with a house party. I didn't know Meesh particularly well at the time, though we've since become good friends. She was going out with my friend Del, who I'd done a run of Scottish shows with (he played under the name mistakes.in.animation) and who put on a lot of gigs down in Kingston. I remember being on the train out to the show from London when my older sister called me with bad news.

It's a private and complicated matter, but suffice to say that at this time things fell apart quickly. My father hadn't been the most honest of husbands and my parents were in the middle of separating pretty acrimoniously. My sister was upset and told me of some new, fairly dramatic and final developments. I felt stunned, numb, shellshocked. All of a sudden the house party didn't seem like it was going to be so much fun. I really just wanted to be on my own for a while, but as ever with touring I was constantly surrounded by well-meaning strangers. I didn't even feel like drinking, just like thinking. The road has its own momentum, though and I didn't want to let people down, so the show went ahead.

It so happened that I'd been working on a song in which I was trying to address my disconnect with my father. As often happens, fresh events spurred me on into finishing off the words and the tune in a final sprint of creative energy. I'm usually one for sitting on new tunes for a while after they're finished, mulling them over, double-checking what I think of them and if they're good enough to be revealed to the wider world. But on this occasion it all seemed to come together and make sense. That night I played 'Father's Day' for the first time, stood in the middle of Meesh's living room, with everyone sat on the floor around me, stumbling over the words here and there, teaching everyone the sing-along part at the end. I didn't tell people the background of the day's events, but I think the assembled partygoers understood that there was something slightly darker at work.

After playing, I managed to secure a small back bedroom to myself and I found an old curtain to make into a bed of sorts. I slept wrapped up in it on the floor, by myself, thinking things through, but ultimately glad that the next day I had another show in another town.

SHOW # 82
The Wheatsheaf, Oxford, UK, 15 April 2006

I have a long-standing connection with Oxford. Jon Spira, a friend of mine who made a documentary about the history of the local scene, even dubbed me an 'honorary Oxfordian'. In April 2006, the day after I'd played at Meesh's house in fact, I played two shows supporting a band called Dive Dive at The Wheatsheaf, a classic small venue up a rickety flight of stairs in the centre of town.

As I've mentioned, I'd done a couple of tours with my friends Reuben, working on their crew in between my own tours as a way of staying on the road. In early 2005, on one of these tours, I was setting up the merch stand in Joseph's Well, a venue in Leeds, when the support band started sound checking. Their drummer played a beat-perfect rendition of Zeppelin's 'Rock and Roll' and I was impressed. His name was Nigel Powell and he was the drummer for Dive Dive. As the tour went on I fell in love with their angular indie rock and became friends with Nigel, Ben Lloyd (electric guitar, onstage maniac), Tarrant Anderson (bass) and Jamie Stuart (singer, guitarist and frontman).

A while later, when I was starting to blaze my trail around the UK, I got a little tired of selling CD-Rs comprising songs I'd recorded on my laptop at home with a crappy microphone and my guitar accompanied by ersatz programmed instruments. Thoughts turned, naturally enough, to a proper recording. I did some demos with a guy called Tristan Ivemy, a friend of The Holloways', in London, recorded in his bedroom, one of which ('The Real Damage') ended up on a split with Reuben. But I wanted to do something more substantial and with some extra players, so I ended up giving Ben Lloyd a call.

Tarrant used to live in a big house in north Oxford, on the Woodstock Road, and in the basement he had a little rehearsal room set up. As a band, they'd recorded their first album there by stringing wires up the stairwell to a makeshift control room on the top floor. On the Reuben tour, Ben had mentioned that he, Nigel and Tarrant were interested in recording new stuff and might be up for helping me make a record. So in February 2006, between runs of house shows, I spent a few days down in that basement, teaching Ben, Tarrant and Nigel the parts for a few new songs. In the end we did three tracks together – 'Nashville Tennessee', 'This Town Ain't Big Enough for the One of Me' and 'I Really Don't Care What You Did on Your Gap Year' and two solo numbers – 'Thatcher Fucked the Kids' and 'Casanova Lament'.

The next stage in the process was to talk to someone about actually putting the recording out, rather than just hawking cheap copies at shows like some kind of bootlegger. I had remained close friends with the people at Xtra Mile Recordings, the label that had put out Million Dead's last album and, after some initial caution about my new direction, they expressed an interest in helping me out. Charlie Caplowe, the owner of the label, effectively became my manager and we continue to work together today in both label and management capacities. I presented the new recordings – material light years ahead of what I'd been peddling to date – to the label and they enthusiastically decided to put out a CD EP. I borrowed the title from an anonymous drunk punter at a show I played in Dundee, who'd slurred to me while we shared a cigarette after my set that I was 'campfire punk rock'.

With a finished proper release under my belt I felt infinitely more established and boxes of manufactured CDs entered my packing list for tours from this time onwards. I'd also really enjoyed the process of collaborating with the guys in Oxford and we definitely had an eye towards working together more in the future. To bring all of this together, Dive Dive asked me to support them on their two-night stand, so I took the train over to Oxford to play. For the first time since Million Dead, I started feeling like maybe I had some allies in this mission, both in Ben, Nigel and Tarrant, and in Charlie and Xtra Mile. The idea that all of this might amount to something more solid than just my Guthrie-wannabe wanderings started to seductively suggest itself to me.

SHOW # 86
Whistlebinkies, Edinburgh, UK, 19 April 2006

Around this point in time, I'd embarked on what could be termed a proper full UK tour. I'd played a show in Camden, at Monkey

Chews, a little while before and had shared the bill with a singer-songwriter from Wiltshire called Gabby Young, along with her backing band. We got on well and she had one hell of a voice. A post-show conversation revealed that she had a UK tour booked and coming up soon. She'd asked me if I wanted to come with and I'd jumped at the chance, as it filled up a good month of my time with more shows spread around a wider area. The tour did not, however, go as smoothly as I had hoped. There were a lot of great shows – I remember Swindon and Leeds in particular – but Gabby's enthusiasm was not always matched with experience. She'd booked many of the shows herself without going through a local promoter, so in many of the towns no one really knew that the gigs were happening and turnouts were often disappointing, to say the least. Nothing saps morale quite like an empty room far away from anything resembling home.

We drove north in a hired van and crossed the border into Scotland. Whistlebinkies is a small bar just off the main drag in Edinburgh and it usually plays host to bar bands, covers acts and pay-to-play-type affairs. It's dark and dingy and more often than not the people in the bar have no interest in the music being played, especially if the show is a free one, which in this case, it was.

I remember that night because we had a grand total of one person in the room who'd actually come to see the show and he'd taken the train down from somewhere further north (Aberdeen, I think) for the occasion. As punk rock as one tries to be about everything, rock 'n' roll involves some degree of putting your ego on the line night after night; the paradigm, on paper, involves at least some level of appreciation from a crowd of people. I believe firmly that you should always play your heart out, whether for one thousand people or just one. However, in practice it's hard. I did my best at this show to do what I do as well as I could, but I remember playing with my eyes shut tight, teeth slightly gritted.

Our lone audience member, despite the fact that the situation was slightly awkward, had a good time. I guess it was a character-building experience for me. But looking back through all these shows, the overriding thought I have is that while I'm glad I did this stuff, I'm gladder still that I don't have to do it too much any more.

SHOW # 94
The Watering Hole, Perranporth, UK, 1 May 2006

A few weeks later, the same run had wound its way down to my favourite part of the UK, the south-west. The Watering Hole in Perranporth is a bar on a beach in Cornwall. It wasn't actually accessible by road, so we had to park our van on the kerb nearby and lug all of mine and Gabby's equipment over the sand. The bar was a small, relaxed, hippy kind of place. After a short sound check I went for a quick wander along the beach. I love being next to the sea. The English used to be a nation of sailors, so it makes me feel somehow ancestral looking out over the cliffs into the Channel. The tour had been on for a long while by this point, so getting some quiet time to myself, some fresh wind on my face and even that rarest of commodities, some English sunshine, did much to lift my spirits.

The turnout for the show was pretty good as I remember it and a great time was had by all. Afterwards a bunch of people from the show told us they were having a house party nearby and invited us to join them. I went along, partly just to see what was happening, but also because the invitee was a cute girl I'd noticed at the show.

Now is as good a time as any to talk about this frankly: young men on tour try to get laid; it's a pretty basic fact. The motivations are as simple as you'd imagine, although there is another angle to it. On a tour like this one, sleeping with someone didn't just mean sex, it meant literally that: a chance to sleep in a bed, with only one other person in the room. After months of crashing on floors surrounded by rustling sleeping bags, angular elbows and using your shoes for a pillow, the luxury of a bed with a pretty girl in it and some peace and quiet is hard to overstate.

So, with high expectations, I headed to the party and made some headway (as I remember it and I'm the one telling the story) talking to the girl, who was the host of the evening's celebrations. We were sat together on the sofa, limbs starting to wander quietly around each other, casually resting hands on a leg or brushing back some hair. I was confident that I was going to sleep soundly. Then, suddenly, events took a turn for the decidedly surreal. The doorbell rang and somebody answered the door. In rushed a young guy, a beach-surfer type with short dreadlocks and something trite like a ganja-leaf pendant round his neck (again, my version of events) and he made a beeline for the sofa where I was sat with my new friend.

'Babe, I'm still in love with you,' he announced, rather curtly, in front of a now-captive audience. Given that the said babe's legs were draped over mine as he said this, I couldn't help but feel a little awkward. Things moved fast. She looked shocked, but took his hand when he outstretched it, disentangled herself and stood up to face my competitor. Before I knew what the hell was going on, he kissed her, she threw a small apologetic look at me over her shoulder and the two of them were out the door, into his car and driving off into the night.

I sat on the sofa, the imprint of the recently departed woman pressed into my posture, suddenly feeling pretty embarrassed, quite annoyed and not massively welcome, as everyone else from my crew had departed to wherever we were originally planning on sleeping some time before. My last desperate hope that maybe I'd still be able to sleep in the girl's bed (having scoped out where her room was before) was quickly crushed by the sight of her friend, who'd been giving me evil looks all night, swiftly darting in and slamming the door behind her. The party's momentum had been well and truly crushed and in a matter of minutes everything was winding up. I really had no idea where I was and in the end another, reluctantly sympathetic, housemate said I could sleep on the sofa if I wanted to. Alas, this was the sofa surfer's worst enemy: the short, hard-sided type that was impossible to stretch out on or drape your legs over in anything approaching comfort. So I spent a confused and miserable night trying to find a way to arrange myself so that I could get some sleep, with only my jacket for a blanket, ever conscious of the intangible luxury that was only one slammed door and one romantic surfer guy away.

In the morning I woke up to a dead house. Knowing I had to be on my way to meet up with the tour party before anyone was likely to wake up, I used a trick that has stood me in good stead many a time. Fishing around by the door, I managed to find both a card for a local taxi firm that'd been shoved through the letterbox at some point and a letter addressed to someone in the house, thereby letting me know where I was. One expensive taxi ride later, I was back with Gabby and the crew (who all laughed their arses off at me) and we were on our way to our next stop.

Life on the road is strange. The sense of liberation in part comes from the fact that, nine times out of ten, you won't be in the same city, perhaps even the same country, come the next day. In a way it's a shield against taking responsibility for your actions and it allows you to exist in a state of permanent semi-adolesence, if you so choose, almost indefinitely. Being a thinking human being, I do sometimes wake up in the night and contemplate the way in which people like me can arrive in a town, play a show, interfere in local social circles and then be gone as quickly as we came, leaving a swirling wake that we don't have to deal with. So in a way I'm glad that the surfer guy came back and got his girl, because I haven't been back to Perranporth since and I think that true love should, at the very least, conquer the desire of a Woody-Guthrie-wannabe for a bed.

SHOW # 111
Blagnac Festival, Toulouse, France, 26 May 2006

My second major foray overseas as a solo artist took me to France. Just before Million Dead broke up we had been planning to cross the Channel for a short DIY punk tour. Our contact was a guy called Daniel Chamorro (Cham to his friends), the drummer for a reasonably successful underground French punk band called Guerilla Poubelle. He'd been pretty pissed off with us when we'd cancelled the tour, although this was later tempered somewhat when he realized it wasn't because we didn't like or trust him, it was because the band had ceased to exist. A little while later, we'd crossed paths at a solo show of mine in Kingston. On the strength of that performance (and, I suspect, for the love of adventure) Cham had decided to go ahead and try to book me a solo tour in France using his contacts and what little goodwill he managed to generate while booking the previous nonstarter of a run.

So I arrived in France with my bag and my guitar, preparing to spend two weeks driving around the country, playing small bars and basements, with a French guy I'd met twice, and briefly at that. I was a little nervous before the first show, to say the least, which wasn't helped by Cham being dumped by his girlfriend over the phone on our drive from the airport into town (something he succeeded in patching up later that day, but it still led to a fraught couple of hours). But in the end it was an amazing trip and Cham has become a lifelong friend.

We started the run with a handful of shows in and around Paris, including a stint opening for Hundred Reasons, a band that Million Dead had shared the stage with many times. After that we set out on the open road. I have an image in my mind that captures this tour: the two of us tearing down the motorway in the sunshine, listening to Queen at full blast; Cham teaching me French words and telling me about the wonders of French women; and Cham constantly, constantly chain-smoking bootleg cigarettes. We crisscrossed the country, sometimes playing to small punk crowds when opening for other bands, sometimes literally sitting in the corner of a bar playing for disinterested Gallic drunks. We met a businessman in Belgium who told us a crazy story. The cops had found a dead body by the side of the road with no identification at all apart from the Belgian's business card in his jeans. When the police asked him if he knew the deceased, he said he didn't make friends with people who wore denim. We played a show with Oceansize (I totally fell in love with their music), drank exotic beers with coked-up barmen in the Alps, did mushrooms while laughing at French Nazi punk records and inexpertly tried to scale the heights of chatting up *les Françaises*.

The penultimate show of the tour saw us down in Toulouse at an open-air festival. On arrival it seemed that it was less of a festival in the normal sense and more a kind of village fete. The stage was too high, the sun was burningly hot and, aside from some friends of Cham's, there really weren't that many people paying much attention. The day sticks in my mind, though, partly as a crystallization of that manic time and partly because I played a new song that I'd been working on for a while.

'The Ballad of Me and My Friends' was written as a summary of everything that had happened in the time since the band had finished. In a way it's a pessimistic song, but the message is supposed to be one of hope, of defiance. That day, I played it and not so many people cared, Cham aside. But after the tour was finished, I flew back to London and arrived at Nambucca, where an all-night party was just getting started. I already knew that I wanted to have a crowd singing along on the recording, so that night, as we sat in the back of the bar at about 4 a.m., I taught the people there the words to the end section and we recorded a makeshift version of the song. Unfortunately, it's too ragged – I played too fast because I was shiveringly smashed – but there's something about the feel of it that I love and the cast of characters who were singing along was perfect. In the end we released a version recorded at a later show, but I think one day I might get that first recording out there, as it captures the spirit of the song a little better, I think.

SHOW # 127
Lexapalooza 1, GJ's, London, UK, 17 June 2006

I met Alexa Burrows, or Lex, back in the Million Dead days. She'd come down to the video shoot for a song called 'Living the Dream' and we'd ended up going for a drink afterwards and becoming friends. Lex was one of those people who overflowed with life. She slipped into our friendship group seamlessly and it was like she'd been there all along. She had a shock of pink hair, a roll-up cigarette never far from her fingers and time for everyone's troubles. After Million Dead we remained good friends and through the early days she'd been a constant and dogged supporter of what I was trying to achieve, even if she not so secretly preferred my earlier, heavier work.

Before I met her Lex had fought and beaten a bout of breast cancer. As a survivor she was filled with a burning passion for raising funds and awareness for the Breast Cancer Campaign. That summer she decided to put on an all-day show in her end of south London, at GJ's in Colliers Wood, to make some money for the cause. We'd all pitched in to help, but it was basically her event. I was roped in, both to play a set and to compere the day.

I remember this particular show as being a friendly day but a little shambolic; I certainly was several sheets to the wind before my time to actually play (rather than make up comedy lies about the other acts) rolled around. I had twisted Lex's arm to get my friend Adam Killip (of London's The Tailors, one of my favourite bands then and now) on to the bill and ended up on stage with him, playing second guitar and singing harmonies. I thought it was great, but the general consensus was that I didn't add much. But the day was a good-natured mess and a reasonable amount of cash was raised for the Breast Cancer Campaign. Lexapalooza has continued as a concept since this time (much more on this later), but this day seems worth mentioning as the inauguration of a tradition and also as the only one that Lexie herself was in full charge of.

SHOW # 145
Latitude Festival, Suffolk, UK, 15 July 2006

This was the first year that the Latitude Festival ran. It's a great set-up, one of the most beautiful locations for a festival I've ever seen, set among fields and forests in the Suffolk countryside, miles from anywhere. As it happened, Charlie, my manager, was also employed to run the press campaign for the festival. A little behind-the-scenes horse-trading enabled me to get a slot, albeit an early day show, on the Saturday on the Literary Stage. Nevertheless, a slot at a major festival is a slot all the same.

One of the problems with Latitude is that for those of us without a car, it's not the easiest place in the world to get to. There is a train that runs to a station nearby, but it stops running pretty early and you still have to get a coach to the actual festival site. On this occasion, I found out that The Lemonheads, a band I dearly love, were down to headline the Friday night. So, with a female friend of mine who we'll call Natalie, we decided to get the last train down there that evening, watch their set, camp for the night and be ready for my set the following day. Things did not, alas, go according to plan.

Natalie is an old and great friend and it is not my intention to besmirch her character in any way. However, on the Friday afternoon she decided to get her hair cut – an event that is slightly more momentous for the fairer sex than it is for me (in fact I'd essentially stopped having my hair cut at this point). I sat nervously at the station, counting down the minutes until the time of the last train, waiting for her call or arrival. The time came and went, the train departed and Natalie was still busy being coiffed. No Lemonheads set for us then. I was pretty gutted and Natalie was hugely apologetic. We resolved to head up to the festival first thing in the morning.

The trouble was that the two of us now found ourselves with a free Friday evening in London. Friends of ours were still running indie clubs in London at the time, so we decided to head up to KOKO in Camden to see what was going on. With grim predictability, we ran into some of the more nefarious characters that we know and started getting knee-deep into being seriously messy, mainly in tandem with an Irish friend of mine, who we'll call Paddy. Before we knew what was happening, we were all still awake and buzzing and watching the sun come up. I'd phoned ahead and managed to get Paddy a ticket for Latitude and we had plans for a *Fear-and-Loathing*-style convoy out into the country-side to attack the festival.

Unfortunately, Paddy's car was a convertible that simply wasn't up to taking the three of us and my bulky guitar, so, being a gentleman, I volunteered to take public transport and meet the two of them there. The journey is a mammoth trek at the best of times and seems to stretch into eternity if one is massively buzzing and still awake from the night before. Bizarrely, I ended up sat round a table with a pair of nuns who were off to administer the 'good news' somewhere. I basically talked their ear off about anything and everything in between less-than-furtive trips to the bathroom to top up my buzz. They smiled sympathetically and I suspect were worldly enough to know exactly what kind of a state I was in, despite my believing I'd fooled them.

I finally arrived at the festival and met up with my London companions and my friends who had successfully made it to the site the night before. The show went surprisingly well, despite my being in something of a state (really, I was, I've seen video footage), which was a relief – I didn't feel particularly big or clever being such a mess. Afterwards Natalie, Paddy and I continued raging long into the day and the evening. One of the features of the festival is the flock of sheep in the field by the entrance. For reasons best known to himself, the farmer has a habit of dyeing them a number of different bright and slightly psychedelic colours. On encountering this sight while very much the worse for wear, I sank to my knees in despair, convinced that I'd finally broken my mind. All in all it was a hell of a lot of fun.

Alas, all these things must come to an end and the following morning I awoke, in Natalie's black (black!) tent, in the burning sunshine, dehydrated to the point of feeling like a raisin – a raisin with a crushing headache and a monstrous comedown to boot. It was around then that I realized I had to get up, tackle the entire public transport debacle in reverse and then continue on to Winchester to play a show. The journey stretched before me like forty days in the wilderness, but a booking is a booking and cancellation was out of the question. Looking back I'm really not sure how I made it, but make it I did and with the help of several strong vodka and Red Bull cocktails I played a decent show in my hometown as well.

The lesson from all of this? Don't book tight schedules around a woman getting her hair cut.

SHOW # 155
Fontaine Palace, Liepāja, Latvia, 4 August 2006

After the success of my first solo foray into Latvia earlier in the year, Edgars and I had decided to put together a more ambitious tour schedule for that part of the world for the summer (when it was less likely that there would be insane amounts of snow around). A run of shows came together, starting at a festival called Fonofest in Cēsis, Latvia, and then heading into Finland, Russia, Lithuania and Estonia. As before, Jamie Grime came with me and the two of us set out eagerly on our next Eastern European adventure.

Fonofest was an absolute blast (even after Jamie managed to destroy himself in a shopping trolley on a BMX course – but that's another story) and afterwards we headed north. In Finland I played a festival by a lake in the ethereal endless light of the northern summer night at Lohja. Then we headed into Russia. This was very much brave new ground for me. For a start, I needed a visa to get into the country, which wasn't the easiest thing to arrange. We took the train to St Petersburg and met up with Vetal, our Russian contact (more on him and Russia in general later) and Denis, his partner in crime. After one show in St Petersburg and two in Moscow, we boarded an overnight sleeper train and headed back to Latvia.

We were the only two Westerners on the train and although Vetal had put us on the train and showed us where to sleep, we still felt out of our element. The other passengers in our carriage were certainly curious as to why two English guys would be there. Apparently there's a much faster but more expensive train that runs the same route in about four hours, as opposed to the sixteen or so we were looking at on the more domestic service, in a battered wooden carriage that had more than a whiff of the Soviet Union about it. Nevertheless, our fellow travellers were not impolite and we ended up having a conversation with a skinny and bold fourteen-year-old Russian kid called Dimitri, who was sleeping on the bunk below us. He told us he was on the final leg of his journey back to Latvia (where he lived) from central Siberia, where he'd been visiting his grandmother. The train journey from her house to Moscow took *three days*. Suddenly our current predicament felt a little easier to handle. Dimitri enjoyed practising his English with us and introduced us to his sister, who was also on the train. We ate our packed suppers and settled down to get some rest.

We were woken at the border crossing at about 6 a.m. the following day by a Russian female border guard checking documentation. If I was writing a Carry On film about Russia I couldn't have made up a more over-the-top stereotypical character. Looking like a man in drag, she was stocky, officious and started shouting at us in a crazy Russian-English hybrid language. She was very excited to find two British passports among her haul. After looking us up and down she practically ran off the train to go tell her uniformed chums in the little wooden hut by the side of the track. After some frenzied consultation, they raced back on to the train and pointed first to Jamie and me and then to our rucksacks and my guitar.

'Buggush!' she roared, with a triumphant smile. Jamie and I were at a loss as to what this might mean, but also mindful of the fact she still had our passports in her pocket. We shrugged in an innocent, trying-to-help kind of way.

'Buggush!' she shouted again and by now pretty much everyone else in the carriage was up and observing us with amused interest. I was starting to get a little panicky – I really don't like dealing with authority figures – and trying to decipher what she was on about. After a few more rounds of this, suddenly it hit me – 'Baggage!' She wanted to inspect our bags. We happily rolled them out and let her have a poke around. She seemed a little disappointed not to find rolls of dollars or stolen Russian state secrets or stowaway Russian child brides or whatever. After stopping to consider her options for a while, she then put her hand out towards us angrily and said, 'Two hunnerd roubles!'

Clearly she was looking for a bribe. Given that I'd been half-expecting to have her strip-searching me by now (and the fact that she was asking for about £4), I was minded to pay it. However, before I could get the last of our currency out of my pocket and start searching for the right denomination, up jumped Dimitri, half-clothed and quivering with fury.

'Nyet!' he cried, the chime of righteousness ringing in his voice. Jamie and I then stood there in dumb disbelief as a semi-naked fourteen-year-old kid harangued the forces of oppression on our behalf. We had no idea what he was saying, but he said it at some length and with a lot of finger pointing. The other people in the carriage were clearly swayed by his oratory and started to cheer individual points. It felt like we were slipping into a scene from some kind of Russian version of *Braveheart*. Finally, in the most unexpected twist of all, when he was finished, panting with the exertions of justice, the guard threw our passports on the bunk, span on her heels, walked off the train and waved us on our way to Latvia.

It turned out that Dimitri, as a patriotic Russian, was incensed at the fact that this woman was essentially confirming the negative stereotype that many in the West have of Russians (or at least their officials) as being corrupt. He had furiously told her not to steal from us and, seeing the mood on the train turning against her, she'd retreated. I've genuinely never seen a skinny kid have such balls in the face of authority and he remains a hero to me.

This little encounter was not, however, the craziest part of this trip. That came a few days later, on what Jamie and I christened 'The Worst Day On Tour Ever'. A day that has yet to be bested.

Our story begins in Estonia.

The previous evening I'd played a show in a bar in Tallinn, the breathtakingly beautiful capital of the northernmost Baltic republic, to a small but enthusiastic crowd, alongside a local hip-hop crew (who were so Aryan it almost hurt to look at them). The plan for the following morning was to take the bus to Riga (in Latvia), where we would meet up with Andzs, our great friend, and together the three of us would drive south over the border into Lithuania, where I would play at a festival. It sounds like a marathon and it was something of a challenge on paper, but the Baltic states are pretty small and we'd planned things to a T, so we were reasonably confident that we'd complete the journey just fine.

The best-laid plans . . . First of all, on arriving at the bus station we were told that the bus was fully booked – despite their website saying you couldn't book seats in advance. The bus was crammed, but we spotted a few spare seats. As this was the only bus going that day we needed to be on it, so we just shoved handfuls of confusing Estonian currency into the driver's hands until he waved us onboard, where we set up camp, hoping not to be moved.

That part of the journey, then, went off OK (apart from getting stopped by a drug patrol with sniffer dogs at the border and me almost losing my passport as we disembarked the bus in Riga). We hiked across town to Andzs's flat and after a short wait headed out of the city in his car, which then duly broke down.

Thankfully Jamie is actually a proper, real-life mechanic and can fix things to a degree that makes MacGyver look like, well, like me really. So after half an hour of scraping and grunting under the bonnet, a fix to a broken pipe (or fuel line? Or was it the radiator? Fuck knows – I don't get on with cars) was hammered together and we set off again, albeit a little slower than before. A few hours on, now in the late afternoon and pretty far behind schedule, we arrived at the border crossing.

Now, there's a fair amount of historical animosity between the Lithuanians and the Latvians, so I'm not sure we were expecting bouquets of flowers from the border guard, but when he took the passports from our car and spotted two British guys and one Latvian, he actually laughed and went and sat back down in his little hut. After a perplexed silence of a few minutes, Andzs went to investigate and see what the score was. Using the little Russian he knew he was able to ascertain that the guy basically thought we were arseholes and we'd need to pay him good to get our passports back.

Andzs was furious (much like Dimitri) but this guy seemed to be made of sterner stuff than the Russian guard and there wasn't an audience either, so I doubt any amount of shouting, whether from someone clothed or not, would have made much of a difference. In the end we caved and said we'd pay him. Unfortunately, he'd resolved to only accept Lithuanian currency, of which we had none, having not yet got into the country. He happily told us about the nearest ATM, which was twenty miles over the border. We dejectedly drove to get some cash, paid him and we finally got our documentation back and set off on our way.

By now we were running seriously late for the festival, so I phoned ahead to the promoter to let him know that we were still en route. He sounded a touch distracted but said that he'd find space on the bill for me whenever I happened to arrive. So, with Jamie at the wheel, we floored the gas and raced south . . .

Whereupon we hit a deer.

Apparently, there's a long-standing problem with deer wandering on to motorways in Lithuania. I'd have thought that the humble fence might be able to do something for them here, but then what do I know? Well, I know this: I was sat in the back seat reading my book when I heard Andzs and Jamie up front scream with pure fear, half a second before there was a massive crunch that threw the car across the road. Things moved in slow motion, but I had no real idea what had happened yet, so I opted for frozen terror rather than anything more practical. Thanks to some heroic wrestling with the wheel by Jamie, we managed to skid to a stop by the side of the road with the car the right way up.

There was a small, uncanny silence, broken only by hissing steam and something, somewhere, dripping. The bonnet had a massive dent on one side, neatly edged with blood and fur. There was no sign of our victim. After a moment's pause, we all started getting out of the car in a half-panicked, half-automatic kind of way. Miraculously, everyone was fine – the car was not. The car, I should mention, belonged to Andzs's brother; in fact, it had only belonged to his brother, after a prolonged bout of saving, for about three days. It was a functional car no more.

The immediate problem facing us now was that we were in Lithuania rather than Latvia – or to put it another way, we were in the country where we had no roadside assistance, versus the land where we did.

After some slightly dazed messing around with mobile phones and Andzs's pidgin Russian, we eventually managed to make the authorities understand that we were at the side of the road in a dead car near a dead deer (Jamie found it and confirmed that it was now decidedly an ex-deer).

Two lackadaisical cops eventually rolled up in their car, smirking furiously, looking for all the world like buddies of our friend at the border crossing. After more torturous linguistic negotiation, it became clear that they were more bothered about the deer than us. After inspecting the carcass and agreeing with Jamie's diagnosis and checking that none of us were in a similar state, they started getting back into their car to leave.

We protested, quite vehemently, that it might not be beyond the realm of possibility for them to help us. This seemed like a novel idea for our uniformed friends, but after some discussion they decided to give us a tow. We were hoping they could tow us back to the border, spit us over the line and let our insurance kick in. No such luck. After ripping out the seatbelt from the back seat, cutting it into a tow rope using a Zippo lighter and fastening our wreck to their squad car, they towed us . . . twenty miles further into Lithuania . . . to a shit-heap motel run by a friend of theirs, who decided that he had special room rates for Latvians and Brits.

After the cops had departed we decided not to stay in the motel (our love for the local culture being somewhat diminished by this time). Andzs called his brother, a man I can only describe as a saint. On hearing of our plight (and that of his new car), he calmly sighed and agreed to come and get us, from his home in Cēsis, a mere four hours' drive away, in his dad's car. We settled down in the remains of his car to await his arrival, scowling through the cracked windshield at the motel owner.

It was clear we would have to let the festival know that there was no way in hell that we were going to make it. However, during a quick phone call to the promoter he told me that the festival itself had been violently shut down by a massive police presence after someone got fatally stabbed. So even if we hadn't hit the deer, we would probably have met those arsehole cops anyway as we'd have likely been arrested at the festival.

Andzs's brother arrived in the middle of the night and wearily roped our wreck to the back of his borrowed vehicle. The four of us then drove, slowly, back to Cēsis, which took about six hours; I remember watching the sun coming up over the horizon. We pulled into his driveway at about 9 a.m., shunted the dead car into a corner and then considered our options.

The thing was, we had another show booked that evening in Liepāja, a coastal town in Latvia about as far away as you could possibly get from Cēsis and still be in the same country. There was, however, a bus, leaving shortly, that would get us there in time for the show. Joy of joys! Jamie, Andzs and I, now moving with the dead automation that comes with lack of sleep and resignation, trudged over to the bus station, bought our tickets and got ready for an eight-hour haul in cramped seats over potholed roads to our final destination.

When we arrived at the venue, Fontaine Palace (welcomed effusively by our old friend Louie Fontaine), I was filled with a kind of euphoria and pure joy at the knowledge that the journey was over and that I could now, finally, play a show. I don't remember much of the actual gig as I was so tired, but I think it went well. The three weary Argonauts retired to the youth hostel where we were booked in, eschewing any afterparty activity, and slept the sleep of the just. It had been one hell of a day and as I say, it has yet to be topped (or I suppose bottomed), in my experience.

I suppose you might think that at some point in all of this Jamie and I questioned the wisdom of this journey, of our efforts, if not our larger life choices. But in all honesty it never even crossed our minds. To be on the move in distant places, seeing new, strange, wonderful things, experiencing new things and encountering new people – that's the stuff of life to me.

SHOW # 158
Camden Barfly, London, UK, 8 August 2006

After the trials and tribulations of Eastern Europe, Jamie and I flew home, dirty, broke, but a hundred times richer in experience. Those shows had come on the back of a long stretch on the train around the UK and now that we were back I had a handful of gigs left to do before I had a definitive break from touring, the first proper one scheduled in the diary since I'd started out on my own. The Camden Barfly is the quintessential toilet venue. I mean that in both a positive and a negative way – it's seen the greats come through its doors and grace the tiny stage, but it's also seen an almost endless stream of no-hopers thrash and howl against failure within its sticky, stinking, graffiti-covered walls. Million Dead played their first show there in 2001 and I'd been back many times since. With that in mind, I arrived back on English soil with the prospect of this show not exactly filling me with any particular sense of anticipation.

Jamie and I went back to his place in Holloway for a shower and a rummage through bags to see if either of us still had any clean clothes. Once you've put your touring baggage down – the ruck-sack and the guitar case – in a familiar place, it can sometimes be the hardest thing to pick them back up again, even if it's only for a handful of shows. It was a beautiful sunny day and sitting on a deckchair in the garden, I wanted nothing more than just to stay there and fall asleep.

As I was dozing, Jamie, who was still sort of acting as a tour manager at this time, called the venue to see what time we needed to head over for sound check and the like and was passingly informed that the show had sold out. Now, don't get me wrong, it's a small room – 150 people or so – and selling it out is a feat that many have accomplished before and since. But this marked the first time in my 'solo' career that I'd sold out a proper venue *in advance*. One hundred and fifty people had bought tickets to come see me play and they'd had the presence of mind to get tickets before I even got to the venue myself.

Newly invigorated, I grabbed my stuff and we headed over. The rest of the night was a joyous blur. Jamie Lenman, my friend from Reuben, did a short acoustic set as support and I played a great fun show. After teaching the crowd the words to the end section, I played 'The Ballad of Me and My Friends' and recorded it for posterity – that's the version that's on the first album. Jay from Nambucca was there, singing with me. At the end of the night we got paid about four times the amount I was expecting (when you sell out a show you get paid more as you generally have a percentage break deal worked out with the venue). I remember standing in the tiny cupboard of a dressing room with Jamie, just laughing at the amount of cash I was holding, which was easily the most money I'd seen to date from playing solo shows. We split it down the middle and headed off into the night for a chaotic party, during which I spent pretty much all of the money, but somehow it seemed worth it.

That show was a real peak for me. For the first time, all the effort put into traipsing around the country was tangibly starting to pay off; in the days before social media became as pervasive as it is now, it was also something of a surprise, albeit a pleasant one. Afterwards I wandered up the country for a few days, to Northampton, Wrexham and Blackpool for a punk-rock festival. But it really felt like the first phase, the real hand-to-mouth days, were coming to a happy end.

SHOWS # 171 / # 172

London Astoria / Proud Galleries, London, UK,
19 October 2006

I spent September of 2006 back in Oxford, at Tarrant's house, with Ben Lloyd, putting together my first album. After all the road covered, the new songs written and the copies of the EP sold, Charlie and I decided that the time had come to make a proper record. I'd been pleased with the recording method the last time round, so we decided to do the same thing again, but spend more time on it.

Most of the time it was Ben and I working on things together. Nigel came in and played the drums in the basement early on, but beyond that I handled most of the instruments. We had some friends come down and join in, playing violin and cello and singing backing vocals. The songs were pretty much everything I had written at the time, aside from what had been on *Campfire Punkrock.* Older tunes like 'The Real Damage' sat alongside newer ideas such as 'Vital Signs' (written in Moscow), 'Back in the Day' (written in a crowded Travelodge in Scotland) and 'Wisdom Teeth'. There were a few songs we recorded that didn't make the grade – 'Sea Legs' didn't seem to fit somehow and 'Back to Sleep' was a reworking of an idea I'd written for my sister when I was about fifteen that somehow still seemed a little childish to me. Everything has since been released one way or another.

I'd done a few sporadic shows throughout the time spent in the studio – among them a gig in London with Dashboard Confessional and the Farmageddon festival in Cambridgeshire. But in essence I hadn't been touring properly for over a month. Once all the finishing touches for the album were in place, it was a great relief to set out back to London with my guitar in hand, ready for a new stretch on the road – but this time slightly bigger, slightly better.

This particular night I played two shows. The first was at the Astoria, a venue that looms large in both my musical history and the musical history of London. It was the main 2,000-capacity room in the capital and over the years I'd seen hundreds of bands play there, from punk to indie to spoken word and back again. Million Dead had played one appalling and two great shows there; this was to be my first solo appearance on the hallowed stage. I was opening a show for a band called The Automatic, who had invited me on tour (more on that later). This was the biggest solo gig I'd played to date by some distance, even though I was the opening act of four. I remember being a little nervous as to whether what I was doing would translate properly on that kind of scale. In the end it went well, I had a good show. Despite being on my own onstage and being almost completely unknown, I managed to make some new friends; in fact, the novelty of a solo acoustic act on a more rock-oriented bill seemed to work in my favour. Afterwards I packed my things and jumped on the Tube to head north.

The second show of the evening was in Camden at a venue called Proud Galleries, an arty space in the centre of the old Stables Market. This occasion was set up as Xtra Mile Recordings' birthday party. I came rushing through the door and had time to dump my belongings, grab a drink and tune up my guitar before it was time to play again – this time to a much smaller but more receptive crowd. A photo from the show graces the inside cover of *Sleep Is for the Week*.

After finishing my second show of the evening, I had a quick drink with friends before heading back down south to The Automatic's official afterparty, which was in a high-class, rock 'n' roll hotel, the K West, in west London. Going from the one environment to the other, from close friends to industry hangers-on and wannabes, felt a little disconcerting. But I felt ready to take on that other, more phoney, more self-obsessed world and defeat it on my own terms.

A very drunk Paul Weller was at the party and tried to steal my hat and kiss me.

Weird night.

SHOW # 175
Bristol Academy, Bristol, UK, 22 October 2006

The tour I did opening for The Automatic in autumn 2006 was, I suppose, one of my breaks. I often get asked what my *big break* in music was, as if there was one binary moment when I went from being a broke and hungry unknown to a bloated figure of the establishment. I've never really felt like the music business works like that, not for me personally or, for the most part, for other people either. There's so much work and dedication, so much sweat and tears that goes into making a successful career that it seems crass in a way to try and pin the whole thing on one moment.

Having said that, this tour did me enormous favours and definitely advanced me along my path a fair distance. The Automatic were, at the time, probably the biggest indie rock band in the UK. Their radio hit 'Monster' was everywhere and this tour was their moment when they smashed into the public consciousness, playing to thousands of hyperactive kids every night for a few weeks. It so happened that the members of the band included in their number some Million Dead fans who were aware of what I was up to now. Against the wishes of their booking agent and management, they managed to get me a small opening slot on a bill that already had two other bands on it and gave me a bunk on their tour bus as well. I remain eternally grateful.

The tour was a big step up for me, both in terms of the size of venues I was playing at and crowds I was playing to (even as the first on) and the level of music-industry people I was dealing with. In Million Dead we'd started bumping up against the bigger league of players, the booking agents and managers and major label executives and so on, so I had some foretaste of it all, but not much. This was the tour where I started thinking that maybe I should get myself a booking agent to represent me – partly to be taken more seriously by the other players, but also so I didn't have to deal with the bullshit directly myself. I suppose you could argue that was a cowardly approach to the matter, or even that I should have stuck with booking my own shows through DIY promoters. However, I've never made any secret of my ambition – though I'd define it as being the ambition to play to more people, but never to compromise along the way. By doing things this way I've been able to take my music all round the world, to many more people, but I can honestly say I've never had to do anything I didn't think was the right thing and never had my arm twisted artistically or otherwise. I'm pretty proud of that fact.

Anyway, enough testy self-defence; back to the story. The tour was great. I finally felt like I was starting to climb back towards the level that I'd been at with my old band (though I was by no means there yet). The Bristol show, a few days into the tour, was particularly memorable. I was playing pretty early after doors, but there was a crew of die-hard Automatic fans who were coming to every show who had started to twig that I was someone they wanted to watch, so they'd started making sure they were there for my set every night. Their enthusiasm went a long way to winning other people in the crowd over as well and on the merch stand after my set I made a lot of new friends.

After the Bristol show, Pennie, The Automatic's keyboard player, and I sat up late in the back lounge of the bus talking. The drive was only over to Cardiff, a matter of an hour at most. I'd just got a CD from Ben Lloyd with the finished mixes of my debut album on it and as we got drunker I was *that guy* and insisted on playing it back for my friend. He was effusive in his praise and much inebriated hugging took place. As we got more intoxicated, we ended up climbing on to the roof of the bus as it rolled along the motorway, clinging on to the sides and whooping with fear and delight. Once we arrived at our destination, the two of us sat up there with a bunch of laughing-gas canisters and some balloons, inhaling the gas to get high and light-headed until the first murmurs of dawn started creeping into the edge of our conversation and we decided to finally get into our bunks and sleep. A night to remember.

SHOW # 197
Vibe Bar, London, UK, 26 November 2006

Despite my new-found dash of professionalism, I was still prone to the occasional lapse into drink- and drug-fuelled chaos at this time: I was not yet totally cleaned up. After the Automatic tour finished I went back to my old routine of spot shows here and there around the country, joined up by looping meanderings on the UK train system, although at this point there were a few more people coming to the shows. In late November I went down to Brixton for the evening to play at a regular south London night called Sadder Days, an alt-country affair run by my friend Adam of The Tailors.

It's worth recounting how I met Adam and the role he played

in my thinking about music. A few years before, while still in Million Dead, I'd been in Nambucca for a pub-quiz evening. My team had come joint-first with a group of country musicians, the aforementioned Tailors, who were all dressed and built like lumberjacks. Jay, who was running the night, decided that the tie-breaker for the prize pot (£100) would be an arm-wrestle, on stage, in front of the assembled quiz crowd. Being the only guy on my team I was compulsorily volunteered for the contest, despite the fact that I am certifiably rubbish at arm-wrestling (I do pub quizzes instead, OK?) and the fact that Adam, for the other team, clearly wasn't. So it was that I found myself being swiftly humiliated, not once but three times (Adam charitably suggested we do best of three after my first total defeat), in front of a sizeable crowd. Adam, being the good soul that he is, decided it was only fair that we split the winnings over the bar and so we spent the evening drinking and talking about music. After revealing something of a new-found interest in Springsteen and Neil Young, Adam grabbed a guitar and we ended up seeing in the dawn sat on the roof trading songs by The Lemonheads, Counting Crows, Gram Parsons and Townes Van Zandt. I've learned an awful lot about music from Adam and owe him something of a debt.

So on that night in November, I headed down to Adam's event. At the time I was even talking to him about me joining The Tailors, as they'd just lost a member. In the end it didn't work out, though I still hope we'll write some music together someday.

The gig was a lot of fun. I played to a crowd made up of pretty much every alt-country enthusiast in the capital and it went down well. After The Tailors headlined the night, we ended up retiring to Chad's house, Chad being their Canadian guitarist. We also had my friend Cahir, of the band Fighting With Wire, in tow (a maniac from Derry in Northern Ireland who is on my crew these days). The night spiralled ever onwards towards the dawn. I managed to get myself mugged by a small gang of local kids while popping out to get more party supplies, losing my wallet and my phone (as well as having my face beaten roundly in), another dumb middle-class kid falling foul of Brixton in the middle of the night. But the party kept rolling. In the end, we had to concede that it was definitely the next day and The Tailors had themselves an afternoon show in Shoreditch at Vibe Bar, so we all piled into a van and drove east for the gig.

En route it was decided that I would play a few songs of my own and also that I would play with The Tailors for the day as well. I've always been the kind of player who learns other people's songs fast and I knew (and still know) a whole bunch of their material, so it wasn't too much of a challenge for me to slip in with some rhythm guitar and backing vocals. The show was in a yard by the side of Brick Lane, the stage being the side of a trailer open to the elements. We were all feeling pretty terrible by the time the show came around, despite copious amounts of vodka and Red Bull, and I'm not sure we acquitted ourselves with much finesse. There weren't so many people there anyway, so I think we got away with it.

After the shambles of a show, we sat in the afternoon sun contemplating our fate and when and how any of us would actually get any sleep. Cahir went to the bathroom and ended up escaping through the back door of the bar to go home, rather than concede his weakness before the group – a classic Irish departure. The Tailors thanked me for my participation and prepared to head back south. I, however, had to make it up to Harlow, just outside north-east London, to play a show of my own at The Square, a legendary venue that has been there for many years and that has played host to most touring acts in its time. This fact had slightly slipped my mind and I had to borrow some cash off friends to even get there, my wallet being currently in the hands of some crack-addled arsehole. So with weary resignation I headed out to the station and to Essex. In the end the evening show went fine and I managed to find somewhere to sleep the sleep of the dead for a good fourteen hours or so.

It's important to me to mention that I didn't spend the entirety of my time at this point in my life getting wrecked and partying. Or at least that wasn't my sole motivation. Through all of this the desire to play, to make music, to communicate, was the burning beacon on the distant cliff-top that kept me moving forwards, that inspired me to get off my broken, drunken behind and get the train to the next show to play. The shows, far from being a means to an end, were in fact the only thing that pulled me through my tendency to self-obliteration. They still are.

SHOW # 200

Meonstoke C of E School, Meonstoke, near Winchester, UK, 19 December 2006

It feels slightly strange writing up this show immediately after the intoxicated mayhem of the previous entry. Suffice to say, I didn't mix that kind of behaviour with this show – I did have a good while off in between to sort my head out!

My mother was a state primary-school teacher for forty years. She taught at the local village school, at the end of the road from the house where I grew up, in the small Hampshire village of Meonstoke, not far from Winchester. She taught me recorder as a five-year-old (not much of which actually stayed with me, it has to be said). In the intervening years she'd become a full-time teacher there and one of her longer-term projects was to get me to come in and play for her class.

Obviously this wasn't going to be a normal gig for me, playing songs about love, loss, drinking, etc. I suppose it was more a kind of exposition of my instruments, aimed at a primary-school audience. So I gathered up a banjo, a guitar, a mandolin and a harmonica and headed down to the school. I have to say, after all the shows I'd done up to this date, and for that matter since then, this was about the most nervous I've ever actually been to play before a crowd. I figured that sharp, barbed quips and 'your mum' jokes weren't the most appropriate responses to being heckled by six-year-olds. I've never been all that confident around small children, so I was really quite worried as I set up my stuff in the main hall, waiting for the kids to come in.

In the end it was a lot of fun – I played them as many different noises as I could make with my little array of instruments, from fingerpicking to thrash guitar and everything I could think of in between. They loved it. After playing a few safely conservative traditional tunes, I was even called back for an encore of sorts, deciding to play some of the more lyrically obtuse early Dylan songs that I know. Afterwards a number of the kids announced they'd decided to get guitar lessons on the strength of my performance, so I guess maybe I did something right.

SHOW # 201
Club j'Est, Moscow, Russia, 31 December 2006

For New Year's Eve 2006, I wanted to do something a little different. New Year's Eve always strikes me as being an amateur's night for partying. Those people dedicated to the cause of inebriation don't need an excuse as flimsy as a calendar rollover to get thoroughly, insanely wasted – that can happen on a Tuesday if you want it to (well, a Tuesday into a Wednesday and maybe a Thursday too). My friend Craig has a theory that the real, dedicated drinkers are the ones at the bar on 2 January. I'd spent the last few New Year's Eves getting wrecked with friends in London, which is fun, but it's always expensive and after a while it starts getting a little predictable.

An email arrived from Vetal, my friend in Moscow, asking if I fancied coming back to Russia to play a show on 31 December at the venue where he worked, called Club j'Est. I'd been there before in the summer with Jamie, during our manic trip around Eastern Europe. The first trip to Russia had been totally incredible. It felt so good to be somewhere that was decidedly un-European, somewhere far away from the world I know and feel comfortable in and still be playing songs. Russia is a fascinating country and the history and politics geek in me had revelled in the chance to see the place first-hand and educate myself. We'd met indoctrinated ultra-nationalist punk kids and super-cynical BBC-addicted indie kids, crazed Chechen veterans, blank-faced authoritarian cops, ageing alcoholic venue owners and everyone in between. While the handful of shows I'd played had been great, it was interesting to be in a place that didn't feel entirely safe for English boys like me and Jamie. I'd really enjoyed myself and had been thinking about going back as soon as possible, so when the email arrived, I called Jamie and we both jumped at the opportunity.

Vetal met us at the airport. He's tall, gangly and gregarious and is something of a legend to many bands that have done a DIY tour of Russia. He's a great promoter, that much is obvious, but he's also arguably several cards short of a full deck. He has a taste for home-knitted Christmas jumpers that defies any rational explanation. His collection of music is miraculously encyclopedic, for someone living where he does. His hair is flat-out insane. And his sense of humour is utterly bizarre – on our previous visit, he'd seen Jamie's spoof 'Beaver King' (in the style of the Burger King logo) shirt and laughed until he couldn't stand up. This was *before* anyone had explained to him the possible double meaning of the word 'beaver'. Once that information had been imparted, his brain pretty much had a meltdown and he didn't speak for about two days. Jamie gave him the shirt as a present.

New Year's Eve in Russia is quite the occasion. Being a largely Orthodox Christian part of the world, Vetal explained that in Russia they are culturally given to celebrating Easter much more than Christmas, which seems to pass pretty much unremarked. Add to that the eighty years of state-imposed atheism and Yuletide is an almost total nonevent. The only party of note at the end of December is New Year's Eve, so people out there tend to celebrate it with gusto.

Now, it's a well-known stereotype that Russians enjoy a touch too much vodka. I have to say that on the basis of our first trip out there in the summer that this is largely not the case with the younger generation. There were plenty of sozzled old people wandering around, but Jamie and I had been relieved by the reticence of our hosts when it came to alcohol, as compared with the horror stories we'd heard. They actually seemed to have something of a bee in their bonnet about the stereotype, resolving not to be ruined by drink as their parents, or maybe grandparents, had been. However, all of this admirably rational consideration seems to go right out the window when it comes to New Year's Eve. This is something Jamie and I discovered the hard way.

On the night itself, it was decided that I'd play two sets – one just before midnight, the other after. On paper, this seemed fine and the first set passed without much incident, the full room of Russians seeming to enjoy themselves immensely. So far so good. However, after sitting back down at the table with Jamie, Vetal and Denis, we started drinking properly. At first it was just 'sticks' of vodka –

long strips of wood with holes bored into them all along the length, with a shot glass full of vodka in each hole, up to about twelve or so. These would arrive at the table to much cheering and be demolished by the assembled company pretty quickly, in between more cautiously sipped beers. Next up, however, I was introduced to the wonders of Yorsh. Yorsh involves taking a full pint of beer, sipping an inch or so of the liquid off the top and then dropping a shot of vodka into it, before downing the entire cocktail as fast as possible. The *coup de grâce* is the smashing of the empty glassware on the floor, while shouting 'Yorsh!' (and feeling slightly unstable). Denis demonstrated the technique to me and I rather meekly protested that it would only take about one and a half of these things to finish me off properly. This was weighed up by the board and judged to be 'pussy talk', so rather many more than that went down the hatch.

Things get a little hazy from this point onwards. I have vague memories of my second set, including an English friend (Sam McCarthy), who randomly happened to be there, making a rush for the stage and singing a song with me. After that, nothing much at all remains in my recollections. I have, however, been informed that the following took place, much to my personal, and arguably national, shame.

Sometime after the second set had wound up, I decided that the time had come for me to have myself a lie-down – sometimes when I'm hammered, a homing beacon of sorts kicks in and I just know that I have to get horizontal as soon as possible to ward off impending disaster. In a genius piece of drunk logic, I realized that, it being winter in Moscow, the cloakroom was packed full of big, fluffy, warm coats and jackets. So in I snuck. I made myself quite an impressive bed from the assorted clothes that I found and drifted off into the land of nod.

However, the evening's celebrations came to an end, as all such good times must, and the people in the club started heading for the cloakroom to get their coats and set out for home. They were dismayed to find a wasted Englishman sleeping soundly on their garments, but in their politeness tried to get them out from under me without disturbing my slumber. Apparently, I wasn't having any of that and started to try to fight off the intruders who were stealing my bedclothes. This was made all the more awkward by the fact that, though most of them didn't speak enough English to understand me, they all knew who I was having just seen me play two sets. Eventually, poked and prodded one too many times, I demanded to know where Jamie was, announcing that if he was there I'd leave quietly and let everyone get their coats too.

Jamie, however, had already left the club, adopted by no less than three young Russian beauties who were taking him back to their flat to have their wicked way with him. On hearing that I had been left alone by my compadre, I jumped to my feet, rushed into the club, leaped up on to the bar and shouted 'Communist bastards! I'll fight you all!' while rather pathetically waving a plastic cup. At this point, Vetal and Denis decided that for my own safety the time had come to intervene and they tackled me off the bar and into a waiting taxi, which took me home to sleep and wake up feeling quite perfectly appalling, both physically and morally.

The next morning, we awoke slowly and remorsefully to the slightly alarming news that Jamie was still missing in action. As exciting for his libido as the turn of events was, he was now somewhere in Moscow with three girls who did not speak English or know either of our hosts. The language barrier can be pretty formidable out there and with hostile cops and a different alphabet to contend with, wandering around unsupervised can actually be pretty dangerous. So we were concerned. Sometime in the afternoon, my phone finally rang and it was Jamie. In the event, he'd made it back to their flat but had been copiously ill (thanks to all the Yorsh) in, or rather on, their kitchen before they'd managed to make it to the bedroom and when he did make it there he fell asleep. He woke late and hungover to three less-than-impressed Russian girls urging him, in unfamiliar language but unmistakeable tone, to get the fuck out of the flat.

Operation Get Jamie Home now kicked in in earnest. Keeping him on the line, we told him to walk around until he found a Metro station. He succeeded in doing this pretty quickly. Then Vetal took over and instructed him on where to find the name of the station he was at. He did this, but there was the problem of the different alphabet. So Jamie tried to describe the letters to me, 'Backwards R, N, kind of a square thing, backwards N . . .' and I attempted to write down the letters as best I could. Eventually Vetal and Denis figured out where he was. From that point it was fairly easy to explain to him where he was on the Metro map and then direct him on how to get back to where we were. Finally, we were all reunited sometime in the early evening, hungover and relieved, just before I had to play another show at a club called Bilingua, where I got mistaken for Edward Norton by some Russian hookers touting for business. But that's another story.

SHOW # 209
Nambucca, London, UK, 15 January 2007

After the Russian New Year, I headed back to the UK to prepare for another exciting milestone – the release of my first proper album. *Sleep Is for the Week* had come together nicely and we'd released 'Vital Signs' as a free download on Christmas Day. The album title came from my friend Lex – it was her favourite party catchphrase, usually accompanied by 'Eating's cheating'. We were all set for an early January release. It felt good to get a proper body of work out there, as the EP had been around for a while and it was nearly two years since Million Dead released their last full-length.

To celebrate the release day, we decided on a typically over-the-top promotional scheme. There used to be a chain of record shops in the UK called Fopp (remember record shops? Anyone? No?) that had four branches in central London. It was decided that instead of just doing the one in-store performance to promote the new album, I'd do one in all four of the Fopp stores, before heading up north to Nambucca for a private (ish) release party. We set up a deal whereby if people came to all four of the in-stores, they'd get an invite to the party in the evening.

So we set out; five shows in one day. The first show was fun, not perhaps the busiest gig I've ever played, but satisfyingly well-attended for a show in a shop on a Monday morning. The film *This Is Spinal Tap* has given every musician everywhere an enduring fear of the in-store appearance; like many other things in the film, it rings painfully true. We're always convinced that no one is going to show up, leaving us sat behind a desk like chumps with a record-label guy telling us he did 'too much promotion'. Anyway, as the day rolled on, more and more people started joining the party and the pre-gig stops in nearby pubs were generally attended by people coming to the show, so a real sense of camaraderie built up as the day went on. At this point in my career the line between fans and friends was pretty blurred, given the small numbers involved and my tendency to hang out with everyone after the show, whether selling my own merch or not. So there was a friendly vibe to the day.

Finally, feeling a little drained, we finished the last in-store show at the Tottenham Court Road branch, before telling pretty much everyone where the party was and jumping into a cab to head up to my old stomping ground, Nambucca, accompanied by old friends and new who were generally clutching newly purchased copies of the album. The evening was fun, although I was totally exhausted and didn't play so much at the last stop – I let Jay (Beans On Toast) and Sam (Get Cape. Wear Cape. Fly) handle most of the live performance duties. I can't remember where I ended up sleeping that night, but I do recall feeling more and more like a proper, established musician now that I had an actual album available in real-life shops.

SHOW # 212
Port Mahon, Oxford, UK, 20 January 2007

As well as preparing for the release of the new album through the medium of in-store shows and other such promotional activity, I'd also been preparing for a new tour – a tour that was going to be something slightly different from anything I'd done before. A full UK headline tour, with a backing band in tow.

Through the guys in Dive Dive I'd met Joanna Ashmore, a booking agent who worked (at the time) at ITB, a pretty sizeable agency. She booked their shows and expressed an interest in talking to me about my future plans. At the same time, I'd been thinking about how to put together a band to play with live. The obvious first port of call was to talk to Nigel, Ben and Tarrant. They were receptive to the idea and after much toing and froing we settled upon a scheme. We would do a full UK headline tour to promote my new album, booked by Joanna, featuring Dive Dive as the main support act and also as my band.

Ever since this little project began I'd had the idea of playing with a band. Springsteen's E Street Band and Neil Young's Crazy Horse were obvious inspirations. But at the same time it's not like

I'd only ever been inspired by solo artists – Counting Crows, The Weakerthans and many more had always featured heavily in my thinking about music. As much as I love playing live on my own and as much as that remains the skeleton of what I do and I will always return to it, it can be quite limiting to have just the one instrument on stage, both artistically and sonically. In the Dive Dive guys I'd found three excellent players for electric guitar, bass and drums. I also wanted to have some organ and piano parts in the mix as well (they were on the recordings, after all). Jamie Stuart, the fourth member of the band, gamely volunteered to play some keys in the set, even though they're not, to be charitable, his main instrument. So it was that the first version of a band came together. The tour was booked and on sale. We even had an advert in the *NME*.

We thought it might be an idea to have a warm-up show of some kind, to test the band out on a real stage in front of a real audience before departing on the tour proper. This is when Equitruck came up. Truck Festival is a long-running institution on the Oxford music scene, an independent, underground and thoroughly awesome annual bash. Around this time, some of the people involved came up with the idea of having a show called Equitruck, which would be held exactly half a year away from the festival proper. Seeing as the Dive Dive guys are such pillars of the Oxford scene, it made perfect sense for Deadly (the promoter) to ask them to play the show. And as he knew we were working together, he asked me to join as well. Hey presto, we had our perfect opportunity for our first ever full-band set.

The Port Mahon is a fantastic, if cramped, venue in the Cowley district of Oxford. The show was an all-dayer, running from midday to the bitter end, and we were on halfway up the bill. We had to load our equipment on to the small stage through a crowded room in a very short space of time. It'd been a long time since I'd done a gig that involved anything more than my acoustic guitar and it'd been a very long time since I'd loaded a band's worth of equipment on to a stage in such DIY settings. It felt like coming home, reminding me of hardcore shows that Million Dead, or even Kneejerk, had played many years back. The show, as I remember it, went off OK – there were no dramatic fuck-ups, but perhaps we were not yet the tightest band in showbiz. Nevertheless, this stands in time as something of a milestone for me and afterwards we were ready and hungry for the road.

SHOW # 234
The Borderline, London, UK, 13 February 2007

The tour was a blast – twenty-two shows in roughly the same number of days, with my old friend Jay (Beans On Toast) in tow as well. We'd been up and down the UK, playing to crowds of between fifty and 150 people a night. We'd had great shows in Aberdeen, Manchester and Leeds; empty shows in Carlisle, Coventry and Bristol. I'd played solo dates at Keele University and in London, and we'd played possibly the hottest show in all history in Cambridge. We'd been gelling more as a band as time went by. I'd been selling T-shirts and records at the merch booth each night, making new friends and a bit of extra cash to pay for the petrol to get to the next town. Dive Dive had been killing it as well, while Jay had decided to see if he could score drugs in every town on the run (with some serious degree of success), meaning that he was pretty broken by the end of it all.

The London show was scheduled for The Borderline, a historic venue in Soho. It was here that bands like Counting Crows and Rage Against the Machine had made their live debuts on our small island. I'd been to see a lot of bands there myself over the years – in particular I remember seeing Josh Rouse there, a blinding show that turned my head musically as to what one man and a guitar could achieve.

The venue officially holds 275 people. We arrived and loaded in, a little drained from the previous three weeks of charging around the country, but ready for a grand finale. Ticket sales were healthy – it was already scheduled to be the biggest crowd of the tour, and you never knew, more people might turn up on the night too! In the event they did and I remember that the final count was 273 people in the room, although Joanna insisted that this meant we could tell people it had sold out. Jay and then Dive Dive played great sets and we prepared to go on one more time.

Two things stick in my mind from that show. We were opening the sets with me playing 'The Real Damage' on my own, which meant that I'd take the stage solo at the start of the show. As I walked on that night, right there in the front row was my dad, who I hadn't seen for a long time. That was pretty strange for me, not least because the song 'Father's Day' featured prominently in the set. It didn't ruin things for me, but it threw me off a little right at the start. I'm not sure I played 'Damage' particularly well, I wasn't feeling as focused as I wanted to. But, in a perhaps slightly clichéd way, I was overtaken by a desire to prove myself, here on my own turf. My performance of 'Father's Day' that night was pretty savage, as I remember it. I didn't see him after the show.

The other thing I remember from the evening was my very own Bob-Dylan-in-Manchester-Free-Trade-Hall moment. Halfway through the set, someone in the crowd started yelling 'Lose the band!' at the top of their drunk voice. Much as I feel everyone is entitled to their opinion, it was pretty rude in the context and a series of devastating quips (hey, I'm telling the story here) put them back in their place. With the benefit of hindsight, taking the comment a little more seriously, this was obviously a time of transition for me, getting used to playing with other people on stage, honing that sound, fine-tuning the machine that would eventually grow into The Sleeping Souls. People are entitled to prefer my ragged solo fumblings from 2006; but I knew where I was heading and what I wanted to sound like and I wasn't going to be distracted from the path by heckling. After all, plenty of people told me not to play solo acoustic music after Million Dead split.

All that aside, it was the biggest headline show of my career to date and I judged it to be a success. I knew that the band needed more work from all of us to bring it up to the standard that I had in my head, but for a first foray into that territory, I was satisfied. After London we played a few more shows, finishing up tired and triumphant in Oxford's Zodiac (the old one). The beginnings of a new template had been laid out and new people had been successfully integrated into the master plan.

SHOW # 239
Bar Mary, Porvoo, Finland, 18 February 2007

After the UK tour was done, I took precisely zero days off before heading on my next jaunt, to Finland. I'd been there once before, on my summer adventure with Jamie in 2006, when we'd played that small festival in Lohja. We'd had fun, though perhaps I hadn't broken the Finnish music market completely. I was keen to go back again, although I must confess to something of an ulterior motive. In Riga, Latvia, at the end of our trip, I'd met a Finnish girl who I was rather taken with. We stayed in touch and I'd been looking for an excuse to get out to her home country in the hope of seeing her again. After hitting up some vague contacts in that part of the world, I managed to get a few shows (well, two) in the diary. After bidding a temporary farewell to the band I got on a plane with my guitar and headed north-east.

The first show was literally a case of me being sat on a speaker in the corner of a trendy joint in Lohja. I can't say I remember it as being the most rewarding gig of my life – most people seemed to be a little confused by my presence and slightly annoyed that I was making their conversation harder. But my pretty Finnish girl was with me, so it felt good to be there all the same. The next day we took a coach heading east, to Porvoo, a small but fairly gentrified town on the route to the Russian border. The gig that night was set for a place called Bar Mary, run by an eccentric chap called Jocke, who lived nearby in a houseboat that was up on blocks by the side of the frozen river. Speaking of that, it was unbelievably cold in Finland in February. I know that sounds like an obvious thing to say, but God damn it, I'd never felt the insides of my thighs freeze before or my nose hairs sticking together with ice as I breathed in.

Jocke kindly met me and my lady friend off the coach in his van and drove us into the gorgeously quaint town to check out the bar before the show. It was then that disaster struck. My guitar was in its battered case in the back of the van. This was the guitar that I got for my sixteenth birthday – it was nothing particularly special, a Jim Deacon as I recall, but a guitar that had travelled many miles with me, with which I had played every show to date, which I had restrung and cleaned and patched and polished countless times and which was very close to my heart. Jocke took us inside, leaving the van in the street, and gave us a quick tour of the bar. We then took a minute to sit at the bar and try a traditional Finnish shot of alcohol to warm our frozen cockles. When we went out to the van at first sight everything seemed normal, but as we got in to drive back to Jocke's place to get some food, he glanced over his shoulder into the back and said the fateful words: 'Hey man, where's your guitar gone? It was right here, wasn't it?'

It was . . . or at least it had been. Now there was no sign of it and on closer inspection the back door of the van was slightly ajar, with the telltale scratch marks of a crowbar around the lock. In the ten minutes that we'd been inside the venue, someone had come along, jimmied open the back door and taken my instrument – my friend.

Panic set in, and not just for me. Jocke kept insisting 'There is no crime in Porvoo!', which, to be fair, seemed like a reasonable statement. The chocolate-box houses and neat driveways gave the place an air of affluence and there didn't seem to be any rough estates on the edge of the town. On the other hand, the facts were staring us in the face. Jocke got his phone out and started driving around. In a matter of half an hour he had either visited or spoken to the owner of every bar in Porvoo, telling them to be on the lookout for anyone carrying a bulky guitar case covered in stickers. He also spoke to the local police chief and even managed to get a journalist from the local paper to meet us back at his place to conduct an interview, which would be run in the next day's edition, complete with a description of the lost guitar.

In the end, the hunt was fruitless – I've never seen the guitar since, much to my sadness. Apparently, the one source of criminal activity in the town is due to its proximity to Russia. Long-distance truck drivers, crossing the border regularly, pick up stolen goods and bus them into the markets in Moscow or St Petersburg and come back the other way with cheap manufactured Russian speed. So I guess my old faithful axe got sold in some Muscovite car-boot sale and who knows where she ended up. I still think about her every now and again and hope that at least someone's playing her.

The rest of the day had something of a pall over it, understand-ably. Jocke managed to source another guitar for me to use at the show, so I did in fact play for a decent-sized and enthusiastic local crowd – he'd done his work as a promoter. Afterwards, we stayed the night in his bizarre houseboat and in the morning I got up early and walked on the ice of the frozen river in the snow-muffled silence, something I'd not done before. It was a strangely detached experience and helped me come to terms with the loss.

As much as I try not to be materialistic about things – after all, we take nothing with us when we die – it's still pretty hard, as a musician, losing your old friend. Shortly after we headed back to the airport. I said farewell to my Finnish lady and I don't think I ever saw her again either; we both knew it wasn't working out by then. In travelling around the whole time, I often feel like I'm leaving little things by the roadside as I go – whether it's a washbag left in a hotel (I always lose those), an instrument in Finland or a girl who wanted something more fixed than I could offer. Each one is a small thing, survivable in itself, but I do occasionally wonder what they all add up to over time. Maybe one day I'll do a world tour of trying to find the things I left behind. It'd be a long trip.

SHOW # 245
Side Cinema, Newcastle, UK, 2 March 2007

After getting home from Finland, I'd headed south to Brighton to meet up with my friends The Holloways. At the time they were indie darlings, riding around the UK on their bus playing triumphantly packed-out shows. They'd asked me to come and play with them in the Republic of Ireland and of course I'd said yes. But there was a gap in my schedule before those shows started, so I ended up getting on their tour bus a few days early to hang out, party and hitch a ride over the sea. The gigs were fun, if a little messy, and I also had an interesting time buying myself a new guitar in Stoke-on-Trent. I rang directory enquiries, got the number of a guitar shop and called it, only to find out that the owner of the business had died and I'd managed to ring up in the middle of a meeting about funeral arrangements. Hungover as I was, this was not the news I wanted or expected to hear. I managed to get one in the end, something cheap and nasty to tide me over until I could sort a more permanent replacement for my missing baby.

After the Irish shows were done, including a short headline run in Northern Ireland, I was homeward bound, but decided to make one more stop on my way back to Winchester, this time in Newcastle, for a special occasion. The previous summer, my friend Rachel Brook (the Rachel whose house I had played a show at just over a year ago) had accompanied me on tour for a short while, armed with a video camera. This was back in the heart of the trains, floors and rucksack days. She'd been a trooper, putting up with my wayward behaviour for a week or so. She had edited down the footage that she shot into a short film called *All About the Destination*. After some consideration, Xtra Mile decided it would be good to release as a DVD, documenting the very early stages of my time as a solo artist. We put the package together, with extras including music videos (made both by me and by fans), live footage and more, and it was set for release.

To celebrate the release, Rachel decided to have a screening of the film at a local Newcastle cinema, the Side, followed by a short show and talk by me. I agreed, albeit slightly nervously. This was me out of my element, under the microscope, and I hadn't yet seen the film, so I wasn't sure how I came across. I took the train over to Newcastle with trepidation.

In the event, the film was great, although I found it slightly hard to watch. I'm less guarded when talking, even on camera, than I sometimes think I am and it was surreal to sit in a theatre with a bunch of strangers watching myself be quite personal, quite revealing, on a massive screen. It was honest though and people enjoyed it. I'm glad that Rachel made the film and that it's still out there for people to see. It gives an impression of what those days were like for me, even if, by the time it was released, they were starting to fade into the distance and I was moving on.

The other reason why this show is of note for me, is that it was the 245th solo gig that I played, in about a year and a half. That's noteworthy because, in our entire career, Million Dead played 245 shows.* In a way we achieved a lot more in that time than I had up to this point. However, it seems strange to me that we played so few shows. We toured as much as we could at the time and it felt like a lot back then. But here I was, passing the previous high score already. It was one of many small steps I took that made me feel like I was starting to emerge from under the shadow of my past – not that I'm in any way ashamed or down on what we did; it's just that I don't want to be defined by it for the rest of my life. Now, of course, I've done so much more than the band ever did. But at the time, this was something worth marking.

SHOW # 247
The Sanctuary, San Antonio, TX, USA, 14 March 2007

For a kid born and brought up in England, listening to rock 'n' roll, skate punk and hardcore and playing in bands, America looms large in the imagination. There's something magical about the idea of being on tour in the USA; but at the same time, the vast

---

* I have since worked out that Million Dead played 247 shows; but I didn't know this at the time.

country that has exhausted so many of my countrymen before me is a slightly daunting prospect. Million Dead made it over a handful of times for one-off showcase gigs, never for a tour. I have to confess that, at this time, I really didn't know much about the place (not that it stopped me, like many a petulant armchair theorist before me, from having strong opinions about it). But there had been a plan in the works for a while to get me over the pond and now the time had finally come.

I met Jonah Matranga on a tour of the UK in 2004, though of course I knew who he was already, as he'd played in bands like Far, New End Original and Gratitude. He was opening a bill that included Million Dead and Funeral for a Friend, playing solo in front of an emo and hardcore crowd with just his acoustic guitar. I remember at the time thinking he had balls to be doing what he was doing and though it didn't occur to me until much later, there was probably some subconscious note-taking going on deep in my brain. We'd met up again in the UK for a few shows after the demise of my band and in the summer of 2006 we'd released a split vinyl through Welcome Home Records and Xtra Mile. After all that, it made sense to talk to Jonah about the possibility of me going over to the USA for a run of shows and, as always, Jonah was nothing but helpful.

A gazillion emails later, we had ourselves a bona fide plan. We pencilled in a run of dates for the two of us and a friend of Jonah's called Joshua English – a songwriter originally from Boston who now lived in Portland, Oregon – who had been in the hardcore band Six Going On Seven. We'd start in Texas, with the South By Southwest (SXSW) festival, head west across the desert and then drive up the coast to the Pacific Northwest. Simple.

The start of the tour was complicated a little thanks to some financial hitches. Flights into Austin TX, home of SXSW, around the time of the festival (or anywhere nearby) are prohibitively expensive. I can't remember the exact details, but in the end the easiest and most affordable way to start the tour was for me to fly to Oregon on the West Coast, where I met Josh for the first time, at the airport. He's very tall and has a lot of tattoos and one of the driest senses of humour I've ever encountered; in short, he's awesome. I spent the night at his place and in the morning he and I hopped our way back down the great country towards Texas.

My first ever solo show in the United States was set to be in San Antonio, as a warm-up show before the festival. There are a lot of people trying to play warm-up shows in the area before SXSW, so Josh, Jonah and I were to play on a side stage in a large building called The Sanctuary, where a lot of other (more metal) bands were playing.

Jet-lagged and a little sick of being on planes, Josh and I met Jonah at the airport and headed into town. I wandered around, gawping like a tourist, thoroughly enjoying myself. The other two were a little more battle-hardened, but happy to be on the road nonetheless. I managed to contain my desire to pee on the Alamo, took some snaps, grabbed some food and headed to the venue. The stage times were a little later than we would have liked and the crowd not exactly stadium-sized, but the excitement of being on virgin territory wiped all of that from my mind. I remember the crowd being cool and friendly and the show going off without a hitch.

The problems began after Jonah had finished his set and the time had come to settle up with the promoter and hit the road. This being a pretty hand-to-mouth affair, we were tour-managing ourselves, so Jonah and I went to meet the guy with the cash, Angel, to get the money we had agreed for our three-act package, which, as I remember it, was about $400. That would be about enough for us to get some food, put some money towards the rental car and have enough gas to drive across the vast and empty expanse of West Texas to our shows after the festival. Not exactly a king's ransom, in other words.

In fairness, I'm pretty sure what happened wasn't Angel's fault – he seemed like an understanding guy and I've met him since and he was cool. I think he'd been instructed to short-change us by his boss, who we never did meet. Anyway, the fact of the matter is that he offered us around half of what we had been promised. Jonah and I were, predictably, not having any of that and we started to kick up a fuss. Touring people get worked up about this kind of thing: at one point in time I did in fact have a piece of paper in my guitar case with the dictionary definition of 'guarantee' written on it. The nature of the road is such that, if the show doesn't do as well as planned and money is tight, the promoter is still obliged to pay the agreed sum to the acts who played. After all, they're far away from home and getting by on small change; he, if nothing else, will probably be going home to sleep in his own bed that night.

We had no plans to leave without getting paid what we'd been promised and Angel had clearly been told not to pay us any more than he was offering. By about 2 a.m. we'd argued ourselves into a stalemate and I walked dejectedly outside to the car, where Josh and a Texan friend of his were waiting for us. They asked me what had been going on inside and I explained that we'd been ripped off but there was, apparently, nothing to be done about it. The Texan seemed to think that this was giving up too easily. He reached into his car and produced a small hand-held shotgun from the passenger glove box. 'Want me to sort this out for you?' he asked, nonchalantly.

I don't think I'd ever seen a gun other than an air rifle prior to that, certainly not one so clearly designed for, shall we say, inter-personal use. I decided that being party to some kind of shoot-out on my very first American tour date was probably not the best plan, so I declined his friendly offer.

Angel said he'd see if he could sort us some more money in the morning – always, in my experience, a total pile of crap. We slept on the floor in a student house-cum-squat that was next door to the venue. There was no sign of him in the morning, so we wound our weary way back up to Austin for the SXSW shows that we had planned, a little shorter on cash than had been anticipated. It was a pretty memorable baptism of fire in the ways of touring the USA, but I'm pleased to say that it didn't put me off – far from it – and for the most part it's a country that I deeply love playing in, travelling around and learning about. The rest of the tour was a great experience. We played some awesome shows, making our way over to the West Coast and then up towards the Canadian border. Jonah jumped off in Northern California, Josh and I made it up as far as Seattle, making friends along the way. I've been back around the country many times since then, but that first US tour has a special place in my heart.

SHOW # 267
Frog, Mean Fiddler, London, UK, 14 April 2007

I've already mentioned Nambucca and the crew of people who were based there. As well as running the pub, the main activity occupying their social and professional lives at the time was Frog. Frog was an indie club night that took place every Saturday at the Mean Fiddler (also known to the older among us as the Astoria 2), a 1,000-capacity club that used to sit right in the centre of London at the bottom of Tottenham Court Road. The club was pretty ground-breaking at the time – Frog was certainly the largest indie night in the capital

– and it played host to a number of bands that went on to become stars in the early 2000s' indie rock scene, such as the Kaiser Chiefs and The Libertines. Being friends with the people who ran the place, I'd often show up on a Saturday night. Tré Stead (who today works as my tour manager) ran the door and would wave me through to the backstage area, where I'd spend the night hanging out with Dave, Jay and others, usually getting pretty wrecked.

Every week the club would have a band play. Sometimes it was an uneventful set from an uninspiring guitar band, replete with skinny jeans and stylized haircuts. Sometimes it would be an old favourite playing something of a secret show (I remember Ash coming through and absolutely storming the stage). Sometimes the shows had the tinge of mania that can accompany a band that everyone knows is about to explode.

During the time I was in Million Dead, Dave, who was largely in charge of who played at the club, was pretty honest with me, as a friend. We were way, way too heavy and abrasive for the genteel indie kids who came to his club (and indeed for his own taste) and he made it clear that I shouldn't expect him to book us, despite me being a friend of the promoter. True to his word, we never did play and I think it was a good decision on his part – I can't imagine we'd have gone down well with the regulars. However, now that I was not only playing a different style of music, but also had my band together (Dave was concerned, rightly, that a solo set might not capture the kids who came out to dance to *NME*-approved club tracks), the time was right for me to play.

The show itself wasn't much to remark on. We played well and went down OK with the crowd. I remember that I shaved myself a moustache not long before going on, for reasons that have been lost in time (it was certainly a terrible idea, I looked like nothing so much as a pederast). But it was an important show for me because it was the only time I ever played that stage, at a venue that I went to more times than I can count, but also because I played Frog. On that particular social scene I'd long been the musical outsider; when everyone was excited about Babyshambles, I was listening to Converge. It felt like a measure of acceptance from my friends that we played and acceptance on my own terms, given that I had hardly started playing angular skinny indie rock in the meantime. The night was all the more poignant, retrospectively, because it was one of the last for Frog. The club night came to an end not long afterwards, for reasons that it's not my place to go into here. It was the end of an era in a way and I'm glad that I was able to be part of it, both personally and with my music.

SHOW # 280
Bush Hall, London, UK, 2 May 2007

After a short break following the Frog show, I headed back out around the UK again on a more official tour, complete with the band, a nice splitter van, backline and shows booked by Joanna. In truth it hadn't been that long since we'd done the initial tour for the release of *Sleep Is for the Week* and we were visiting some of the same towns and playing in similar-sized venues. In a way it was part of the problem of not having a proper release organized for any other territories in the world – the logical next step seemed to be to hit the road again, even if we were repeating ourselves.

The tour was OK, as I remember it, but not stellar. We did have the joy of playing with a band called Blah Blah Blah. They were a London-based three-piece outfit that I still regard as one of the great lost bands of that time. They had a unique mixture of indie rock with almost music-hall sensibilities, mixing up snippets of

Madness, Chas and Dave and everything in between. They never did take over the world, but I still suspect they should have done. Justin (Jay Jay Pistolet, later singer for The Vaccines), Jay (Beans On Toast) and Captain Black (a Nambucca-linked band) were also on the bill at various points.

We started in Manchester and headed north to Scotland, coming back down through Newcastle, Liverpool (playing at Korova, a venue we did a number of times and that I came to loathe – nice club for dancing, terrible venue to play), Sheffield and Cambridge. The London show was at Bush Hall and was placed about halfway through the tour. Afterwards we continued down to the south-west, then back up to Oxford, before wrapping up, tired, in Norwich.

For booking agents, the London show on any tour is kind of a barometer. The shows there are usually the largest on any given run and deciding which venue you'll play there often sets the tone for the rest of them. Last time I'd been around we'd played a successful (almost) sell-out show at The Borderline. It made logical sense, from a booking point of view, to try and up the size of venue for this run, climb one more rung up the ladder. With that in mind we picked Bush Hall, a beautiful 500-capacity theatre in Shepherd's Bush, west London.

Unfortunately for me, the world was not quite in agreement with our perception that we'd climbed a little higher in the months since the album had been out. At the time, *Sleep Is for the Week* had been a moderately successful record, in an underground, DIY kind of way. Some people had liked it, the reviews on blogs had generally been OK and a certain mass of people were keen to come to the shows. But things were not exploding exponentially – far from it. So I remember this show for being a little disappointing, in the sense that it felt like essentially the same number of people (if not actually the *very same* people) as at the last London headline show, in a larger venue, leaving some aching gaps in the crowd.

I guess what I'm trying to say here is that it was by no means a given at this point (or any other, for that matter) that things would continue to build in the way that they subsequently have, or that I would actually break through into playing larger venues with more people in the end. It's easy to feel like it was all an inexorable process looking back, but it really wasn't. I remember feeling at one point on this tour that maybe this was it, I'd had my shot and maybe it was time to think about what to do after music. It wasn't a good feeling at the time but it felt like the sensible, grown-up thing to do – adulthood nagging at my sleeve. Funnily enough, the other thing happening at this time was that the songs that eventually became the album *Love Ire & Song* were starting to come together in my head and I suppose there's one chorus on that record in particular that springs to mind writing about this. I certainly didn't want to have to sit down, let's put it that way.

SHOW # 299
Academy 2, Manchester, UK, 28 May 2007

After the slight lull in my fortunes and mood around the UK head-line tour, I was pulled out of my torpor by old friends and pushed forwards on to new ground. Million Dead crossed paths with Biffy Clyro a number of times; we were both part of a weird hybrid underground rock scene in the UK in the early years of the twenty-first century. Through a mixture of industry wrangling and friendly cajoling, I managed to get myself a solo opening slot on their forthcoming UK tour to promote their new record 'Puzzle', which was set to move them out from the underground and into the dazzling light of the mainstream. Also on the bill, between me and Biffy, was Yourcodenameis:milo, a band from Newcastle that had toured with Million Dead some years before. In short, it was something of a reunion of old friends.

On paper, being a solo player with an acoustic guitar opening for a band known for having ludicrous amounts of guitar wattage blasting the audience could seem like a tough gig. In the event, I had a superb tour. There was enough of a critical mass of people who at least vaguely knew who I was from the old days to make sure that the crowds weren't actively hostile when I started playing. By the end of my set, most days, they were firmly on my side. I was selling my own merch at the shows, as ever, and I remember copies of *Sleep* flying out hand over fist after my set each night. In a way it felt like a lot of people were there who had been wondering if anyone from Million Dead was up to anything these days, but they'd missed the promotional work and the touring that I'd done to date, or else hadn't put two and two together to make the connection.

The Biffy guys were great to me, as ever, a very nice bunch of guys all round. There was a degree of debauchery between shows, but it wasn't as manic as might have been expected, which was a good thing both for my health and for my shows. Opening up for an established band in big rooms (1,500 people or more) is actually something I really enjoy (especially when things tend to go my way!) It's a challenge to stand in front of a room on your own and win people over to your cause. If you're successful in the endeavour then it's immensely satisfying.

The last show of the tour was in Manchester. For the most part, I'd been catching a lift with the Milo guys on their bus, but this being the end of the line I needed to sort myself somewhere else to stay after the show before returning south in the morning. One of the great things about spending a lot of time on tour is that you generally acquire a list of people you know in each town of the UK, the people you habitually put on the guest list and hang out with when you come through and who you can comfortably ask for a floor or sofa to sleep on. My usual list of Manchester co-conspirators was, for whatever reason, running a little dry on this occasion, so I ended up calling a sister of a friend of mine who was a student in town to ask if I could crash round. She said sure, no problem, so on paper at least everything was set to go.

In the event, I was really tired after the show was done and very much in the mood for heading to bed sooner rather than later. I let my host know this during the day and she was fine with it. However, after a passable set, my friend's sister and I headed out of the venue to a nearby bar, where we sat waiting for some other friends of hers to show. They took their sweet time and were stoned as hell and up for a long night out when they arrived, which my host thought was a wonderful idea. Doing my best to not be ungrateful, I gritted my teeth for as long as I could, but after a while I was losing myself in that weird mix of tiredness and irritation that comes when all you need to do is lie down and you can't.

Sitting in the bar, listening to the inane chatter of my drinking companions, I started doing a little bit of tour maths on the back of a beer mat and something interesting occurred to me. I'd sold a lot of CDs on the run and had done pretty damn well financially. Playing first on doesn't pay much at all, but if you can successfully catch tour bus rides and sleep on floors where needed, you can come out of the tour comfortably in the black. My calculations showed that I was about £60 in profit and as I sat there in the bar a gloriously seductive idea started to creep into my brain. I could go and get myself (whisper it) a *cheap hotel*. One where I could go, right now, sleep until midday and then head for the train station. Once the thought had suggested itself there was no fighting it and in no time at all I was outside smoking a cigarette and calling a hotel on my phone to make a last-minute booking. A room secured, I made my excuses (not perhaps as graciously as I would have liked, looking back) and headed for the luxurious privacy of a Manchester Travelodge.

As I lay there in the large, soft, white, double bed and the soothing silence, I felt pretty good. I was now the kind of musician who could afford to get himself a hotel room, all to himself, at a moment's notice. It felt like I'd already hit the big time.

SHOW # 302
Scala, London, UK, 4 June 2007

When I was growing up and first stumbling across punk rock, I also ran headlong into the exciting world of anarchist politics. The vivid rush of listening to Propagandhi furiously articulating their rage tapped into my pre-existing love for Rage Against the Machine. Pretty soon I had a red and black star badge on my jacket and was on the train to London attending book fairs, squat discussions and the like. Before long I was marching in anticapitalist demos through the City of London with groups like Reclaim the Streets. As I got older, I started getting a little jaded with the whole thing, slightly bored with the staid social scene and rigid orthodoxy of the protest movement – but that's a story for another time.

On my first solo EP I wrote a song called 'Thatcher Fucked the Kids', which was a pretty formulaic leftist rant on an obvious topic. In some ways I was, subconsciously or not, trying to ingratiate myself with a certain scene. In that I was successful. I remember playing a gig with Attila the Stockbroker (a thoroughly lovely chap, but we're not quite on the same page politically) in Leeds and after I played the song he actually got onstage to shake my hand. That was all very nice, but the fact of the matter is that at the time I was starting to re-evaluate my view of politics generally and move away from the simplistic sloganeering of the lyrics of that song. Bad timing on my part, I suppose. Without going into the details too much here, as I've got older I've become more interested in finding ways of channelling my initial disregard for authority into more practical avenues. I also got very sick of the Left generally, not least the total disregard for the history of the twentieth century, which, in my view, tells you everything you'd ever want to know about the dangers of enforced collectivism, regardless of the colour of the shirt they're wearing.

In the midst of all this, I'd been having some conversations with the guys who run the Stop the War Coalition (STWC). I was and remain opposed to the Iraq War of 2003 and joined the march against it, so it seemed to make a lot of sense to work with them on some benefit shows, which I was happy to do. In this instance, I'd got a call from them to ask if I'd be interested in playing on a STWC bill with Tom Morello, guitarist for Rage Against the Machine, now playing in his new solo, protest-singer guise as The Nightwatchman. Of course, I instantly said yes.

The day of the show rolled around and I felt like I was in pretty esteemed company, playing as I was with Tom, Ed Harcourt and a number of other prestigious musicians. Scala is a fantastic venue, one that I hadn't played before. It was shaping up to be a good night. Just before I was due to take the stage myself, the organizers asked if I would mind if someone made a short speech to the assembled crowd before my set. I said no I wouldn't mind. And that's where I started to feel a little less comfortable with the whole thing.

An earnest guy from the STWC took the stage and started talking about the ongoing wars in Iraq and Afghanistan. At the time, Tony Blair was on a kind of world victory lap, visiting other world leaders just before stepping down as prime minister. The speaker told the crowd that Blair was 'leaving office early, in disgrace, because of our efforts!' That struck me as delusional, to say the least – he was leaving early, but pretty much everything else about the statement was transparently false. He then called for the immediate withdrawal of all Western troops from everywhere, especially the Middle East. I felt that given the situation in Iraq at the time, regardless of the morality of our entry into the conflict, that was tantamount to a call for genocide – the Sunni and Shia sections of the population were at each other's throats plainly enough as it was and I believed that the Western military had a moral responsibility to deal with the mess they'd created.

The speaker wrapped up his talk, introduced me to the crowd and I dutifully did my best to play a good set. But I was troubled. I felt uncomfortable playing after a speech I strongly disagreed with and more generally it didn't sit well with me to have the politics so totally overriding the music. I want to be a musician, that's basically all I ever wanted, and right then and there it felt like I was in fact providing protest muzak, background noise for sloganeering about the 'revolution'. I left the show early, feeling like I wouldn't be agreeing to play a similar gig anytime soon.

In the event, my politics have shifted more since that occasion and I now feel much more confident in my opinions on the world, calling myself (if I really have to call myself anything) a libertarian. That puts me at odds with some of the public statements I've made in my life, both in Million Dead and arguably in songs like the aforementioned 'Thatcher'. I guess that's part of growing up; it's just more awkward to do in the public eye and with that eternal and infernal record, the internet. I've also taken more than my fair share of flak in the press for all of this, which isn't much fun, but I've stood my ground.

All of that said; one thing that I do stick by is that I'm not a budding politician hiding behind a guitar, using music as a conduit for radical philosophy. I'm a musician plain and simple. If you're looking for more than that, you're talking to the wrong person.

SHOW # 305
The Bridge House, Copsale, UK, 8 June 2007

It's a point of honour for me to be generally contactable. That's why I have my email address on my website, why I sometimes work my own merch, why I'll talk to people at shows. It's probably a Henry Rollins-inspired thing more than anything else, but it's important to me. Another part of that is also having contacts on my website for my booking agents, press people and so on. As a result of this, Joanna gets an awful lot of people emailing her about me playing somewhere and she does her best to respond. Some of them are, despite the best intentions of the good people sending the emails, beyond the realms of possibility, such as offers to play in tiny pubs in remote corners of the UK. And sometimes they're just plain ridiculous. For the record: I can't fly home from the USA on my one day off in a tour to play a fourteen-year-old kid's birthday party in Wapping, sorry. Having said all of that, just occasionally things work out and when they do they can be awesome.

The Bridge House was a pub in the very small village of Copsale in Sussex, halfway between Brighton and London, which was run by a robust Irishman called Brian and his wife Rachel. They were among the people who often emailed Joanna, with little hope of a response, asking me to come and play. They were nothing if not persistent and eventually there was a moment where playing there made sense. I can't actually remember what the original Bridge House booking was, but I do remember that it was something that worked geograph-ically, but which then had to be pulled for some reason – I think I was ill. Being, as I try to be, a man of my word, I then decided it was important to reschedule the show. And so it was that, after a gig in Bath, I found myself driving with Ruth towards Copsale.

Ruth is an ex-girlfriend of mine. We went out for a long time at university, had some pretty wild ups and downs and have come out the other side as friends of a kind. She lives near Bath and after the show there the night before I'd stayed on her sofa. As she had nothing on the next day, she offered to drive across the south to my next show with me. I hadn't realized quite how small and remote a place we were trying to find. We missed the exit from the main road more than once and eventually found a quaint and slightly ramshackle pub sitting on the outskirts of Copsale, which is little more than a hamlet.

We pulled up and met Brian, which is always quite the experience first time round. Brian is an Irishman, a folk singer, a physically big guy and a force of nature. He's travelled his island thoroughly with his guitar, playing shows wherever they'd have him, and lived to tell the tale loudly, circuitously and entertainingly to pretty much anyone within earshot. My first reaction to him was a mixture of fear and incredulity, but over the course of the day, and many more since then, we've become good friends. He even played some accordion on 'Love Ire & Song'.

The pub was small and adorable, quintessentially English. It could hold maybe a hundred people and I was surprised to learn that the show was basically sold out. Given the remote location I'd been wondering if anyone would come at all, but it turned out that Brian had both a regular clientele and a pretty direct route for promoting shows to local indie kids. I also found out that my friend Dan Martin, from Brighton, was going to be opening the show (in his guise as Amongst the Pigeons). I have to admit that at the start of the day I'd been a little dubious about the show as a whole, but as time went by I was getting more and more into the swing of things.

Above: Onstage at the London Underworld with Million Dead, 22 September 2005.
Below: Graffiti (by Ben Dawson) on the dressing room wall at The Joiners, Southampton.

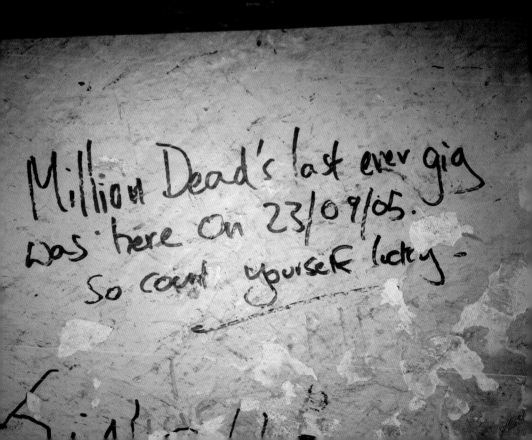

The French / Belgian tour 2006.

Left: Onstage in Tolouse, playing 'The Ballad' for the first time; whole crowd in shot.

Below: The legendary Chamoule holding up some French lyrics for me to sing.

Below: Restringing my guitar onstage mid-set at Nouveau Casino.

Above: Playing the freezing carpark outside The Fenton, Leeds in 2006.

Right: Onstage (with a bass!) at Nambucca in the midst of some lost weekend. The photo was taken by Laura Marling.

Opposite page, clockwise from top Left: Leaning on Justin Pistolet's shoulder in Devizes, 2006; Jamie with the destroyed car after our accident in Lithuania (not funny at the time); Jamie and I arriving at our destination, Liepaja, after the longest day on tour ever; Looking up the local lingo onstage in Moscow, 2006; Onstage, accompanied by the audience, at the end of a Barfly show in Camden, summer 2006.

Clockwise from the top. Finishing up at the Roundhouse before Biffy Clyro in 2007, a job well done; Live at Cave 9 in Birmingham, AL on a very early US tour; *Love Ire & Song Tour*, 2008: Nigel, me, Graham, Ciara, Tarrant, Ben, and a dog; Hanging with Andzs, the man who brought me to Latvia; My first ever show in New York, at Matchless. In shot: the whole audience, hence why I ditched the stage.

Above: Giving it a bit of the old Freddie Mercury at the Scala in London, 2008.

Right: A lovely poster from my hometown venue, the Winchester Railway Inn, the last show of the *Love Ire & Song* tour.

Below: With Charlie Caplowe – my manager since day one and the man behind Xtra Mile Recordings.

Left: The awful tattoo I did on John Berna's chest in Austin.

Below: An early incarnation of the band, on the set of the 'Long Live The Queen' shoot: Ben, Chris T-T, Me, Tarrant, Nigel.

The first Revival Tour, at the Blender Theater, NYC: Tim Barry, Chuck Ragan, Me, Ben Nichols.

The show was, in the end, awesome. Brian played some songs (of course), Dan was great and then I played a good fun show to a packed-out crowd, throwing in a whole bunch of new songs to boot. Dan recorded the show for posterity and I imagine he'd be happy to share the bootleg with anyone who asks – I've seen it floating around the internet somewhere. After the gig was over, Ruth and I sat in the bar with Brian and some of the locals. We ended up drinking whisky and swapping songs and stories of the road well into the night, before finally making it to sleep in an upstairs room, thoroughly sozzled but very happy – happy for a good show, for a great time with new friends and for a memorable and platonic evening spent with an old flame who knows me far too well.

As I mentioned, Brian and I have become friends since then, though he now lives back in Dublin. The Bridge House, alas, closed down not too long afterwards, a victim of poor budgeting and local council intrigues, although not before I'd played another show there in March 2008. I still think of the place fondly from time to time.

SHOW # 320
Maker Festival, Cornwall, UK, 29 July 2007

For any professional musician in my corner of the music world summer is festival season, for better or worse. In more recent years, every summer I've found myself spending the majority of my time standing around in fields, trying to figure out what time I'm playing on which stage, everywhere from Tennessee to Latvia. Back in 2007, things were a little sparser. There are a lot of smaller festivals (especially in the UK) with which to fill your time. These can be awesome or they can be weird as hell. This show fits neatly between those two extremes.

I'd been asked to play at the Maker Festival by Oli James, an old friend from Plymouth who had put on Million Dead shows many years before, as well as some of my very early solo shows. The festival was run by a friend of his and took place in a dramatic cliff-top farm in the south-western toe of England. We were booked for a full-band set and duly prepared for the occasion.

The festival itself was reasonably well organized – not quite as efficient as a German one, but a damn sight better than some field-based clusterfucks that I have had the misfortune of experiencing. Everyone knew where all the stages were, the timetable was generally being adhered to, there was a backstage area and everything was coming up roses. The only thing that was slightly troubling was that our stage, inside a large marquee tent, didn't appear to have anything in the way of security.

Security guards are easy to vilify. It's true that the profession attracts a lot of meat-head thugs who positively revel in the opportunity to beat up skinny Cure fans *and* get paid for it at the same time, and who fulfil the stereotype with reckless abandon. Having said that, there's a good reason why they're there at shows and festivals, they more often than not do a difficult but necessary job and more of them are cooler than music folklore would have you believe. The reason why it's good to have security at shows is that there are plenty of punters at gigs who are, to be charitable, on the fringes of normality and sanity, and who have some bizarre and often violent ideas about interacting with both the people and the equipment onstage. As a skinny Cure fan making music, it's often reassuring to know that there's someone who can actually handle themselves in a fight standing between me and the crazier audience members.

This particular gig turned out to be one where we really could have done with some muscle to protect our soft, delicate, musician skulls. The crowd was: a mix of people who knew my songs and were enjoying the show; people who had no idea who I was but were interested in checking out new music; people who happened to be there but were basically drinking beer and talking to their friends; and out-and-out festival weirdos. That's a pretty normal mix, but alas the weirdos were off the leash that day, as there was no security around to keep them in check.

During one song, a guy pulled himself up out of the crowd to stand on the stage. He was quite a sight – long, filthy dreadlocks, combat shorts and trainers but no shirt, looking like he hadn't slept for a day or two thanks to some chemical assistance and smelling like an entire Grateful Dead audience compacted into one person. He was clearly out of his head (although I suppose saying that implies that he'd once been *in* it, something that his fashion sense would seem to belie – those dreads take a long while to grow) and started dancing around next to me while I was playing. I'm usually all in favour of crowd participation, but this guy was just being an exhibitionist dick.

At this stage a security guy would normally come to the rescue, but alas! Security – there was none. Playing and singing at the same time occupies most of my mental energy, not to mention both hands and my mouth, so it can be hard to signal to someone that you want them to, you know, fuck off. I doubt the guy was really in the mood to get any kind of message anyway. After a little while he started shimmying his way across the lip of the crowd barrier, shaking his booty directly in front of me. By this time my irritation had reached breaking point and in a gap between verses I walked forwards and kicked the back of his knee so that he fell down off the barrier and into the crowd. I had hoped that this might be the end of the matter, both making clear my opinion of his dancing and also practically bringing the routine to a close. However, in what I regarded as a clear betrayal of what Jerry Garcia would have wanted, the guy pulled himself back out of the crowd and came swinging for me, holding my guitar stand as a weapon. The guys in the band and I all simultaneously decided that this was where a line was being crossed and we downed instruments, Nigel leaping over the drums to grab the guy before he could brain me.

Much kerfuffle and confusion ensued. Oli and some of his friends came racing to the rescue, but thanks to his righteous ire and/or the drugs, the guy took some serious subduing. In the end about five people had to hold his thrashing torso still so that he could be carted off the stage and out of the festival, all the while trying to punch out anyone he could get his hands on and screeching some pathetically ill-informed shit about 'fascism' and 'pigs'. Apparently he was eventually arrested but gave his name as Donald Duck – which could, for all I know, be the truth. Meanwhile, we continued with the show, a little shaken, but feeling like the forces of sanity and hygiene had come out on top.

This kind of thing is, at the end of the day, an occupational hazard in my line of work and I don't want to make too big a deal about it – this was just the most memorable occasion. I'm not one for having my own personal security – that would be ridiculous – but we do tend to play shows with slightly more competent bouncers these days.

SHOW # 334

Reading Festival, Reading, UK, 24 August 2007

The summer of 2007 was long, hot and chequered for the band and I. We played some good shows, we played some bad ones, we got rushed by a couple of hippies, but everything came to an awesome climax with the Reading and Leeds festivals. The first festival that I went to was Reading 1995. I remember seeing Beck and Hole on the main stage and being generally overwhelmed by the whole thing. After that I went back as a punter many times, including a few years going down with the Frog crew, who used to run the Thursday club night at the Rivermead Leisure Complex next to the festival site. Million Dead played in 2005, one of the last shows we did and a bittersweet career highlight for the band. So when the booking was confirmed for me to play there as a solo artist (with the band, which was at the time a nameless four-piece: me and Ben, Nigel and Tarrant), I was overjoyed. We had a slot in the middle of the afternoon on the Carling Stage. It was the smallest of the tents, but it didn't matter – we were playing the festivals and that's all we cared about.

Looking back through all these shows for the purpose of writing about them, the more I think about it, the more certain turning points start to become apparent. In fact, I tend to think of them more as consolidation points. It's like I get to a certain level, then start feeling out into new territory, seeing how far I can push things for a while; like a save-game point in a video game. Then eventually something happens that brings all the work together and settles me down on a slightly higher rung than I was on before. The show at the Camden Barfly in the summer of 2006 was certainly one of those moments. This was another. I'd spent the intervening year playing everywhere I possibly could, opening for other bands, playing small headline shows, weird festivals, wherever anyone would have me. I also felt like the band was slowly coalescing into something more like what I wanted it to be – we were playing better, playing *with* each other, getting tighter, more cohesive. The new songs I had were better than the ones that came before – practice might *not* make perfect, but it certainly made me *better* at songwriting. And then to cap it all off, we played at Reading and a multitude of people came to see us.

I think you try to be pessimistic about the number of people who will be at your stage during your set at a festival. It's instinctive self-defence, in that if you assume no one will bother wandering over then you won't be hurt if they don't and if anyone does you feel like you're up on the game. I have no idea how many people came to see me that day, but it felt like thousands. It was almost certainly the largest crowd I had played to (who were there specifically to see me) to date. I was a little overwhelmed, it felt like every single person who'd been at every shitty little show had all turned up *at the same time* and that everyone was looking around wondering who the hell all these other people were, realizing that their little secret was shared by a lot of others. It was glorious. The career jitters from earlier in the year at Bush Hall disappeared like mist in the morning sun.

PART TWO

SHOW # 347

Clwb Ifor Bach, Cardiff, UK, 19 September 2007

After the triumph of Reading, it was time to get back to the normal business of touring. Earlier in the year, an idea had been hatched between Jonah Matranga, Josh English and I, about them coming to the UK so we could reprise our American adventure. In conversation a concept had arisen. The three of us all used to play in heavier hardcore or post-hardcore bands and were all now playing acoustic music. At the time that career path was rare and was more remarkable for it. We decided to do a tour that emphasized this, so the Softcore Tour 2007 was born. The line-up comprised the three of us plus Jacob Golden, a singer from California who was a friend of Jonah's and who had been in the band Birthday, who you could just about describe as post-hardcore, at a push. To commemorate the tour, we put together a CD featuring each of us playing two acoustic covers of hardcore songs. I picked 'Pay to Cum' by Bad Brains and 'Fix Me' by Black Flag. The schedule for the tour was pretty hardcore itself – seventeen shows in a row without a break.

The four of us drove around the country in a splitter van, with four acoustic guitars and Graham Kay. Graham (or G Man, or the Grinch, or G-Bold, or . . . you get the idea), as I mentioned much earlier, had been Million Dead's sound guy. Since the summer he'd started coming out with me for shows with the band, doing both sound and tour managing. It felt good to have an old hand back on board. Despite the almost constant Geordie moaning he's damn good at what he does and remains central to my crew today.

The shows were a blast. They were well-attended and the crowds were enthusiastic. I was playing a lot of new material, as part of the point of the tour for me was to try out new stuff and see how it felt in front of a crowd, so songs like 'Substitute', 'Photosynthesis' and 'Love Ire & Song' got their debut outings at this time. The four of us on the tour got on well, we sold a ton of the limited-edition CDs and we were duetting at the end of most nights with a cheesy cover or two – Guns N' Roses or Abba mostly, as I recall. We covered a lot of ground and had a great time.

The show at Clwb Ifor Bach in Cardiff was pretty typical of the tour in many ways, but it sticks in my mind for sad reasons. Lexie, founder of Lexapalooza, Million Dead stalwart and my good, old friend, had been ill again with cancer. This time, she didn't pull through. The details are not mine to share here; I'll just say that I managed to see her one last time before the tour started and I knew then that I wouldn't see her again. She passed away, the funeral was arranged and I knew that I had to be there no matter what. It fell on the day of the Cardiff gig, so I ended up getting a train down from Newcastle to south London and afterwards travelling over to Cardiff for the show. I knew she wouldn't have wanted me to miss the gig, but it wasn't an easy one to play all the same, emotional and exhausted as I was. Graham, the other players and the crowd were all brilliantly supportive, but it was hard to sing that night, especially 'The Ballad of Me and My Friends' at the end. Lexie was definitely there in my glory days when I sold my soul and the memories of my time with her are cherished and will never leave me. I'd say rest in peace, but she'd never want to be that passive – if there's a beyond, she's at the bar keeping everyone entertained.

SHOW # 373

Pete's Candy Store, Brooklyn, NY, USA,
12 November 2007

After the Softcore Tour was done I jumped on a plane and headed back to the United States. A little while back, a random email had arrived in my inbox from someone called Casey Lee, from Naples, Florida. Casey had heard my music somewhere and wanted to know if his label, Good Friends Records, could put out a 10" vinyl of *Campfire Punkrock*. I excitedly said yes. As part of the deal Casey invited me over to the USA to play some shows with his band, Fake Problems. I jumped at the chance and a slightly ramshackle run of dates was cobbled together for the autumn.

I arrived in Gainesville, Florida on the Sunday of The Fest, an annual underground punk-rock festival that is legendary. Unfortunately, Sundays are generally the worst day to arrive at a festival as everyone is wiped out from the wild partying of the night before. I met the Fake Problems guys, lifelong friends-to-be, and played a small show in a bar to them and a handful of other people. After The Fest was done we careered around Florida for a week or two, with Casey's brother's band, Barlights, in tow, playing house shows and community centres. It was a great time, real American punk touring. We finished up in Naples, which is in the south-west of the peninsula. The last show finished with a titanic party, so it was lucky that I had a few days' rest scheduled afterwards.

I bade a fond farewell to the Fakey Ps and made my way up the coast, via basement shows in Harrisonburg, Virginia and house shows at university halls in upstate New York and Massachusetts. The run had been enjoyable, but all the shows were on a small scale, the drives were exhausting and I'd been drinking a hell of a lot as we went along to sustain my optimism. By the time I arrived back in New York I was exhausted.

I had two shows scheduled for the day I got back. The first was opening for a band called God Fires Man, which included Arty Shepherd and Joe Grillo, two old friends of mine who had toured with Million Dead in their former band, Gay For Johnny Depp. I played to a smattering of people in a typical toilet-circuit club, before jumping in a cab and heading across town to Pete's Candy Store for my second show of the evening.

Pete's had been sold to me, by the person organizing the show, as a classic Brooklyn folk dive, a great place to play. I guess that's true, but as with many 'classic' venues, it can often be a pretty depressing experience playing there when no one shows up and the staff have the attitude that comes with working at a venue with a reputation. In fact, the reason Joe had got me on to the bill earlier in the evening was so that I would at least play to some people while I was in his city.

So, as you might have guessed, the show at Pete's was not exactly packed out. In fact, the sum total of the crowd was my holidaying friend Rachel (she of the house show and the documentary), her local friend and another couple. Four people in the room made the PA system seem a little surplus to requirements, so instead of plugging in I decided to fall back on the natural sound of an acoustic guitar. I made my way to one of the tables in the middle of the room and sat down on one side, with everyone else across from me. I played whatever songs they wanted to hear, told stories, chatted between songs and generally had a great time. This actually sticks in my mind as one of my favourite shows – I was playing for the love of it, really relishing the songs, dropping some of the showmanship that edges into playing music when confronted with a large crowd and just enjoying myself.

A small, strange but fun footnote to this show: unbeknown to me, one of the other people in the bar that night was a writer for

Playgirl magazine. She enjoyed the show and for quite a long while afterwards I always got glowing reviews in that publication, which was nice, if a little surreal.

The next morning I boarded a plane to California to meet up with Charlie, my manager, and play a few shows in Los Angeles. I had a good gig at The Hotel Cafe and everything felt like it was back on track. This American run was definitely one to file under 'character building', but of all the shows, it was the one at Pete's that stays with me the most.

SHOW # 383
Brixton Academy, London, UK, 31 December 2007

I got back to England and spent December flitting around London, playing a few shows here and there and catching up with my fragmented social life. Most of my friends had either got used to my sporadic comings and goings by this point or had faded out of my life. That's a price you pay as a touring musician, though I don't want to overstate the hardship – the friends you do have are as close as can be and the upsides of life as a touring musician greatly outweigh the downsides for me (and if they didn't, I could just stop). Nevertheless, a little effort in catching up with people goes a long way, so I often spend my short breaks at home grabbing drinks, coffee, food or whatever with disparate groups of friends.

For the celebration of New Year, I'd been booked to play a slot at Brixton Academy, a cavernous and historic venue in south London. The night was being put on by XFM, a UK radio station that's been very good to me over the years. I was set to play a half-hour solo set in between various DJs. Kid Harpoon was also set to play. Kid is a friend and I maintain to this day that he is a transcendently brilliant singer and songwriter, one of the best I know. Around this time was when he was at his best, in my opinion, but alas the stars did not align for his own solo career (he's happily now a respected song-writer for, among others, Florence and the Machine). Naturally, I had plans to head off into the night after the gig, so I invited a bunch of close friends down to hang backstage and watch the show.

The gig was pretty much an unmitigated disaster. I was tired, nervous about the size and make-up of the crowd and irritable. Before my stage time came around I'd had a fair bit of time to kill at the venue and had, unwisely, started down the road to oblivion that I was planning to advance along later in the evening – in other words, I'd started drinking hard, and more besides. Added to all this was the fact that the billing was pretty uncomfortable, to say the least. The punters at the sold-out night were there to shake their drunken booties to indie club classics like The Killers and the Kaiser Chiefs. What they quite specifically were not there for was a largely unknown skinny drunk guy with just an acoustic guitar stumbling fractiously through half an hour of songs they were not familiar with. As every minute of the set wore on I felt worse: tense, strung out, feeling like I was losing the fight, slipping slowly over the edge of a cliff of indifference.

The show was over quickly enough (though it didn't feel like that at the time) and I scuttled offstage and back to the dressing room to start on the serious business of cleaning the stink of defeat from me with the medicine of alcohol. Afterwards, the rest of the evening was frantic – I ran into my friend Dan Smith (who is now the singer in the band Bastille) and dragged him up onstage while I played guitar with Kid for an REM cover. I spent the actual countdown to the New Year in a cab with some friends heading for a party on the other side of the city. It was an OK night (and following day) I guess, but all through it the memory of the gig was sticking in my craw.

It was a strangely appropriate way to end the year. On the one hand, I was playing a show at a huge venue, sponsored by a major radio station, to a large crowd of people. These, if anything, are the signs of success, of things heading in the right direction. But I was still pretty off kilter in my personal life – my family a mess, my love life worse and my 'partying' (this always strikes me as a particularly insidious euphemism) a problem. I was heading somewhere, but not without stumbling all over the track. The main thing driving me forwards was the new songs I had in my back pocket, new songs that felt like they were special.

SHOW # 397

Pappy & Harriet's, Pioneertown, CA, USA, 24 February 2008

In between shows on both sides of the Atlantic in the second half of 2007, I'd been working on making a new record. There were various things about the process of making *Sleep Is for the Week* that I'd really enjoyed and wanted to reprise; and there were some things I wanted to change. I had enjoyed working on the songs with Ben a lot, but it didn't seem like it would be possible to occupy Tarrant's house in Oxford again, not for such a long time, and to be honest I wanted to spend a little longer for this session and, if possible, to get away from the distractions of the road and what passed for my social life. I felt like the new songs I had deserved my full attention and focus.

Back in Hampshire, near where I grew up in the Meon Valley, my friend Simon's parents lived on a small farm. They had recently converted a dilapidated old barn into a large, modern outhouse. It had one large open-plan room, a small bedroom, a bathroom and a kitchen. I'd seen it over Christmas 2006 at a party and had instantly thought that it would be a good place to record.

It was in the countryside where I'd grown up, it was pretty isolated and it felt like the perfect place to shut ourselves away for a while. After some negotiation, we booked ourselves in for two separate sessions in between tours, in October and November.

Ben and I went down there together and lived in the studio. We took all the equipment with us – a mixing desk and a pro-tools rig, plus Ben's collection of microphones. Nigel came down and played some drums, and visited us again later to play the piano and organ parts. Various other friends came and went, adding upright bass, strings, backing vocals and the like, including The Holloways and Jase from Unbelievable Truth. The sessions were relaxed but focused and over time the outlines of *Love Ire & Song* came together.

Once the recording was finished, I took the files to my friend Tristan, who I'd worked with before, for him to mix them. He did his work in London in January and pretty quickly we had a finished record on our hands. I wasn't entirely sure whether it was better than the previous record in terms of songwriting, but I was confident that it sounded better and other people seemed to like it, especially Nigel and Ben. Charlie and Xtra Mile were also pleased, so we set about getting ready for the release.

It was decided around this time, in the lull between finishing the record and release, that I would go to Los Angeles for a while. The record industry is, it has to be said, a little obsessed with America. I suppose there's a good business reason for this: it's the largest music market in the world. All the same, the obsession with 'breaking' the place always seemed a little overcooked to me. I'm more than happy for America to keep functioning smoothly. Nevertheless, my management were keen for me to get out there again to try to sort a proper deal to distribute and promote my music on that side of the pond. LA is where it's at for music, so we set up a bunch of showcases and other shows, booked a motel room and I got on a plane.

In all I spent about a month in California. Much like London in the UK, the fact that LA is *the* place to be for the music industry in the USA means that it's crawling with people on the make, with hundreds of different dead-end projects classed as 'great opportunities', with artists and bands desperate to catch anyone's attention. The Rodeway Inn Motel on Sunset and Highland where I was staying was pretty run down and as I don't drive (I know, I know, I'm planning on starting lessons as soon as I've finished writing this book) I was basically stranded there when I wasn't actively being bussed around for shows, meetings and interviews.

I can't say it was the happiest month of my life. Some of the things we were doing felt good and at the start Charlie was out there with me, but after he headed home I had a fair few evenings of playing what were essentially glorified open-mic nights, or sitting alone in my room wondering why the hell I wasn't at home.

After a few weeks of solitude, Chris T-T arrived. Chris is a folk singer from Brighton, England, and someone I'm happy to call a close friend. His manager at the time, Stephen, was based in LA and he wanted Chris to come over for a similar testing of the waters. It made sense for us to hook up and play some shows together, a pair of beardy Englishmen zooming up and down the coast. Packed into Stephen's car with our guitars, we played Sacramento and then drove down the Pacific Coast Highway to play another show at a hippy student house in Isla Vista. We filled out the bill at some LA nights and even managed to play the same venue in Oxnard twice in a week (for reasons that now escape me). I'm not sure that we were laying the foundations for Beatles-style American success, but we had a good time and became closer friends.

Towards the end of the run we headed out into the desert of the Joshua Tree National Park for a couple of shows. I'd never been into the legendary expanse before and was keen not only to check out the scenery, but also to try and get some mescaline and trip out, Hunter S. Thompson style. Unfortunately, the drug now seems to be as scarce as facts backing up Gonzo journalism, so we had to settle for some hash cookies that a friend had legally procured, thanks to a little weed medical permission slip from the state government.

After a pretty uneventful show in Yucca Valley, we hit our motel out in the desert. The scenery, the emptiness, was breath-taking, the panorama of the stars a real sight to see for us city dwellers. We ate the hash cookies and spent the night staring up into the beyond – well, some of us did. Chris had something of a freak-out trying to decide whether he should sit down or stand up, or indeed kneel, which kept the rest of us entertained.

The next day we drove on to Pioneertown, to Pappy & Harriet's. We were all a little wiped out from the ingestion of the night before. The place is somewhat mythical for me, being mentioned in the Counting Crows song 'Mrs Potter's Lullaby'. However, the gig left much to be desired. We later found out that the girl doing sound, and indeed pretty much everyone at the venue, had managed to find the mescaline I'd been looking for and had taken it all. That at least would explain the utterly bizarre delays and reverbs they kept putting on my voice and guitar, before running for cover away from the swirling noise. No matter in the end, as there can't have been more than ten people there, none of whom had come for the show. I finished my set with gritted teeth and resignation, doing my best to remain profes-sional and entertain Chris and Stephen at the very least. I headed back to the UK shortly afterwards, America remaining firmly unbroken.

SHOW # 404
Bar I Love You, Riga, Latvia, 16 March 2008

Back in the UK, momentum of a kind was building for the new record. Mike Davies at BBC Radio 1 was playing 'Photosynthesis' on his punk show, thereby making it the de facto first single from the record, and tickets for the album tour were starting to sell. Before embarking on the proper promotion, I headed back to Latvia for a short run of shows. This time round, Ben Dawson, drummer of Million Dead, came along for the ride. He's one of my oldest and best friends, and it was fun to invite him out to experience the Latvian chaos.

Latvia was awesome, as ever. On our first day there, Ben and I found ourselves on a bus to Liepāja with an American Jehovah's Witness. The poor kid made a valiant attempt to engage us in a conversation about the divine, but hadn't reckoned on Ben's militant atheism and total failure to give a shit about upsetting him. Believe me, four hours is a long time when your friend is philosophically deconstructing a teenager like he's picking wings off a fly. Nevertheless, it was nice to be back in the country, seeing old friends and having a blast.

The main reason for us being there was a big gig in Riga organized by *Veto* magazine, through the good auspices of my old Latvian pal Andzs. Ben and I actually rehearsed a couple of my songs with him on drums for the occasion, and a song by Kneejerk, the band that we'd been in when we were sixteen and that had prompted our first invite to the country many years before. The show was in a big club, was professionally organized and it went off fine, though I have to say it lacked some of the chaotic charm that I associate with that country. Thankfully chaos was restored the next night at a bunker squat show in Cēsis. Finally, before our flight home, we headed back to Riga for one more show in a small bar.

The show at Bar I Love You was utterly unhinged. Ben and I decided to drink White Russians, but the poor barman didn't seem to know what they involved. After some negotiation, and realizing that they had all the necessary ingredients, Ben was behind the bar mixing them for us. It only occurred later to us that, in a former Soviet country, Russian drinks (even if in name only) might not have been the best idea. My old friend Karlis showed up, ready as ever to do battle with alcohol, and took an instant liking to Ben. I played in the basement and the show itself was OK, but my throat was pretty fucked from the night before, though people sang along – but it was afterwards that things got really out of hand. The last I saw of Ben was him lying in the gutter outside, shortly after having been sick on the DJ (classy), with Karlis stood over him, pouring red wine into his mouth and shouting 'Drink, you soft English bastard!' Meanwhile, I have some haziness in my mind as to the sequence of events of what happened to me, but I do remember waking up in an office at about 4 a.m. on a sofa without some of my clothes and with company.

Man, I miss Latvia sometimes.

SHOW # 434
The Railway Inn, Winchester, UK, 24 April 2008

Ben and I returned fuzzily to home soil. After an album launch party and a few warm-up shows, I was ready for the release of *Love Ire & Song*. The record came out on my little sister's birthday, 31 March, and on that day the band and I embarked on a twenty-four-date tour of the UK to let people know about it, starting at the Brudenell Social Club in Leeds.

At this time we had a girl called Ciara Haidar playing keys in the band. The new album had even more piano work on it and it was getting increasingly incongruous playing as a four-piece, either skipping the parts completely or using a sampler to trigger them. Ciara sang backing vocals on a few songs on the record and was (is) a great keys player, so it made sense for her to play with us, as well as for her to open the shows with her own solo material. Also along for the ride was Andy Yorke, who had played with Nigel in Unbelievable Truth in the 1990s. At this time he was coming out of a self-imposed musical exile and starting to record and play shows again. I for one was honoured to have him with us.

The tour visited the same kind of venues that we'd played on the two UK band tours we'd done to promote the previous record, but this time round something felt decidedly different. Shows started to sell out and did so before we even got to the towns in question. There might only have been two or three hundred people at the gigs, but now they knew the words and people started badgering me to get on the guest list to sold-out gigs. Things were definitely starting to change – and for the better. On top of all of that, the reception to the new album was considerably more positive than I had dared to hope.

Two-thirds of the way through the tour, Ciara jumped ship, having been offered some much larger shows with Kid Harpoon and The Kooks. I can't say that I was over the moon about it at the time, some heated words were exchanged, but looking back I understand. All the same, this left us without a keys player for a few shows. After a slight panic, I had a brainwave. I called Chris T-T – who, as well as being a great songwriter himself, can really play the piano – and after some emergency between-show rehearsals, he joined us for the last few dates of the tour.

In London we sold out the 100 Club on Oxford Street, a venue steeped in music history. Many famous jazz and rock 'n' roll bands played there back in the day and the Sex Pistols tore the place up in 1976. My gig at the 100 Club stays in my mind more clearly than most to this day. Things felt so exciting, so full of promise. I opened the show with a short abbreviated acoustic cover of a song called 'Rock 'n' Roll Singer'. It's originally by AC/DC, but personally I prefer the delicate, laconic version that folk singer Mark Kozelek recorded and that's the style I chose to play it in. It felt appropriate to the moment, the softly spoken lyrics of simple, innocent, adolescent ambition, which felt somehow a little closer to being real that night. With Chris in the band, everything was really starting to gel and suddenly the horizons that I could imagine for what I was doing started expanding rapidly.

The final show of the tour was in Winchester, at The Railway Inn. The Railway is pretty much the only music venue in my hometown, a place where I'd seen many shows and that I'd played countless times, both solo and in previous bands. I'm very fond of the place. The show was sold out and went great. I was exhausted and I knew I had to fly back to California the next day, but I felt exuberant. After the gig I was hanging out with people from the show, drinking and talking nonsense, and in the fug of it all missed loading out the gear into the van for the band's final drive back to Oxford (I was staying at my mum's in Winchester, before heading to the airport).

The next day I got an email from the boys saying that they were peeved about that. In all, despite us being a much better musical unit, the tour had been pretty hard on Ben, Tarrant and Nigel. It wasn't just the schedule (which was tough, but we'd all done tough tours before). Now that we weren't opening the shows with a set from Dive Dive, their motivation for being on the tour was different. As much as they're my friends and great players to boot, what we do is not like being in a normal band together. They are kind of session players, though I shy away from using that word to describe them as it seems somehow belittling. They're much more than that. But at the same time, the reality is that it's not an equal situation. The motivation for me to be there is obvious. For the others, of course they care about the music and the project as a whole, but it's at one remove.

When you're playing to 200 or so people a night, the amount of money in the budget for paying people isn't huge and I didn't have a massive label behind me pumping cash into the coffers. Essentially, the guys were working their arses off for very little money. Obviously, there was the understanding that we'd keep working at this and get to a place where things would be more equitable, which we have done, thankfully; but that doesn't necessarily mean much in the short term when you have rent and bills to pay.

In short, there was tension between the boys and I, and looking back on it I might not have handled it in the most sensitive way. It took me a little while to grasp the situation from their point of view and this was not the only occasion on which some hard words were exchanged. I guess I'm mentioning this here to show, firstly, that even when everything is rosy during the show, the mechanics of touring on this level can be pretty punishing financially and personally. And secondly, it's important to me that people understand that the boys in the band have been dedicated to working with me since way back when. I couldn't do what I do today if they hadn't backed me up at times like this and I will always be grateful for their belief and hard work. Thanks guys.

SHOW # 437
The Viper Room, West Hollywood, CA, USA, 2 May 2008

Charlie and I returned to the States after the UK tour for one more bout of Los Angeles-based schmoozing. Despite my pessimism about my last stay in the City of Angels, it seemed like we had made some headway. We headed back out for a long weekend of showcases and meetings and this time round things were much more positive. I played a radio session at the House Of Blues and had meetings with a lot of people who seemed more serious than some of the others I'd met out there before. In particular, we signed up with

Caitlin Roffman, an agent at United Talent (and an awesome person to boot), who was now on board to book my shows in the USA.

The final show in California was at The Viper Room, a venue that was once partly owned by Johnny Depp and outside which River Phoenix met his maker. There was a great turnout for the show and it really felt like people over there were starting to take notice of what I was doing; not to quite the same degree as back home, but still.

One other thing happened that night. I met an English girl at the show; she was on a business trip and had a night off and decided to check out The Viper Room without knowing who was playing. Her name was Isabel. It's a date that's marked in my diary still.

SHOWS # 447 / # 448
University Union – Mine, Leeds, UK, 15 May 2008

The next instalment of the never-ending tour of everywhere involved a trip back around the UK, this time opening for The Holloways. I'd done a few solo shows with them before and of course we'd played chaotic late-night impromptu gigs at Nambucca plenty of times. But now I was down for a full UK support tour and I was bringing the band with me (albeit we were a four-piece once again).

The Holloways had had a degree of success on the indie rock scene, with support from the *NME* and BBC Radio 1, and their song 'Generator' was riding high in the charts. Their previous bout of touring had been a great success, packing out venues up and down the country. Alas, in the meantime they had started to fall prey to the terrible luck that often creeps into a band's career. The American record label with whom they had signed had gone into receivership and their rights to their own music had become tangled up in the ensuing legalities. More fatally still, the complications had led to a slowing down in the momentum of their career. For a band, at the stage they were at, that's pretty much everything and losing the drive to go forwards is often terminal.

As a result, the run of shows we did with them was a mixed bag. Some of them were great, but some of them were poorly promoted and poorly attended. I was spending money from my own pocket to take the band out with me and there were some slightly demoralizing moments, seeing the smattering of people at the shows and thinking about how much the exercise was costing me. All the same, it was great to be out on the road with my friends and there were some great shows to make up for the tough ones.

I have a bunch of good memories from the tour. In Bournemouth I played an aftershow gig at the iBar, which ended up being more fun than my set at the gig proper. In Reading some kid tried to steal the hat that I was wearing, which led to a titanic late-night chase through the university grounds and a small punch-up. Most memorably of all, in Leeds, I was onstage with the band and halfway through a great set the fire alarm went off and everyone was ordered outside. Never one to let the moment slip by, I'd taken my guitar out with me so stood on a small grassy hillock among a bewildered crowd, half of whom had not even been at the show, and started to play a few songs, yelling to compensate for not having a PA. At first people were sceptical, to say the least, but after a while people started getting into it and by the time the alarm stopped and we were allowed back in, I'd led the crowd in a sing-along to that old favourite, Abba's 'Dancing Queen'. We ran back inside and just had time to play one more song, 'Photosynthesis', before making way for the main act.

The other thing to mention from this run of shows was that I was spending a lot of time hanging out with The Holloways' crew: their guitar tech, Tom Barber (known as Barbs); their merch girl,

Sarah Crowder; and their tour manager, Tré. They were all people I knew from around the bar at Nambucca, but I definitely got to know them properly on this tour and saw them at work. In time, they would start coming on tour with me and become members of my touring family.

Playing support shows with my band is something I really enjoy doing, because when we get it right (which we often do), we really have it in us to smash through a disinterested crowd and force people to pay attention. It's a challenge and therefore can be more rewarding. We did well on this run of shows and in a way it was a forerunner of later American tours we did where we proved ourselves night after night.

SHOW # 460
The Loft, Xscape, Castleford, UK, 8 June 2008

By this time, *Love Ire & Song* had been out in the UK for a few months, we'd done two tours around it and we were still steadily shifting copies. As summer crept on, my gig schedule was a little less meandering and a little more regimented. Nowadays, things are pretty much always militarily planned, as they have to be with the amount of shows I want to play and countries I want to visit. But back in 2008 things were still shifting from one model to the other. So at the start of June I had a slightly odd run of shows running into the beginning of festival season. I did an in-store in Cheltenham, a club night in Kingston, a house show in Fulham and a small festival in Durham. Most of these were solo shows, so I was back on the train with my guitar, but the shows were larger than they'd been last time I was out like this and the mood was different.

One show on the schedule that I was not optimistic about in

advance was at The Loft in Castleford. I confess I hadn't really heard of Castleford prior to the show. During pre-gig planning I found out that the club was essentially in a large motorway services area with a train station, a hotel, a bowling alley, cinema and, tucked away in a corner, a venue. I was not at all convinced that anyone was going to show up for the gig. Train schedules for the day were such that I arrived in the early afternoon. I checked into the hotel, dropped my bag and wandered over to the club. It was nice enough, a small 200-or-so-capacity room on the top floor of the leisure complex. After a cursory sound check, I met up with my little sister Gilly (who was still living in nearby Leeds) and her boyfriend and we went downstairs to go bowling.

While I was being thoroughly shit at knocking down pins (as per bloody usual), we started chatting with the people in the lane next to us. They were there for the show and were pretty excited about hanging out with me, all stifled giggles and photograph requests. It sticks in my mind because, while I'd experienced people being a bit weird around me before, it generally only happened immediately after coming offstage. Here we were, hours before showtime and these guys and girls were excited. I found it a little odd and it made me wonder how the show was actually going to turn out.

In the event, the gig sold out, much to my surprise. The room was packed with people, all full of energy and excitement, and when I played they sang along with all the songs – the new ones, the old ones, pretty much anything I could pull out of the bag. I was stunned. I'd had packed-out, sing-along shows before, but not in (no offence) *Castleford*. It felt like everyone was buzzing about the songs I was playing and, I'll not hide it, that felt fucking great. This little gig, in a prefab roadside leisure complex called, of all things, Xscape, stands out for me as another moment of realization. People were starting to *like* me.

SHOW # 463

Eton College, Windsor, UK, 18 June 2008

Yes, it's true; I was educated at Eton College.

To people outside the UK, this is generally not much more than a piece of passingly interesting trivia, usually accompanied by a dull question about Prince William. In mainland Europe, America and beyond people have a habit, which I am a huge fan of, of judging people on where they choose to direct their lives, rather than on their past, their education, their class, their hometown, etc. For better or worse, that's not the case in the UK and this is as good a time and place as any to say a few words on the subject.

I got an academic scholarship to Eton when I was thirteen years old. My parents put me up for it. They wanted me to get the best education that was available. They were also, it has to be said, interested in the social aspects of the school. My folks are like that. I'm by no means from anything other than a middle-class back-ground (and have never said otherwise), though I doubt they would have been able to scrape the funds together to send me there without the bursary.

So I went. The educational facilities were amazing. A lot of the kids were kind of snobbish dickheads, although I have to say I find it hard to hold that against someone who is fourteen. They haven't seen the world or emerged from the social bubble in which they've been brought up. If you want to point fingers, point them at the parents. Personally, I felt very socially awkward at school – I vividly remember kids referring to friends of mine from back home as being 'plebs', a disgusting word that I didn't initially understand. In that context, when I came across punk rock it made a huge amount of sense to me – the rage, the defiance, the way it made a virtue out of the necessary agonies and isolation of adolescence.

Reading about Joe Strummer made me feel like it was possible to survive my current predicament.

I'm more than aware, as a thinking grown-up, that I had a privileged start in life. I'm not sure whether I'd send my kids (should I ever have any and should I ever have the cash) to a similar school. I'm politically uneasy about these types of schools to say the least, but then the instinct to do the best by your offspring is both powerful and understandable. Some people might say 'Who cares?' Well, actually there are an awful lot of people who'll happily yell 'CUNT!' at me at the top of their voices because of where I went to school, who'll dismiss me out of hand, shout me down, call me a fraud. As I said, it's a peculiarly and depressingly British impulse. I don't think there's anything I could change about my life that would satisfy those people, which I think highlights the irrationality and stupidity of their hatred. It's a hatred of an abstract idea that's been grafted on to a person and that can never be altered by reality. Judge me on the choices I've made, the paths I've voluntarily taken, not on what was decided for me when I was a kid. One of the things the place gave me was a broad experience of prejudice and a fervent desire never to let that be part of my character.

When I left the place, I was more or less set on not going back ever again if I could help it – I was pretty angry and conflicted about the whole experience at eighteen. But many years later, I got an email from a kid at the school – not anyone I knew – saying that someone had pinned up an article about me from a music magazine on the noticeboard at the school and written this underneath in black pen:

'SEE? YOU DON'T HAVE TO GROW UP TO BE A BANKER.'

That seemed cool to me. I was flattered and it made me feel good to know that maybe there were more kids at the place who weren't sleepwalking into the City. A little while later I got another email, this time from a kid who was organizing the Rock Society at the school. He asked if I could come back to give a talk and maybe even play. I thought about it for a really long time and in the end decided that it was something I would do.

By this time, Isabel, the girl I met in The Viper Room, and I were in a serious relationship. She and I took the train down there. She had had a very different educational experience to me and laughed her way through the whole thing – the uniforms and the etiquette. Her uncomplicated amusement made me relax a little. We had supper with some of the teachers who'd been there when I was a pupil. One or two of them had been supportive to me as a rebellious kid, but most of them thought I was crazy for coming back.

The show itself was OK, a little formal perhaps; they set me up in a stuffy, wood-panelled assembly hall I knew well from my incarceration there. It was lined with marble busts of former head-masters – not perhaps the most rock 'n' roll place to play. I'd had plans to give some rousing speech about confounding social stereo-types and choosing your own path, but it kind of died in my mouth once I was up there – I'm really not so confident in myself that I want to start lecturing teenagers on what to do with their lives.

All in all, I'm glad I did it and I feel now like I really don't need to go back again. If I lost you in this entry, if you're mortified that, like Joe Strummer, I'm not the working-class hero you really wanted me to be, well, sorry. It is what it is.

SHOW # 473
Boring by the Sea Festival, Weymouth, UK, 29 June 2008

Summer, as I've said before, is festival season. Year on year, it's got busier, crazier for me. In 2008, I spent the first half of the hot season bouncing back and forth across the Channel. My friend Cham had joined a band called Jedethan, which also included Dave Condon, a long-haired and loveable New Zealander who had guitar-teched for Million Dead back in the day. Cham had set up a run of shows for Jedethan around France and Belgium, a larger-scale version of our ramshackle trip from back in 2006, and he asked me to come along for the ride. I agreed, before realizing that the trip ran across a number of UK festival calendar entries, not least the behemoth that is Glastonbury. After some head scratching, I had a schedule that was a little intense but looked like it would be fun.

We played at La Fête de la Musique in Paris at the start of the run. We rolled across Belgium playing around campfires, in decrepit old punk venues and even did a gig in a Scout hut supported by a punk-rock covers band, all of whose members were about thirteen years old, who had a kid on bagpipes holding the vocal melodies instead of a singer. Seriously. They did the Ramones, the Pistols, the works, while their intimidating skinhead dads rollicked around drunkenly in the crowd in matching band T-shirts. That was a pretty weird show.

After that gig (in Écaussinnes, around thirty miles south of Brussels), I got an early-morning cross-Channel train back to the UK and met up with the band on the drive from Oxford down to the vast, out-of-control, gloriously disorganized party on a farm that is the Glastonbury Festival. This was my first time going to the festival, having never been before as either a performer or a punter. The guys in my band, particularly Tarrant, are not massive fans of festivals per se and as we drove in through the massed hippy crowds and oozing mud, he was gloomily threatening to call the UN and report a humanitarian crisis.

Once on site, we played a set on the Avalon Stage (it was a slightly ramshackle performance as we hadn't rehearsed recently) and later I played solo at the Left Field in the middle of the night.

There were plenty of friends of mine at the festival and it being Glasto they were all keen on getting out of their heads as soon as possible. I was trying to maintain a degree of decorum, given that I was technically in the middle of a tour, but even with the best will in the world you can't stay sober for long at that festival. I partied my way through the night and into the next day, my putative day off, which turned out to be nothing of the kind as far as my metabolism was concerned.

The next morning I woke early, in a tent, feeling like death and aware of the full horror of the journey ahead of me. First of all, I had to make it off the festival site – no mean feat and one I only achieved thanks to the saintly helpfulness of a passing golf-buggy driver, who ferried me and my guitar across the desolate sleeping festival ground to an exit. From there, an expensive cab took me to the nearest train station, which isn't exactly a main-line affair. About three minor rural Sunday services later I was in Weymouth, where I was due to play a little festival called Boring by the Sea. It's at times like this that I find myself cursing my booking agent (while secretly remembering that it was me who was enthusiastically bolting dates on to the schedule with gay abandon during the planning phase).

It was a gorgeous sunny day and having arrived a little earlier than was strictly necessary I went down to the pebble beach and sat in the sunshine, soaking up the peace and the vitamin D in the hope that it might bring me back to health in time for the set. In the event my plan worked perfectly; it's amazing what a little rest and sunshine will do for the constitution and for morale. The show went just fine, my friend Sam Isaac played a great set as well and I slept happily in a cosy bed and breakfast. The next morning I was hopping trains back to the Continent to rejoin Cham and pals for the rest of the French shows. It was pretty exhausting, but hell, it made me feel alive.

SHOW # 483

2000trees Festival, Withington, near Cheltenham, UK,
12 July 2008

The festival scene in the UK has deep roots – Glastonbury has been with us since the 1960s and there are many other long-running field parties, from Reading to Download (or, as I prefer to call it, Donington). In more recent years, as the live-music scene has grown exponentially, the number of smaller festivals has bloomed commensurately. Some of these have grown into much larger, more established events in their own right, such as Bestival. The proliferation has also led to many not-so-spectacular shindigs, run by people better described as chancers than promoters, which has meant many an afternoon of bands milling aimlessly around a boggy field with inadequate staging, PA, crowds and sanitation.

Occasionally, though, you come across real gems, the perfect small festivals that have a charm and intimacy that the bigger ones lack and a character all of their own. 2000trees is such a festival. Set up by a small group of friends and run in a field in Withington, near Cheltenham, it holds a few thousand people in a cosy farm setting. Each year they showcase the best of underground rock music in the country and the mood is always convivial and welcoming. The festival took place for the first time in 2008 and the organizers contacted me and asked me to play. After I agreed enthusiastically, they suggested that I play a secret (ish) set on the smaller acoustic stage on the opening Friday of the festival, as well as a main-stage full-band set on the second day.

So it was that I pulled up at the farm in a friend's car in the middle of the day, unloaded my guitar and headed for a small tent with a stage, a sound system and a good crowd of people. The first set of the weekend was great. I was really surprised at how many people were there already and how up for it they seemed. After I was done, I had the rest of the day to enjoy wandering the site and checking out bands, then a night to sleep, before meeting my band on site the following morning.

There was a moment in the mid-afternoon when there was no particular band I wanted to see and rain was starting to threaten. I glanced through the programme to see that a certain Jim Lockey was playing right then on a stage that had shelter to the sides. Not only that, but he was described in the blurb as sounding like me. Curious, I set off to get myself out of the rain and to check out the alleged competition.

I'm pleased to say that Jim and his band (Solemn Sun) were ace – Gloucestershire's best-kept secret – and they've gone on to become firm friends and touring partners in the years since. I introduced myself after their set and we ended up hanging out for the rest of the day, and indeed the night, and, well, let's be honest, into the next day as well. The night was filled with a set of camp-fire sing-alongs led by a group of kids who had set up 'Camp Reuben' in honour of the fact that my old friends Reuben had been booked to play the festival but had, alas, broken up in the mean-time. I think I ended up playing long into the night – it was hard to tell exactly how long, given the circumstances.

The dawn came grimly through the English summer weather to find me, Jim and a few others still wandering the grounds looking for adventure. After a brainwave, we managed to get someone better rested and more sober to drive us into nearby Cheltenham, where we grabbed some food and even a shower back at Jim's place. It was then that I remembered that I had an in-store appearance booked at local indie record shop, Rise. We hightailed it over there just in time for my third set in two days, where I played to a small but happy crowd. We returned to the party, refreshed and ready for more. The second day of the festival kicked off with some great bands and by the time my own finally arrived I was in good spirits and we played a great set on the main stage, despite my lack of sleep. Four sets in two days with no sleep – not bad.

As we all prepared to get in the van and return to Oxford for the night, I climbed out of the deep mud leaving my trainers behind me in the mire (where they may still be, for all I know) and took off my sodden jeans, much to the alarm of the guys in the band, before settling down for the journey. It'd been a great weekend and the start of a relationship with that festival that endures to this day.

SHOW # 491
The Duchess, York, UK, 6 August 2008

Because of the proliferation of festivals, doing an actual normal tour in the summer months is generally considered to be something to avoid. People tend to spend their cash on the festivals and often don't have enough time, money or party spirit to venture out to normal shows. That said, there are occasions when it makes sense, especially for artists from other countries; if they can fill in the gaps between festival dates with local shows, so much the better. In the summer of 2008, the singer Evan Dando was booked for just such a filler run and Joanna and I managed to get me on the shows as the opening act.

Dando basically *is* The Lemonheads. They're one of my favourite bands and I rate him enormously as a songwriter. I was really excited to get on to the bill for the shows, although a number of people had warned me that the man has a bit of a reputation for being a handful. I was ready to deal with that, though. Simply sharing the stage with him for a short run of solo shows (just over a week, in fact) was great for me, something to put on my CV at the very least and a chance to watch a master up close and in action.

Evan was accompanied by his English tour manager, who we'll call Chris. Chris is a nice guy, but a little long-suffering in his care for his American charge. For the first few days, Evan was friendly enough, although he was clearly a little more interested in where he was going to score that day than in talking to some kid who was opening the shows. Chris occasionally asked for my help in tracking down disreputable people in the towns we were in and as long as Evan got what he wanted, things went off OK.

On arriving at the York show, where the Dando touring party had, for once, beaten me to the venue, Chris took me aside and asked the standard question: did I know anyone in town? As it happened, I had a phone number or two for people who indulged in illicit things who might know someone who could help, and I cautiously agreed to see what I could find out – with the proviso that, it being early in the week, it was not a guaranteed deal. Chris said fine, and I made some calls. My sound check and my set came and went without a hitch – the crowds on these dates were generally new faces for me, but polite, curious and mostly appreciative. As I was packing down, Evan asked me where the gear was. I just told him that I hadn't heard anything.

This didn't go down well at all. Evan swore at me angrily, claimed I'd promised him a score and kicked his way back into the dressing room. I was a little taken aback. Chris shot me an exasperated but apologetic look. Evan took the stage shortly after and played a short, unfocused and unfriendly set, before storming off to head to his hotel without a backwards glance.

I guess they say you should be careful about meeting your idols. This experience was something of an eye-opener for me. As anyone who has read this far into this book will be aware, I've been no stranger to illicit substances in my time and have indulged out on the road; I'm no angel and I'm not one to point fingers in any case. But there was something so nihilistically focused about Evan's quest for getting high (and it really didn't matter if it was weed, coke, pills or whatever) and something so viciously self-centred about his anger when I didn't, as he saw it, deliver the goods, that was really shocking to me. It made me think again about that whole world, which sounds slightly lame now that I say it out loud, but it's true. I was a little sad to see someone I so respected as a writer be such a dick to people around him and, most of all, to play such a disrespectfully poor show for the people who'd paid to be there. It all sat uneasily with me because of the work ethic that I subscribe to.

I thought pretty hard about whether to include this story here, as I don't want to sound like I'm putting the boot in. Far from it – Evan remains an incredible writer and when he was on form on that tour he was a joy to watch. But the true facts of being lost in drugs, when encountered up close, just aren't pretty and it's not a road I want to go down myself. Since then I've been a lot cleaner on tour – never perfect, of course, but a lot more mindful of treating my audience with the courtesy they deserve. Sometimes you need to see someone else make your mistakes before you can correct them in yourself.

SHOW # 499
Regent's Park Open Air Theatre, London, UK,
24 August 2008

The summer of 2008 was a great one for me. It was a transitional time; everything was shifting from the old, ramshackle way of doing things to a set-up that was better organized, more efficient and on a slightly larger scale. I think I had the best of both worlds at this time.

After the tour with Evan Dando, the band and I did a bunch more festival appearances before the season wrapped up. Since the

UK tour in April, Chris T-T had been occasionally holding down the keys in the band. It was an absolute pleasure playing with the guy – he's a fantastic musician and a great friend. But I think we all knew it wasn't going to be feasible in the long term, as Chris has his own career and his own songs to tend to and share with the world. So as August ran down, there was a slight sadness in the knowledge that these would be the last shows we did with this line-up. Thankfully the shows on offer were great. We played at Beautiful Days – the Levellers' festival down in Devon – and also on the Lock Up Stage at the Reading and Leeds festivals.

The Lock Up is run by my old friend Mike Davies, the punk DJ at BBC Radio 1. It was another massive step up for me to be at those festivals, for the second year running, with significantly larger crowds than the year before. While the shock of their scale was less than it had been in 2007, it was great to feel that everything had moved up a gear. In 2008 I was the only person to play at both the long-running Cambridge Folk Festival and on the punk stage at Reading – and may still be the only person to have done that as far as I know. That's something I think I'm allowed to be proud of.

The last show of the summer was the day after Reading, a booking that was always going to be a little trying for my voice and constitution. Seth Lakeman was making an appearance at the Open Air Theatre in London and I'd been asked to open the show. Seth is a fantastic folk singer and songwriter from Devon and it was a great privilege to play with him. The venue itself is a wonderful place – a steep amphitheatre right in the middle of London's finest park. It being a folk show, the full band had not been invited to play, but Chris and I put together a duo set, with him on piano, which seemed like a fitting end to his official time in the band. The sun was hanging low in the summer sky as we took the stage and my ragged vocal chords rose to the occasion for what I remember as a magical set.

Quite the summer.

SHOW # 500

Lexapalooza 3, Nambucca, London, UK, 6 September 2008

I've already written about the first Lexapalooza, which took place back in 2006. The second one was held in 2007. Lexie was very ill at the time so most of the organization was handled by Evan Cotter, a close and old friend of mine. I couldn't make it as I was in the USA. Lexie passed away soon afterwards. In the aftermath of her death, Evan decided, along with a few others, to keep doing the Lexapalooza festivals, partly to continue raising money for the Breast Cancer Campaign and partly in memory of the friend that we'd all lost.

This was the first of the festivals to take place after Lexie left us. Evan sorted Nambucca as the obvious venue and put together a great line-up of bands and singers. I was technically not supposed to be playing extra London shows at the time as I had a gig at Scala coming up (more on that later). But there was no way I was missing this event for a second time, so I was booked as the not-very-secret headliner for the day.

I think of this event, in a way, as being the first proper Lexapalooza. It had all the things that I've come to love about the day: a firm crew of awesome people running the show, managing the stage, selling cookies at the cake stall and generally having a ball; and a varied line-up of old friends and new acts. The day is usually pretty drunken, as we all figure that Lexie would not have wanted it to be any other way. It's always a blast, we raise a load of money and we all shed a tear here and there for the one person who's missing from the party.

By the time my set rolled around at the end of the day I was far from being sober. During the day Evan had been selling song requests for my set and a large bagful of slips of paper was proffered to me once I got onstage to help me direct my set list. Alas, the people at the show had used the occasion to call for songs I don't play so much any more and alcohol had the predictable effect of hampering my memory for old words and chords. As a result, my set was chaotic, with more than one false start and abandoned song. But the vibe was so great that it didn't matter and at the end of the night I played 'Long Live the Queen', the song I'd written for Lexie's passing. After she checked out, back in 2007, I'd written the song very quickly. The words came together one afternoon when I was in Paris, sat on a bench in Montmartre looking out over the city trying to come to terms with my loss. Since then it had become (and remains) something of a crowd favourite, which is simultaneously gratifying and disconcerting. In the end I'm reassured by the thought that, at a guess, Lexie would approve – or at the very least find it funny. Somehow it was both very hard and very easy to sing that night.

The festivities continued into the small hours and I ended up catching the first Tubes back across London with Isabel in the morning, feeling ropey as hell and trying not to make eye contact with more fresh-faced travellers. It had been a great party. As it happened, it was also the last time I would ever play at Nambucca, though I didn't know that at the time. Looking back, it was a good way to say goodbye to the old place.

SHOW # 507
The Warhol, San Antonio, TX, USA, 27 September 2008

The state of my career has always been a little behind in the USA compared with the UK for the obvious reason that I started touring my home country well before I went over the Atlantic to the New World. This has actually usually been something of a bonus for me

– switching between playing shows at different levels and with different atmospheres helps keep me fresh and my faculties of entertainment sharp. So after some increasingly healthy touring and a great festival season back home, I boarded a plane to rejoin my old buddies Fake Problems in California for a run of shows that was a little more hand-to-mouth.

Also in tow was a band called Cobra Skulls – a great punk 'n' roll combo with an obsession with skulls and, well, cobras. After a couple of shows on the West Coast we headed inland into the desert. I made my first visit to Las Vegas (where I shivered with fever after the gig and singularly failed to do any gambling). We played a seriously ropey last-minute show in Anthony, New Mexico, in a youth project a mere stone's throw from the Texan border, to a handful of kids who seemed to be trying to decide whether it was worth robbing us.

Eventually we rolled into San Antonio, the site of my first American show in March 2007. This was to be Cobra Skulls' last gig on the run with us, although the Fakey Ps and I were continuing all the way to the Florida coast. As with many of the shows on this run, we were a little hazy as to where exactly we'd be staying the night, but we were resolute in our faith in the punk community's ability to provide (and I have to say that it has rarely let me down). We played a fun show to a half-full room before getting stuck into the serious business of drinking with friends who were soon to part ways.

At some point in the evening we arranged to stay with a Hispanic guy from the show called Pepé. Pepé was (and indeed is) an enthusiastic punk kid who simply could not get over my accent. The English accent is a curio to many Americans and can often be used to great advantage. An English friend of mine was once accused by a girl in a bar in Brooklyn of faking his accent in order to get laid (even his passport wouldn't convince her that he was a genuine

Brit). Pepé just thought it was hilarious and adopted me, much the worse for wear, as his evening's entertainment, feeding me sentences to repeat in my mother tongue at regular intervals through the night. We all made it back to his house in the two tour vans. The photos I found on my phone the next morning featured Devin, the Skulls' singer, wearing lipstick, so we were clearly having fun. Come midnight, it became John Berna's birthday. John was the Problems' tour manager at the time, so the festivities were given an extra boost. At some point in the night we fell asleep in a motley heap in the front room of Pepé's house.

The following morning, we woke gingerly. When crashing round at strangers' houses on tour you often have to get up a little cautiously and re-evaluate the situation. One resident's late-night opinion that eight sweaty strangers sleeping on the floor is a great idea can often be overturned by his or her housemates (or indeed their own sobriety) come morning. So the more sensible members of our party were scouting things out, creeping into the kitchen to find Pepé. Derek Perry (of Fake Problems) and I, meanwhile, were in the bathroom, shaving ourselves comedy handlebar moustaches, which made us look like a cop duo from a 1970s' TV show. Were we still drunk? Well, maybe.

Meanwhile, the scouts had found our host, apron on, happily preparing a barbecue for his considerable extended Mexican-American family. Derek and I stuttered our apologies, feeling like idiots, while our whole party quickly started gathering our things and preparing to skedaddle out of the way (an almost instinctive activity to the road dog and one well-practised), embarrassed at having gate-crashed a family day. Pepé, however, hastily informed us that the meal was essentially being held in our honour, the family had been invited over to meet us and that we were to stay and enjoy the food at our leisure before the day's short drive to Austin. So we stayed and continued John's birthday celebrations, heartily eating some incredible food before winding on our weary way. Pepé has remained a touring friend ever since.

One of the great things about taking to the road on the underground punk circuit is that you end up with friends like that in every city of the world – people you see once a year, but who are always happy to drop what they're doing to help out their itinerant friends, to take you to the decent local bar after the show and to let you sleep on their floor. In the UK, that's something that is a little less remarkable, given the size of the country and the fact it's where I come from (or maybe I just take it for granted). When you're many miles from home, on the other side of the Atlantic or even further afield, you learn to appreciate it more. In a way I feel like these people are the unsung heroes of independent touring. Without them the road would be a harsher and less survivable place. One time when I stopped by, Pepé gave me a little Catholic postcard with a picture of the Archangel Michael on it as a good-luck charm and protector for life on the road. I keep it in my wallet.

Whenever I'm at home I always try and put up any bands passing through, to vaguely rebalance my karmic debt.

SHOW # 519
Blender Theater, Manhattan, NY, USA, 13 October 2008

The shows with Fake Problems took us to the East Coast – 3,000 miles along the I-10, from sea to shining sea – and then up through the endless flatness of the Midwest, finishing up in Lansing, Michigan. After the sweet sorrow of our parting, I boarded a plane to New York City for a few shows on a different tour, shows that would turn out to be pivotal for me in the USA.

Chuck Ragan is one of the singers from Hot Water Music, a Gainesville punk band that soundtracked my youth, as they did for pretty much anyone else into that scene in the late 1990s. At one point I had a little picture of Chuck – singing live, all veins bulging from the neck and pure passion washing down his brow in sheets, torn out of a No Idea Records mail-order catalogue – stuck up on my bedroom wall. Hot Water continue to tour from time to time, but sometime in the early years of the first decade of the century Chuck decided to pick up his acoustic guitar and start writing country and folk songs on his own – a move that I can very much identify with.

In 2008 he put together a new idea for a tour – Revival. The idea of Revival is to take singers, mainly but not exclusively from punk backgrounds, and throw them together for an acoustic, roots-based tour. It's a different kind of tour – there are no real delineated sets, everyone shares songs and the stage and it has more the feeling of a travelling revue than anything else. The first run included Chuck, Tim Barry (lately of Richmond, VA's Avail) and Lucero's Ben Nichols and Todd Beene (pedal steel), as well as Jon Gaunt (fiddle) and Digger Barnes (upright bass) as a sort of house band. On top of that core line-up, they were picking up extra players along the way. Revival as a concept and a tour continues to this day, but it can't be denied that the shows that first year had a special kind of magic to them.

I was asked to play four of the shows – Asbury Park (NJ), New York, Hamden (CT) and Washington DC. I'm not entirely sure how Chuck came across my music and what I was doing, but he had decided he liked it and offered me the gigs. I accepted gladly and took a bus down to New Jersey; I was very excited to play.

The first show was at Asbury Lanes, a classic punk venue in Asbury Park on the North Jersey Shore. I wasn't really too clear on how the Revival shows worked at first. I didn't know anyone else on the tour and generally felt like a little bit of an impostor, surrounded as I was by musicians who were older and better travelled than me and to whom I massively looked up. These were also the best-attended and biggest American shows of the tour to date. The Lanes was packed out with 300 or so people and it was with some serious trepidation that I took my turn in the spotlight. In the event, it was one of the most affirming shows I've ever played – the crowd went crazy and after half an hour the room was mine. It was then that I realized that these were to be game-changing shows for me.

That, however, is not the reason why I wanted to write about the gig at the Blender the following night. It was similarly epic for me, even if the surprise was slightly less than it had been twenty-four hours earlier, but it became significant for a different reason. After my set I wandered into the crowd to see how things were going at the merch and to make some friends. I ended up chatting to an English guy called Will. Unlike everyone else at the show, he'd come to see me play. Neither of us really knew too many other people, so we became conversational and drinking partners for the evening.

We were discussing life, the universe and everything when Will said a curious thing to me. He said he loved reading the stories about the characters in my songs, it seemed like a charmed life to him and he wished he could inhabit that world, have those kinds of experiences. I said there was no real secret to it – I just try to seek out interesting people and places; life comes to those who look for it. I genuinely don't think I have any special pass-word or secret key to life. Anyone can do what I have done, or at least embark on the journey. He shrugged and said 'Maybe' and we talked about something else.

At the end of the gig, a general plan was formed by the Revival touring party. Jesse Malin, the former singer of D Generation, had joined us on stage (he and I sang a Hold Steady cover together) and was now inviting us to join him at his bar, Niagara, in Manhattan. So after everything was packed down we were gathered on the pavement outside the club flagging down a small fleet of cabs to take us across town to our designated watering hole. Will was still with me, shooting the breeze and suddenly we found ourselves together at the front of the taxi queue, looking at an open yellow door.

Will hesitated, not sure if he was really invited to come with us. I looked at him and said, 'This is it man, this is the moment where you choose. Either get in the cab and come adventuring, see where the night leads us or go back to the youth hostel and keep listening to records and imagining what might have been. So get in the fucking cab!'

Will did get in the cab and came to the bar and we all had a memorably raucous evening. The Revival crew were there, as were the Gaslight Anthem boys and Matt Skiba from Alkaline Trio. Will in fact, I think, managed to cop off with one of the bar maids (though I've never been sure about this). I ended up winding my way back to the tour bus and the next day I got an email from Will saying that he'd wandered back to where he was staying through the empty New York streets as the sun was coming up, buzzing from the night.

I think the story stays with me for this reason: I spend a lot of time talking about something I believe passionately, which is that life is what you choose to make it, for the most part, and more often than not all you need to do is seize it by the throat and demand more from it. This is probably the most obvious, succinct example of this point that I can give. Even if it was nothing else, it was a beautiful night, a moment in our time not to be forgotten.

SHOW # 531

The Rescue Rooms, Nottingham, UK, 31 October 2008

I came back to the UK just in time to start the second official headline tour for *Love Ire & Song*. It was another reasonably long run around the country, fourteen or so shows in about as many days, with the band in tow. By this time, Chris T-T had bowed out of playing the keyboards for me – he had his own musical commitments to attend to, not least opening for me with his own backing band, the Hoodrats, on this run. I'd been concerned that this would lead to another protracted search for a band member, but luck was finally on my side. On the previous tour of the year we'd met Matt Nasir, a prodigiously talented musician who had been playing for Andy Yorke. He's one of those guys who is just better at everyone else's instrument than they are (the piano is actually his third calling, after bass and guitar) and he's a fun guy as well. So I asked him if he'd be interested in joining me, Ben, Nigel and Tarrant. He said yes. Though we didn't come up with the name for some time, this established the firm line-up of The Sleeping Souls, the band I am more than happy to play with to this day.

We also had the first proper incarnation of my road crew on this tour. Graham was tour managing and taking care of the live sound, Barbs was guitar-teching and stage managing and Sarah looked after the merch in her own idiosyncratic way. The family had grown.

The venues on this run were notably a step up from the previous jaunt – averaging about 400 people to a show rather than 200 – and they were all selling out in advance. The first gig was in the large room at The Cockpit in Leeds. We'd decided to change the set around and open with 'The Ballad of Me and My Friends' (a song that had tended to be a finisher). I remember walking on to the stage from the door at the back at the start of the set and being met by a wall of noise as the crowd sang along. As a band we were starting to properly gel together and become a relentless musical proposition. The London show was at Scala in King's Cross, the venue I'd played for the Stop the War Coalition more than a year before and, again, it was a sell-out. I felt like we were on top of the world.

This was a UK tour where London wasn't the last show. I

always think that's a bit of a drag – you expend all your energy playing and socializing and then have to force yourself not to coast through the remainder of the dates. That's not because I think London is inherently better than anywhere else in the UK; it's just that it's usually the biggest show and it's the one most of my friends come to. After Scala we had a few more shows, including Winchester (where we were a little tired), before driving north to Nottingham to play The Rescue Rooms.

I suppose my immune system wasn't in the best shape at the time, but I'm reasonably sure the actual culprit was a chicken and mayonnaise sandwich from a garage near Oxford. During sound check I felt a little drained. As showtime rolled around I felt increasingly weird, but there were 500 people waiting for a show so I went on nevertheless. As the set list slipped by I knew that something bad was about to happen – my guts, my head, everything was starting to swim. We blasted out the song 'A Love Worth Keeping', which has a long high note at the end. When the note was done I knew I was as well and after a few bars of the next song ('Father's Day', as I remember), I suddenly took off my guitar, threw it to Barbs at the side of the stage, ran into the dressing room and heaved my guts into an ice bucket.

It really felt like I was throwing up my own pelvis; like I was pushing every single thing held in my thorax out of my throat. The gig was over. After I was done throwing up I lay on the floor – grey, sweating and shivering. I felt awful, not just physically, but also because I'd let an audience down. I'd never abandoned a show mid-set before and it hasn't happened since. Nigel courageously let the crowd know that I was quietly dying in the next room and people filtered out, confused and angry (at least in my fevered imagination).

That night the band headed home while Barbs and I checked into a hotel next to the venue. I was alternating between being freezing and unbearably hot and he, great friend that he is, was on watch to make sure I didn't quietly shuffle off this mortal coil during the night. The next run of shows, including Ireland, was clearly not going to happen. The marathon run of gigs on both sides of the Atlantic (plus the sandwich) had done for me.

It was a sad way to end the tour, but I suppose the great thing about this job is that the road stretches ever onwards. There are always more shows to play.

SHOW # 539
Grabenhalle, St Gallen, Switzerland, 23 November 2008

I was, in my solo career, a latecomer to the European continent, I'm sorry to say. With the exception of my slightly manic runs to France and the Baltic, it wasn't until this point, late 2008, that I started playing shows across the Channel. Looking back now I think it's a shame it took me so long. I think maybe I had some underlying fear that the music I was making, particularly if I was playing without the band, wouldn't translate (quite literally) for the crowds in Europe. I know now that I shouldn't have been so judgemental or so dismissive of people's capacity to understand English, or at least the more universal language of music.

Joanna had put together a slightly ramshackle tour, which was hung around a few key pegs – some dates in the Netherlands with the Levellers (more on them later) in particular – and a run of shows in Italy had been put together by Eric, an enthusiastic local promoter. Chris T-T was along for the ride – to play keyboards with me for some of my set and to play his own songs as well. Chris was also down to drive, given my lack of skill in that area.

We took the Eurostar to Paris to play at La Flèche d'Or at a trendy new bands showcase kind of night. As per usual with those kinds of events, it was poorly organized and attended. I have a soft spot for Paris nonetheless (not least thanks to an ex-girlfriend I may have mentioned in a song) and it was good to be back. Unfortunately, the whole excursion was then nearly sunk by a fuck-up with the rental car we were using to get around for the whole tour.

There then followed a panicked evening of problem solving. As stressful as it was, I often think that it's moments like these that remind me why I love a life of touring. You have to be completely alert, open-minded, resolute and proactive. The problem has to be solved, there's no safety net, no buffer zone – you have another city to be in the following day. Somehow or other we got it sorted and in the morning we headed for the Netherlands.

We did two shows with the Levellers and then headed south on our own to Switzerland, where promoter Martin Schrader had organized some low-key headline gigs. Martin is, in my opinion, the best at his job in the country and we continue to work (and drink) together now. Switzerland is a quite unbelievably beautiful country, so Chris and I had a whale of a time checking out the fields, mountains and the architecture in Lucerne and Basel.

The third Swiss show was in St Gallen in a venue called the Grabenhalle. It's a big room, but we played through a vocal PA on a small stage in the lobby, a better setting for an acoustic show. It was also better, though still a little roomy, for the crowd that showed up – about ten people. Being the professionals that we are, Chris and I had a nip of whisky and then threw ourselves heart and soul into our respective sets. The small crowd was delightfully appreciative. As I finished I looked out of the windows of the building to see that a huge amount of snow had fallen in the time that we'd been on stage. In fact, as the stage had a large plate-glass window behind it we'd been framed by a scene of falling snow as we'd played. After the gig we didn't so much disappear backstage (actually there wasn't one) in a puff of glitter and dry ice, we more just kind of stepped forward into the crowd to hang out with our new friends.

Chris and I and the small audience made our way out into the biting cold together, the two Englishmen rather more filled with wonder at the scene than anyone else. Nevertheless, it was strikingly beautiful, enough to silence us all for a little while. I stood at the top of a hill, knee-deep in fresh snow, with the sweat of a gig freezing rapidly on my brow, next to good friends – old and new, the intricate, archaic rooftops of the old town stretching out before me and thought that I was lucky.

After St Gallen, Chris and I took a long train ride through Austria, where we got ripped off by the promoter at a show in Vienna. On the plus side I met some remarkable people at the show – two Englishmen and a girl from New Zealand, who were living in Budapest and making their living through gambling, pool sharking and throwing house parties at their squat. I christened them The Grifters and they made it into a song I was writing at the time about the road. Finally we flew to Italy for some slightly weird shows and then made our way back home, resolving to return to Europe as soon as the opportunity arose.

SHOW # 561
Proud Galleries, London, UK, 19 December 2008

When I was a little kid, throwing myself first into metal and then into punk and hardcore, my older sister had bombarded me with other types of music, most of which bounced harmlessly off my angry adolescent carapace. Some of it got through, however – the sisterly trinity comprises Tori Amos, Counting Crows and the Levellers. The Levellers have never been a fashionable band, but like pretty much all Levellers fans I couldn't give a tuppenny shit. I've loved the Levs for a long time, so it was something of a dream come true when I was asked to do some shows opening for them, first in the Netherlands (which I've just written about) and then around the UK.

The tour featured me playing solo, then a Czech punk band called Divokej Bill, then the main event. The shows were in big venues around the country. Like most bands of their size, pedigree and longevity, the Levellers have fans that are not always, to put it kindly, all that interested in checking out new, unknown acts, so I knew I had my work cut out for me. For this run I took my old friend Tré – Nambucca resident and former tour manager of The Holloways – with me in a hired car as we tailgated the tour bus up and down the motorways.

I had a great time on the tour. As well as the joy of making friends with a band I grew up idolizing (and they are truly lovely people) and getting to watch them night on night, I also went over pretty well with the crowds and added a whole new group of fans to my team. In Lincoln I ended up playing a second set in a pub around the corner for some people who'd come to see me and missed my set; in Southampton we had a massive Christmas dinner on the floor of the Guildhall before the doors were opened to the public. It was a good run.

In a spectacular piece of logistical planning, someone had tacked a few extra dates on to the end of the tour that meant the itinerary included a gig in Inverness the day after a show in Oxford. That's just about doable in a tour bus, where you can combine travelling and sleeping time, but if you're driving it's murder. So after the Oxford set, Tré and I packed up quickly and drove towards Scotland, planning to make as much time as we could before we got tired, then turn in for the night in a hotel, before finishing the drive in the morning.

As we tore north through the night, windows down and radio blaring, Tré got a phone call. It was from Ally, a DJ and promoter who was also living at Nambucca at the time. He asked if she was in the pub – she said no, she was on tour – and he said that was a relief, because the building was on fire. As in, it was burning down.

We pulled off the motorway at the next available exit and found a cheap hotel somewhere in Lancashire. I checked in while Tré frantically spoke to everyone she could get hold of on the ground, trying to find out what was happening to her home. The whole place was in flames and seemed to have already passed the point of no return. We settled in for the night, Tré heartbroken and glued to her mobile, me feeling slightly useless and also sad as the full extent of the damage unfolded to me, second-hand.

The following day Tré dropped me at a train station and I made my own way to Inverness. The Levellers agreed that I could travel on their bus for the remaining two shows of the tour while Tré went home to salvage what she could. The next few days passed me by in a grey blur; it was much worse for her and everyone at the pub, all good friends of mine who'd lost everything in the fire. There's still some debate about what actually happened, though this is not the place to discuss it, but the bald facts remained – Nambucca was gone and a lot of my friends were essentially cast out on to the winter streets of London.

As is often the case, in the midst of tragedy humanity chooses to reveal its good side. Nambucca was more than just an indie pub in north London – it was representative of something, something anarchic, communal, decadent, hopeful and chaotic. Many of the people who had passed through its doors as punters and residents came together to help out those who had been made destitute. Clothes were provided, living space was found. Hell, even the local dealer gave everyone a free round of his wares. It was heart-warming and tragic at the same time.

For my own part, I had a London Christmas show already booked for the day after the end of the Levellers tour, at the Proud Galleries in Camden. The show had been planned as a charitable event and was sold out. Once the full horror of the situation with the pub became clear, I called the charity that had been the intended recipients of the cash raised (Shelter, a housing and homelessness charity) and asked if they would mind me cutting out the middle man and giving the money direct to people who were having trouble finding places to stay over Christmas. They readily agreed, so the show became a benefit for the Nambucca refugees.

It was an emotional night. I played solo. It wasn't so long after the Scala headline show, which had been a triumph for me and the band, and on a personal level it felt like a reconfirmation of that achievement to have the 400-capacity room crammed to the rafters – not least because everyone from the pub was automatically on the guest list. Tré also made it to the show and we had an emotional reunion. The crowd roared their way through my set, singing along with pretty much everything I could think to play. At the end, the 'Ballad' ripped a fresh hole in everyone's heart as we sang about 'another Nambucca show' knowing there would never be one.

The dust has long since settled on all that now. There's another bar of the same name in the same place, but it's not the same people and it bears no relation to the memories I cherish. The people involved have gone on to other projects, other bars, other lives. I think we all still pause, though, when we're on the upper Holloway Road and think about the times we shared. A lot of people have a glorious moment in their lives, some halcyon days, and mine were spent there.

SHOW # 563
London Astoria, London, UK, 14 January 2009

It was, it seems, the season of farewells. The Astoria, as I've mentioned, was a central venue for London and for me personally. Sadly, after many years of swirling rumours, it was finally confirmed that the entire block in which the building sat was to be demolished to make way for a high-speed railway line across London. Naturally, it was decided there should be a final show, a last blow-out, so a random, last-minute bill came together.

On the night itself I found myself giving quite a few interviews as the British music press came together to mark the passing of an era. Everyone wanted me to give lofty, nostalgic, bittersweet quotes about what a travesty it was that the place was closing down. I found it hard to oblige. I was still reeling from the end of Nambucca a few weeks before and, as much as I loved the place, the Astoria was kind of a shit-hole – it hadn't been done up in many years, not least because of the constant threat of arbitrary closure.

But there was another, deeper reason: rock 'n' roll is, at base, an ephemeral art form. It's an explosion of youthful energy; it's all about the moment – a Polaroid picture rather than an oil painting (I might have mentioned this in a song). It was never supposed to be about monuments and museums, about permanent records. It's about that one night where everything came together, the band tore up the stage, you danced and kissed a pretty girl and watched the sun rise with a bottle of whisky and some good friends. To me, trying to constantly lock down places where rock 'n' roll happens seems to run against all of that, to miss the point. Even Nambucca, which was so much more than just a venue, had to end somehow or other. And sure, it's a problem to have one less venue to play in. But rock 'n' roll is a rebel idea, something that is supposed to thrive in adversity, not be sanctioned and subsidized by the author-ities. To all the people bemoaning the passing of the Astoria, I said, 'Let's go out and find the new place that will be like this and we can be the tedious old farts at the back telling everyone it isn't as good as the old days and we'll be dead wrong, just like the old-timers were who castigated us when we were kids.'

The gig was a weird one. Because it was so last-minute, the bill felt thrown together (because it had been) and there wasn't ever a critical mass of audience appreciation for any one act to really bring that feeling of togetherness to the room. A lot of people were there just for the event and I saw guys with screwdrivers taking doors off their hinges while bands were playing. It was oddly anticlimactic, as if the real spirit of the place had already moved along; which, in a sense, it had.

After my set, I could sense the beginnings of a monstrous party coming together. As tempted as I was to hang around, I opted instead for an early night. The following day I had to be up early and head to Europe with the band to play a set in Groningen, in the Netherlands. The gig was a little disjointed – the room was half-empty and due to a family crisis we were a man down (Nigel couldn't make the show). In keeping with the spirit of changing times, it so happened that at that show I met Carolina, who worked for Epitaph Records in Europe, who was mighty excited about my set. It was a meeting that was to have huge implications for where things would head in the future.

SHOW # 578
Underground, Cologne, Germany, 10 February 2009

After my initial foray into Europe with Chris T-T in 2008, I was keen to get back out there and make further inroads. Early in 2009 I got a call presenting me with a fantastic opportunity to do just that. A new (at the time) and up and coming American band called The Gaslight Anthem had a UK and European tour booked and wanted me to be the main support. I have to confess I hadn't heard of them prior to this and if it had been just the UK shows I would probably have declined as I was planning to headline many of the same venues within a few months. However, there was a long European leg of the tour, so after consultation with Joanna and Charlie I enthusiastically accepted.

The first phase of the tour was in the UK, which at the time was buried under an unusually heavy snowfall, which led to the first gig being postponed. For the tour, which I was doing solo (with the exception of the London show), I had arranged to travel with the opening band, another American outfit called Polar Bear Club, who play heavy, hardcore-influenced rock. I hadn't met them before, but jumping in a van with strangers for a long stretch of travelling was something I had a fair amount of experience of by this stage.

After the London show, at Shepherd's Bush Empire, we boarded a ferry and headed for the Continent. The first show was in Cologne. I'd never set foot in Germany before and didn't speak a word of the language, so I was unsure of what to expect. In fact, to be perfectly honest, I was a little nervous. I was playing solo, without the weight of my band behind me. In that circumstance, lyrics are of paramount importance and I really wasn't at all sure if the Germans would understand what I was saying, both literally (could they speak good enough English?) and artistically (does an Englishman have much of interest to say to German punks?). Gaslight's merch guy, Gunnar, was German and he prepped me with a few introductory sentences before I took the stage with some trepidation in front of a packed room.

Within about five minutes I was ashamed of my previous doubts. The crowd was awesome – receptive, attentive, respectful and raucous in all the right measures. I don't think many people had any idea who I was, but by the end of the set the reaction was great and at the merch table that night I sold a mountain of records and shirts, as well as making a whole lot of new friends. Many people with world touring experience will tell you that Germany is one of the finest countries to play in. That night I discovered the truth of that fact first hand.

The rest of the tour was a fantastic ride. We got stranded in Stockholm for four days after Gaslight's van was broken into, meaning that we all missed the ferry to Finland (Polar Bear Club and I, seven people in all, spent the time sleeping in a single hotel room, which was intense). We got hammered in Munich, met old friends in Vienna, had an altercation with arsehole venue staff in Milan, crossed paths with Katy Perry in Amsterdam (well, sort of – we were playing at the same venue) and finished up exhausted in a bar in Dublin. Along the way I made new friends not only in crowds across Europe, but also with the two bands and their crews. Gaslight have gone on to become a major part of my story and I remember this first tour with them with great fondness. As for Polar Bear Club, well, we shared enough cold floors and cramped van time to make us as close as anyone I've toured with. Gunnar put out some of my records on vinyl in Europe (on his label which he, y'know, named after himself, Gunnar Records).

All in all, one hell of a trip.

SHOW # 604
Friends Bar, Austin, TX, USA, 20 March 2009

After the Gaslight tour, I headed back out to the USA, back to Austin for another shot at SXSW. My previous visit, two years before, had been good fun, but from a purely business point of view had not achieved all that much. Things were very different this time around. Charlie and I were working hard at sorting out a record deal for me in North America and had been having a lot of the long, suggestive, faux-enthusiastic conversations that characterize contractual flirting and negotiation. In particular we'd been talking to a Californian label called SideOneDummy, who looked after Gaslight and Fake Problems, among others, and the legendary punk-rock label Epitaph. We set out for Texas with an exciting but uncertain prospect before us.

After a pretty tumultuous journey to the USA (involving cancelled flights, rerouting via San Antonio and a late-night bout of driving by my saintly Texas friend Adrienne), I was happy to get back to Austin, a town for which I have a lot of love. The morning after my arrival, still exhausted from the journey and jet-lagged to boot, I drove to the outskirts of town to a small rehearsal studio to meet some new friends. The guys at SideOneDummy had suggested that it might be fun (and affordable) for me to play some shows with an American-based backing band and to this end had contacted a friend of theirs, Steve Soto. Steve is an early SoCal punk old-timer, having formed and played in the Adolescents in the early 1980s. These days he also has a solo project – Steve Soto and The Twisted Hearts – and they had happily and kindly volunteered to back me up for some shows.

So it was that I walked into a rehearsal studio to meet my new band. A lot of the old country singers regularly play with 'pick-up' bands, but it was not something I'd done before (or since, for that matter). I was pretty nervous and not sure whether we'd sound any good at all. But I'd sent a selection of songs through to the guys with some chord sheets and it was delightful, if slightly surreal, to count off the numbers and have them all come in pretty much note perfect. We ran through our short set a few times, settling into playing with each other and relaxing in each other's company. A few hours later, we were ready to go, which was great because our first show was that afternoon.

I should say at this point that playing with those guys was

great fun and I'm thankful to them for helping me out. But at the end of the day, playing with The Sleeping Souls is in another ballpark. There's no substitute for the years we've put in together and for their musicianship. They're the band for me – the best band in rock 'n' roll as far as I'm concerned.

Over the following couple of days I had what I suppose is a 'classic' experience of SXSW. I played a lot of shows, made a lot of friends, got wined and dined by plenty of record-label people and did a lot of partying. The shows with The Twisted Hearts all went well. I saw The Hold Steady, Two Gallants and Ed Harcourt play blinding shows. I felt a little bit like I was in the film *Almost Famous* – the archetypal depiction of the rock 'n' roll myth – a feeling I don't get so often. It was a great time.

My final show was a solo affair as part of a showcase of British acts in a venue at the end of 6th Street called Friends Bar. I was playing last and in all the chaos of the festival the stage times had run long, so by the time I was up to play I was told there was only time for a couple of songs. There were a couple of hundred people in the room who were dismayed by the prospect, so I resolved to play through the curfew. However, after a few tunes the PA was cut by the tired and inflexible venue staff. I wasn't done playing and the crowd was not done listening, so I headed out into the street with my guitar and started playing in the middle of the road, standing back to back with Jay (Beans On Toast) who was helping me out with fighting the noise of the street by singing and playing along with me. It was one of those moments – a growing crowd surrounding us, traffic stopped, songs howled out at the top of my lungs. Every now and again I meet people who were there and we all agree that it was something memorable, something special.

There's a short coda to this story. By the time that last show was done, and despite the care and attention of the good people at SideOneDummy, Charlie and I had pretty much agreed to go with

Epitaph for my future releases outside the UK. I was in a great mood, all my shows done, good friends around for the party and a record deal in the bag. So I went for gold in the decadence stakes and pretty soon I was several sheets to the wind. I was hanging out with Fake Problems and a mutual friend, Derek Martinez, a tattooist from Austin who runs a shop called Lucky 13. We decided after a while to head back to Derek's place and drink cheaper beer and party in more private confines. However, Derek's place was also where his tattoo materials resided and soon some pretty silly drunk tattoos were under way. Thankfully Derek is straight edge and doesn't drink, so he was able to keep some kind of order amid the chaos. Nevertheless, I managed to tattoo some of my lyrics ('Dead but never dying' from 'Vital Signs') on John Berna's chest and Derek inked a small outline of the state of Texas on my left bicep, where it remains (obviously) to this day, a small reminder of a remarkable weekend.

SHOW # 608

The Viper Room, West Hollywood, CA, USA,
26 March 2009

Thankfully, after the SXSW debacle I had a drive across the vastness of West Texas in which to recover. After Austin, The Twisted Hearts, Look Mexico (more on them shortly) and I played a show in San Antonio. I remember going to sleep on the back bench of the van as we set out after the show, just before midnight, driving west. I woke up a full ten hours later, bleary-eyed, feeling cramped and sweating in the glass-filtered sun, asking where we were. The answer rang dead in the air: 'Still in Texas.' Thankfully I was starting to feel a little better.

We made it to the West Coast, playing a show in Arizona en route. The main stop on the run after Austin was a show at The Viper Room in West Hollywood. My previous stop on these hallowed grounds had been a red-letter day for my personal life, meeting Isabel. This time round I was headlining in the main room (rather than in the broom-cupboard-like basement room), with a backing band, as a label showcase of sorts. We pulled up outside and as we hastily lugged equipment out of the burning sun into the shadowy interior I glanced up and saw my name tacked slightly unevenly to the masthead on top of the building. That felt good.

Later that night, Brett Gurewitz, the founder and head of Epitaph Records, guitarist with Bad Religion and all-round punk-rock legend, came to the gig to check my set and, effectively, give his final seal of approval for me to sign to his label. Epitaph was the mark of musical quality in my formative record-buying years. I used to go to the local Our Price record shop with my scrimped and saved pennies and pretty much buy anything with their logo on the back of the CD. Through them I discovered The Offspring, NOFX, Rancid, the Descendents, Propagandhi and countless other bands that still pretty much define my taste in music. In recent years, under the auspices of their imprint ANTI-, they've also released records by Tom Waits, Nick Cave, Billy Bragg, The Weakerthans and others – in short, the other main subcategory of 'music I like'. In the meetings that we'd had since the start of the year I'd met most members of their team on both sides of the Atlantic and made some firm allies already.

Or to put it all another, much shorter way: when Brett said he liked the show, I was pretty stoked.

SHOW # 614

Bar Deluxe, Salt Lake City, UT, USA, 1 April 2009

On the long, winding road from Texas to the coast and then north to San Francisco, The Twisted Hearts and I had been accompanied by a band called Look Mexico. They are an awesome bunch, originally from Florida but since relocated to Austin, that I met through Fake Problems on some early runs around the United States. In between wowing audiences with their resolutely poppy brand of post-something-or-other, they habitually rode in their own van, which is a wonder to behold. It was originally a minibus for ferrying pensioners around the old-people's homes of the Florida suburbs, but they converted it not only to hold a band (with enough space for most people to properly stretch out and sleep, if needs be) and its equipment, but also to run off vegetable oil. This was both an ecological and a financial measure – most of the fuel was procured by asking around fast-food restaurants just before they closed at night to see if you could get their leftover cooking oil. The van then chugged slowly but resolutely across the wilds of America, making everything in and around it smell of chips (or fries, to my American friends). It was quite the touring vehicle.

The tour continued up the coast from LA to San Francisco, where, after a wild night at Thee Parkside, we parted ways, the Californian Hearts heading south to their homes and loved ones. Look Mexico and I, being rather further from our respective base camps, continued north into the wastes of Oregon. I particularly remember this stretch of shows for being one of the most hardcore bouts of driving and playing I've ever experienced. The northwest coast of the USA is famous for being sparse on shows and thus requires long hauls, but if you're doing it in a chip-mobile with a top speed of sixty miles per hour (less on hills, of which there are many), it gets brutal pretty quickly.

We made it to Portland and had a wild and virtually unprintable night hanging out with strippers in the city. We then headed inland and drove alongside the majestic Columbia River towards Boise, Idaho. There, after an eleven-hour drive, we were greeted by an audience of ten people. A dismaying performer-to-crowd ratio, but they gave us a warm reception. Immediately after the show we considered our next stretch – across the mountains to Salt Lake City in Utah. After some discussion, we decided that we should start driving right away, despite our exhaustion and van-sickness, and get a few hours in before stopping at a motel to grab some sleep and continuing in the morning.

What we didn't bank on was the weather. A spring snowstorm descended on the high-altitude passes just as our fast-food-powered home began the torturously slow climb through them. Visibility dropped to about ten metres and in the swirling snowflakes we caught glimpses of large trucks jackknifed off the side of the road, cars smashed into the central reservation – total desolation. Crawling along at almost walking pace, we shivered together, terrified, gazing out of the windows, desperate to stop but unable to tell if any of the exits would lead to any kind of accommodation.

After a couple of hours, our indecision and slow progress assumed its own logic and as daylight loomed and the snow abated it seemed to make sense to just keep slogging through, however slowly, to reach the relative sanctuary of Salt Lake City. At about 10 a.m. we rolled dejectedly into a car park on the outskirts of the city, near the university, and shuddered to a halt. There was silence in the van. The accumulated long drives, the sleepless fear of the snowstorm, the claustrophobia of the cramped interior – sometimes on tour, it's best for everyone to just shut the fuck up and say nothing. We all lay down and attempted to get some kip, however brief.

On waking, unrefreshed, an hour or so later, a couple of pertinent facts dawned on the assembled company. First of all, we had two shows that day – a matinee all-ages affair at a community centre called SHO, followed by a bar show in the evening at Deluxe. Secondly, we were in Salt Lake City. The home of the Mormons is not, as I had thought, a dry city, but they do have mandated low-strength alcohol – weak beer and watered-down spirits. Given that we were all spoiling for a hard drink, this was something of a problem. Usually bands just drive to a liquor store on the city limits to stock up, but more driving wasn't really a popular option just then.

We loaded in and played the first show to a small but cool crowd of local kids who – like so many people who live in the scattered, isolated towns of the western USA – were just grateful that we'd made the effort to be there. Increasingly crabby and tired, we loaded back out and hauled across town for our second show. This, at least, was in a bar and we were each given enough drink tickets to get a pitcher of local brew. I settled into mine as fast as I could, but was disappointed to find out that, far from getting me hammered, it barely touched the sides and just made me need to pee a lot.

I sat down at a table with a guy from the local punk band who were opening the show for us. The attendance was very sparse – it seemed like we'd drawn everyone we were going to draw at the first show of the day – and I was a little disconsolate. The local offered me his ticket for the band-issue pitcher of beer and I happily accepted. As I was pointlessly chucking that one down after my first failed attempt at drunkenness, I asked him why he didn't want it for himself. 'I know that if I have one drink, I'd be an alcoholic,' he said, quite cheerfully. I immediately assumed he was a recovering drinker and fumbled an apology, but asked if he'd had problems himself, or in his family. 'Oh no,' he continued breezily, 'I've never touched a drink. I just don't want to be an alcoholic.'

Given that I wasn't drunk, I can't blame my crappy logic on the booze – maybe just the tiredness. But it slowly dawned on me that he was a Mormon and thus not someone given to chugging down pitchers of beer, however watered down they were. I guess it was a small culture shock for me. I mean no disrespect to the guy – he was nothing but friendly and his band rocked – but it was a strange encounter for an Englishman so far from home.

I played my set and spent the rest of the night at the bar with the Look Mexicans, trying and failing to get out of our heads on weak drinks in order to forget the fact that we had another ten-hour drive to Denver the next day. At some point Matt (Agrella) pointed out the date – 1 April. We had to laugh.

SHOW # 618
The Wheatsheaf, Oxford, UK, 29 April 2009

By the time I got back from that run in the USA, things with Epitaph Records had basically been settled. We'd agreed a deal whereby they would release my records everywhere in the world except for the UK, which was to remain with Xtra Mile. That was my dream set-up, so I was very happy to say yes. Epitaph were to release *Love Ire & Song* first and then crack on with the new, third and as-yet-unrecorded album.

So the main project on the table when I got back to the UK was to make that record. As ever I'd been writing a lot on the road. Writing is something I find difficult to talk about properly – not because it's uncomfortable for me, but because I lack the vocabulary to adequately describe the process. In some ways I feel like a sleepwalker waking up; I come to with a finished song, but can't remember how it ended up in my hands. I jot down ideas in notepads and on my phone all the time, but the process of massaging those fragments into a recognizable whole remains slightly mysterious to me. I'm fine with that. The process doesn't seem to be broken (yet) and I don't want to examine it too closely in case I do break something.

This time round, in contrast with previous album sessions, I knew that I wanted to take the band into the studio with me. In fact, I wanted to record the music as live as possible and on to tape (rather than a computer) to give everything a raw, unpolished and old-fashioned feel. That meant that the songs, such as they were, needed to be fully rehearsed with the band before we hit the studio.

Tarrant, my bass player, also runs a van-hire firm for bands and has a yard just outside Oxford from which he runs his business. In the yard are some Portakabins and garages, so in early 2009 we set about turning one of the spare ones into a rehearsal room. After much blood, sweat and tears (not so much on my part, if I'm honest, because I was on the road in the States) we had a small but comfortable soundproofed room that was ours to call home. At the start of April 2009 we loaded our equipment in, set up and began arranging and rehearsing a new record.

We spent a gruelling three weeks in that tiny space, powering through the songs again and again, fleshing them out from skeletal guitar-and-vocal compositions into full-throttle rock songs. There was some tension. The conflict between me as a solo artist and us as a band – something that has reared its head many more times in my career – mirrored the cramped physical conditions, but on the whole it was a good experience, our forging as a musical unit and I still feel like you can hear that context on the resulting album, *Poetry of the Deed*.

At the end of the three weeks we decided that we should play some shows in Oxford. Playing new songs live in front of an audience knocks them into shape much faster and more brutally than is possible in the practice room. We arranged four small shows in a row in town and sold them on the basis that we would be playing the new record in full. All four sold out pretty much instantly.

At the first of these shows, at The Wheatsheaf, it worked out that the people from Epitaph Europe would come over from their Amsterdam office, check out the set and sign the final deal. I remember the atmosphere being slightly odd – even though we'd warned people what to expect, it's still a lot to ask of an audience, playing thirteen new songs in a row. It was a tough sell and while the songs felt good, I could tell the moment we were in front of a crowd that there were little tweaks that still needed to be made. Nevertheless the Epitaph crowd were pleased, the deal was signed and it felt like I was starting out on a new phase of this journey.

I went off into another room with the label people to sign the record deal, leaving the guys in the band packing down the equipment. After we were done, I went back to hang out with Ben, Nigel, Matt and Tarrant. While they congratulated me warmly, I could sense something was amiss, though I couldn't quite put my finger on it. I was starting to get really weirded out, when I finally realized that they were all refusing to make any eye contact with me when we spoke – a joke they'd arranged in my absence. It was around this time that the guys in the band gave me a nickname – 'The Product' – designed perfectly to annoy the hell out of me. I love my band.

SHOW # 622
Bar Matchless, Brooklyn, NY, USA, 23 May 2009

After the four Oxford shows, the band and I headed for the studio. We'd chosen Alex Newport to produce the record. He's something of a legend to me, not only because of his studio work, but also because he'd been in early 1990s' sludge band Fudge Tunnel. I was excited about him working on the sound and getting us some-where near the Two Gallants records that he'd made, but I was possibly more excited at the prospect of getting tour stories about Napalm Death, Fugazi and Sepultura. We spent a week playing the songs live in a studio in Norfolk, owned by Dan Hawkins from The Darkness, and then Alex and I hopped on a plane to New York. Alex has a studio in Brooklyn, so the plan was to finish off the vocals and the mixing for the album there.

My first week in New York saw me being studiously well-behaved. My voice takes some looking after and given that we were recording for posterity I needed it to be at its best, so it was all early nights, no drinking or going out and generally being boring. By the end of the first week, the vocals for the album were done and now all that was left was for Alex to mix it while I 'super-vised'. That meant I was off the hook, so I immediately called my friend Arty Shepherd.

Arty has been in a number of awesome underground punk bands, from Errortype:11 through to Gay For Johnny Depp (who opened up on the final Million Dead tour). He also used to work at a bar called Matchless in Brooklyn. I wasn't supposed to be playing any shows while I was in New York, because I had a gig in town with The Offspring in the diary for July, but I figured that a small, last-minute, word-of-mouth-type affair wouldn't hurt. And where better to do it than at Arty's place?

A sign that word was really starting to spread about what I was doing, at least in some parts of the USA, was that the small gig ended up being packed out. After weeks of no sunlight and the weird discipline of the studio it felt awesome to be out on a stage again, with my audience in sweat-dripping distance of me. The show was a blast, new songs went down well and old songs were like old friends. I felt like I was back in the saddle again. The studio isn't really my natural environment. There, you're constantly making decisions about the minutiae of songs that are irreversible – will I sing this line up or down? Slow or fast? Will I drag this part out or cut it short? And the versions you lay down become the permanent record. That always seemed false to me – songs are organic, they continue to grow and change and fluctuate at the edges. The great thing about playing live is that you get a chance to reinvent the songs, night after night, to play a new definitive version to be revelled in for that night only, before being invented anew the next day.

SHOW # 652

Pitkä Kuuma Kesä Festival, Helsinki, Finland,
27 June 2009

When you've finished making an album, thoughts naturally turn to methods of promoting the thing. A big part of that is picking a single, a lead track from the record to send to radio stations and so on. And when you've picked a single, you generally make a music video to promote the song. The whole process really isn't my favourite part of what I do, but it's a necessary evil and within the confines of the process it's possible to have some fun.

As we were preparing for the release of *Poetry of the Deed*, the song 'The Road' was decided on (by me and Charlie – though he's a much better judge of these things than me) as the best tune to introduce the world to the next album. For the video, all I knew is that I'd wanted to work with a director called Adam Powell for some time. He's a busy guy, but this time we finally nailed him down to work on the promo clip. We had several long phone conversations about what direction the video should go in. The song is about movement, travel, touring, the road, so we were naturally discussing a visual interpretation that reflected some of those things. A subtle game of one-upmanship began. Adam suggested a performance video in a number of locations. I suggested that it could be shows in different towns and cities around the UK. Slowly but surely, we started edging towards the cliff, until finally someone blurted out the dreaded words: 'Why not try and do twenty-four shows in twenty-four hours?'

Once the idea was on the table I knew we had to go with it, but organizing such a stunt, let alone actually doing it, was a daunting task. And as is always the way with me, everything was a bit last-minute – we didn't have masses of time to plan or shoot the video. A public appeal on my blog got me an awful lot of offers from people to play at house parties, offices, record shops, bars and the like, and after a bit of logistical trickery we had ourselves a route. The plan was to play one show on the hour every hour for twenty-four hours, playing for twenty minutes or so and then travelling to the next location. Everything was in the Greater London area and I managed to put together a schedule that made some vague geographical sense. The team was also set: we had Barbs driving the van, Adam and a friend running the video and my friend Brad Barrett coming along for the ride, shooting little bits for a behind-the-scenes clip. We were starting and finishing at the Flowerpot, the new bar in Camden that the people behind Nambucca had opened up. We were all set.

The experience of playing those shows is one that I'd file under 'Glad I did it, don't want to do it again, thanks'. Things started well – the first eight shows or so were a breeze, jetting between house parties across north London full of cool, appreciative people. We were filled with cups of tea and the occasional beer, my voice was holding up and everyone was full of vim and vigour. However, as the night went on our first major error became apparent: the schedule ran from 8 p.m. to 8 p.m., which meant that we'd already been up and about for a full working day before we started. As we reached the early hours it became obvious that this was going to be tough. My friend Pete had jumped onboard in an effort to boost morale. Some of the shows, particularly around the 9 a.m. mark, were pretty bizarre – playing to a handful of people in their bedroom while their parents left for work, that kind of thing. Energy levels went from high, to low, to in between, to weird, to unquantifiable.

The home stretch, from about 5 p.m. onwards, got a little easier, as a kind of kamikaze spirit started to infuse the situation. We realized at one point that we'd missed a show somewhere along the line and needed, with some urgency, to add one more performance. My friend Jenny Hardcore (a photographer who has taken many album-sleeve shots for me) happened to be living near the Flowerpot, so I called her and asked if I and about ten other people could drop round and play a fifteen-minute show in her front room. She was, naturally, a little confused, but said yes and thereby saved the day.

Finally we reached the Flowerpot again, to a full room of well-wishers, many of whom had been at previous stops on the run. Everyone, myself included, was slightly incredulous that we had actually made it and the adrenalin and glow of success enabled me to play a full forty-five-minute set to an awesome crowd of friends and fans. After I finished a shindig of sorts got going and I stayed up for another couple of hours, drinking and partying.

This was a terrible idea as I had only one night to catch up on sleep before I had to head for the airport to get a flight to Helsinki. I was playing a new festival there called Pitkä Kuuma Kesä (PKK). I knew that this was my schedule, but in the delirium of exhaustion the realities of that fact kind of slipped my mind. I got to sleep eventually, but my alarm went off a few hours later and it was then that the full force of tiredness hit me square in the face. The cab journey to the airport passed by like a dream and I think I slept through the flight – in fact, I was surprised that they let me on the damn thing in the first place, so incoherent was my check-in attempt. I was met at the airport in Helsinki by someone from the festival. By that point I could barely remember what my name was, so I stared uncomprehendingly at his welcome sign for a while before twigging that he was looking for me.

The show itself actually went OK, apart from the fact that my voice was a little ragged around the edges. There was an appreciative crowd of people waiting for me to play and when I told everyone where I'd been and what I'd been doing in the past thirty-six hours I think they were a little more forgiving. After the gig I was due to hit a bar to catch up with some old Finnish friends, but when I went up to my hotel room to drop my bag and guitar off I ended up falling asleep, fully clothed and with all the lights on, for a good fourteen hours.

The video stands as a pretty cool testament to that little adventure. I've since had half-joking conversations with Adam about ways in which we could top the achievement: the only real suggestion being to try and do twenty-four cities in twenty-four hours, using a helicopter. But I don't know anyone with a helicopter and, to be honest, I'm happy for that one to stay on the drawing board indefinitely.

SHOW #658
Starland Ballroom, Sayreville, NJ, USA, 7 July 2009

One of the more surreal phone calls that I've received in my life happened when I was stopping over at my sister Jo's house in Colorado in April 2009, just after the end of the run around the

USA with Look Mexico. Charlie called me to say that, out of the blue, he'd received a request for me to open up a bunch of outdoor arena shows in America for The Offspring.

The Offspring were one of the punk bands of my youth, just like for a whole generation of kids whose introduction to the scene was through their record *Smash* and Green Day's *Dookie*. *Smash* is still the biggest-selling independent record of all time and I can sing along with the songs on it in an almost Pavlovian fashion. The prospect of touring with The Offspring in the USA was both exhilarating and daunting. These would be miles and away the biggest American shows for me to date; but I'd be playing solo, completely unknown to large, restive, punk-rock audiences and I really wasn't sure how things would go down.

I called my friend John Berna (Fake Problem's tour manager) and arranged for he and I to drive the tour in a hired car. It wasn't a particularly long run of dates, though it did meander down from Canada and the north-east to southern Florida. The tour began in Canandaigua, upstate New York. John and I ended up staying with a guy called Donny Kutzbach, a promoter from Buffalo who had seen me play in Austin at SXSW that year. He also put on a show for me at his venue, Mohawk Place, on an off day. To complete his hat-trick of kindnesses, as we were pulling out of his driveway and heading for Toronto, he asked if we had somewhere to stay that night. When we said no, he gave us the number of his friend Michael, who dutifully came out to that gig (my first one in Canada) and put us up. Michael and Donny are both part of a group called Postcard From Hell, a network of music fans that began as an Uncle Tupelo appreciation society but that has grown into an organization with a will of its own. I think of them as a musical illuminati and I've run into and been kindly treated by their members all over the world.

Playing before The Offspring (and the main support band, Sum 41) was a strange experience. Pretty much no one at the shows knew who I was and my arrival onstage each day was generally greeted with some consternation. In fairness, it was a reasonable reaction to an English guy with an acoustic guitar onstage at an arena punk show. But night on night (or more usually, afternoon on afternoon), I was just about holding my own and making a few new fans here and there. The Offspring guys were all thoroughly welcoming and I was having a good time.

The tour rolled into Sayreville, New Jersey, an army town distinguished by the fact that Jon Bon Jovi grew up there. The Starland is a somewhat dilapidated 2,000-capacity ballroom that sits in the middle of nowhere in a car park. On arrival, I discovered that, while the show had been advertised as being me, Sum 41 and The Offspring, in fact the bill was to be a local competition-winning band, then me, then the headliners. This didn't bode well. As the crowd rolled up, it became apparent that I might be in for a tough show. Not wanting to be unkind, but the crowd that night was overwhelmingly made up of drunk, tough, south Jersey dudes, who were there to drink and mosh to punk tunes they knew, not to listen to a skinny English guy with an acoustic guitar.

My arrival onstage was not an auspicious start – the simple, stark fact of my not being Sum 41 didn't go down so well. The acoustic and English nature of my whole act was also, apparently, not what the crowd was looking for. Half a song in, some people in the crowd started chanting 'USA! USA!' People were heckling, spitting and throwing empty (and some not-so-empty) drinks vessels at me. The mood was ugly. I'm not one for taking that kind of shit lying down, so I decided to rearrange my set a little and play some quieter, more folky numbers, as well as aiming a few barbed remarks at the flag-waver jocks. 'So this is what passes for punk rock in Sayreville, is it?' They didn't appreciate the question.

By the end of my set things were starting to get decidedly

raucous, if not actually homicidal. I made a beeline for my dressing room as soon as I was done, deciding to forego my usual stroll over to the merch table. The promoter came to see me, paid me for my set and then advised that I leave by the back door – probably, like, now. John, my friend Evan (visiting from the UK) and I did just that and headed into Brooklyn to drown our sorrows. None of the rest of the shows was as bad as this, though it was a pretty weird billing all told. That said, in years since I've met plenty of people at my own shows whose first experience of what I do was on this run, so some people were definitely paying attention.

I think this is probably the worst reaction I've ever had from a crowd. I wanted to include this gig here to point out that this touring life isn't all roses. I can laugh it off now and play up how fucking punk I am for lasting it out, but the truth is it's really unpleasant being on the receiving end of that kind of shit and I'm happy it's not something I've had to deal with too often.

SHOW # 664
Titan House, Philadelphia, PA, USA, 12 July 2009

When you're on a tour of large venues opening up for a band like The Offspring, you quite often have to sign up to something called a radius clause. This is a condition that you won't play any head-line shows of your own within a certain time period and distance of the show that you're opening. So, for example, because there was a New York City show on this run with The Offspring (at the Roseland Ballroom), I wasn't allowed to play any other shows in the city for a couple of months before. It's a way of the headline band making sure that they maximize the crowd-pulling potential of their support acts. I'm really not sure how many people I

164 | THE ROAD BENEATH MY FEET

brought to the show in New York, but I can understand the principle behind the clause. What it means is that, practically speaking, if you want to play a show on an off day on the tour you sometimes have to miss out obvious towns and drive slightly crazy distances to reach places that aren't off limits.

The other option, of course, is to play a show off the radar; something not at a traditional venue and that doesn't have tickets for sale in advance, that kind of thing. A house show is perfect. So it was that John and I arranged to stay in Philadelphia on our drive south at a place called Titan House, home of Jon Murphy. Jon used to play for the band Barlights, who I'd shared shows and a van with back in 2007. Initially we were just looking for somewhere to rest our bones between New Hampshire and Baltimore, but once the stop had been agreed, Jon suggested that I could play a set in the house and I readily agreed.

I put the details of the show up on my site and didn't think much more about it. I wasn't expecting much, but if we had a small but appreciative crowd then that'd make for a constructive way to spend my evening. Titan House, like all Philly punk houses (of which there are many) was a pretty run-down place in a less-than-salubrious part of town. But everyone was friendly when we arrived, they had a small PA set up for the gig and everything was set to go well. It was hot as hell, East Coast summer weather.

As the afternoon wore into the evening, people started arriving for the show. *A lot of people.* In fact, after a while it became clear that the little room in which the gig was being held, which basically constituted the entire ground floor of the house, was going to be absolutely rammed full. In order to try and cut down on complaints from the neighbours (and thus visits from the cops), all the doors and windows were shut, with only a pathetically useless ceiling fan as any kind of respite from the monstrous heat. The Menzingers, who at the time were a small local band, though they've now gone on to much-deserved, bigger things, opened with a great acoustic set. By the time I fought my way to the front there were probably 150 people in a small-sized living room – wall-to-wall sweating humanity.

I took up my position at the front. John Berna was crouched at my feet leaning back into the shins of the front row of the crowd in a vague attempt to stop people pushing forwards and smothering my playing. The PA speakers were right next to my head and the sound was distorting pretty badly. But right from the get-go the atmosphere was insane. The whole crowd came together and sang the songs at the top of their lungs from the first chord to the last. At one point my guitar strap broke and I ended up with two people holding it at the right height, one at either end, so I could keep playing. I took my shirt off it was so hot and still sweat was pouring off me. I played for about an hour or so, feeling completely at one with the crowd, blown away by the experience.

Every once in a while I play a show that affirms why it is I do this; that reminds me how lucky I am. This is one of the most memorable, most tangibly electric shows that I can think of that I've played. Since it happened, videos from the night have been on the internet and the people who were there have talked about it incessantly, spreading the word to the point where it gets mentioned in interviews around the world. I still meet up with people at shows across the East Coast who were there and we talk about it like it was a special, magical evening. Because it was. If I could relive just one evening, just one show, this might well be it.

Afterwards we celebrated, drank till dawn and I slept on a sofa in the corner of the room that had previously been packed with people and strewn with empty beer cans. The rest of the run with The Offspring was cool, but nothing, none of the arena shows, quite lived up to that night in Titan House.

SHOW # 675

Y Not Festival, Pikehall, Derbyshire, UK, 31 July 2009

After the Offspring run, I came home again to resume the usual run of summer festival shows. At this point I was still oscillating between solo shows and full-band shows, but the arrangement was more dictated by finances than anything else. It's a lot easier and cheaper for a tech and I to do a show than it is to take four extra musicians and the associated equipment. This was slightly frustrating, because from an artistic point of view I wanted to be playing with the full band line-up, but in the absence of a big label pumping tour-support cash into the operation, I had to make do with the resources at hand.

This particular weekend Barbs and I loaded up a car with guitars and drove north from London for a couple of regional festivals – Y Not and Kendal Calling. I had played Y Not before in 2007 and it was a welcome return. The festival started as a guy called Ralph's birthday party. Ralph, being the proactive type, has grown the event year on year. So what started out as a small shindig featuring friends' bands, has become a serious, well-run, mid-level UK festival. Situated out in the Derbyshire hills, it still has a great vibe to it, like it's a secret that everyone there is in on, that the rest of the world hasn't cottoned on to yet.

Barbs and I arrived at the festival, with Barbs driving our small car carefully around the edges of the muddier patches in the field. We went through the standard festival arrival rigmarole – trying to find some kind of artist entrance or at least a check-in, then trying to find a relevant stage and maybe even someone who knows who you are, why you're there and what on earth is going on. We succeeded in these various missions without too much trouble, dropped our equipment in a storage area near the stage I was due to play and then considered our options.

Camping at festivals is not my favourite thing in the world if I'm honest – I feel like I did quite enough of that in my late teens and early twenties, thanks. If you throw in having expensive musical equipment and a show to play, it's really not a great way to get your beauty sleep. So on this occasion Barbs and I were booked into the nearest Travelodge hotel. That, however, was a good fifteen miles away – like I say, this festival is remote. Barbs fancied having a beer or two at the festival and we had quite a lot of time to kill before my show, so we decided to drive back to where we were staying, check in and then get a cab to and from the festival.

We checked in, decompressed a little and then called the taxi number on the card provided by the receptionist. A car driven by a creaky old guy duly arrived, though it did feel like the taxi firm was basically this guy, with his wife working the phone back home. No matter. We had wheels, we were good to go. We told him we were heading for the nearby festival in the hills, which he immediately said he knew and he set out confidently on the picturesque B roads.

I've never had the best sense of direction, so the fact that it felt to me like we weren't heading in the right direction didn't seem to matter too much. It also felt like we'd been driving for too long after a while, so some gentle enquiries were made as to whether this guy actually knew where we were going.

'Yup, big ol' festival, lots of tents, in the hills, I know it,' he asserted. So we piped down again. A while later he turned off the main road on to a smaller one and then again and again until we were basically driving down a farmyard track. At one point I had to get out and open a gate that was keeping a flock of sheep in the next field. We were driving down an incline into a small valley and as the road finally petered out altogether he pulled up on the side of the road.

'Just up over that ridge, there's the festival,' he said, squinting and pointing to the top of the hill in front of us. It seemed like a dubious proposition to me, but he pretty much kicked us out of the car, took our money and rapidly reversed back the way he'd come and out of our lives. Barbs and I stood in a dell, looking up at the hill and wondering if this time we were finally, well and truly fucked.

We traipsed up to the crest, hoping against hope that the revealed landscape would be dominated by the expanse of tents and parked cars we'd left behind an hour or two before. Alas. On reaching the summit, the achingly beautiful (but festival-free) hills of Derbyshire spread out before us, gently rolling and unending in all directions. Fuck.

After a discussion, some amateur taking of bearings and a fair amount of guesswork, we struck out boldly in what we thought was the right direction, hoping that the next crest, or maybe the one after, would reveal our destination. We had no such luck. We started out calmly checking our watches, seeing that we had many hours before showtime, but after a while the possibility that we might miss my set, wandering haplessly through the countryside, started to become real. When we eventually stumbled across a road we tossed a coin to choose which way to go and hiked for a good few miles until we finally came across a farmhouse, the first proper sign of civilization since our driver had ditched us.

We cautiously knocked on the door, which was opened by a nervous, middle-aged woman, who was understandably a little weirded out by finding two bearded, tattooed men wandering around her front garden. We explained our predicament and she told us her husband would be home shortly and that he knew where the now-near-mythical festival was. He duly arrived and laughed his rural arse off at the two of us. It turns out the cab driver must have driven in pretty much completely the wrong direction and had dumped us like so much dead weight when he realized his mistake. The husband very kindly offered to give us a lift the twenty miles or so back to Y Not, which we gratefully accepted. So it was that Barbs and I, like returning Argonauts, made it back to the festival site, thankfully in time for my set.

The gig was a lot of fun. A great crowd had gathered in the place we'd had so much trouble re-finding. I seem to remember also doing a guest spot with my friends The King Blues that night, in which Itch, their lead singer, encouraged me to try freestyling over a verse of one of their songs (always a terrible idea, my career in hip-hop is clearly a nonstarter). At the end of the night we got a lift back to the Travelodge with someone who definitely knew where they were going, but Barbs had his phone mapping our journey just to make sure.

SHOW # 701
The Yellow Dog Tavern, Winnipeg, MB, Canada,
1 October 2009

I wrapped up the summer of 2009 with a return to the Reading and Leeds festivals, something that was now becoming pleasantly habitual. Immediately afterwards, *Poetry of the Deed* was released, my first proper record with Epitaph. Their international team immediately kicked into gear and whisked me off around the world. After brief promotional stops in Cologne and Berlin, I was back in North America, meeting up with the Gaslight boys for a tour of the USA and Canada, along with The Loved Ones and Murder By Death.

We started in Denver. I was renting a bunk on Gaslight's bus, so I got even closer with them and their crew on this tour. It was a pleasure to watch them tear through the material from *The '59 Sound*, their second record, which they were promoting at the time, night after night. I also enjoyed getting to know the music and the players of the other bands on the bill, especially Dave Hause of The Loved Ones.

We passed through Los Angeles (where I met Tim Armstrong from Rancid backstage, a big deal for me, and played some in-stores and house shows) and then on up the West Coast. Shows in Portland and Seattle allowed me to guest-list friends from earlier, more down-at-heel tours. We then entered the vastness of western Canada, the first time for me, playing in Vancouver, Edmonton, Calgary (where I did an aftershow in the bar downstairs) and Regina.

We pulled into Winnipeg the day before our scheduled show at the Garrick Centre, meaning that we had a much-needed day off in the city. Winnipeg had long held a fascination for me because of the music of The Weakerthans, a local band who have documented their city beautifully. They also happen to be my favourite band. So I spent a little time in the afternoon scouting out landmarks from the lyrics of John K. Samson and taking cheesy tourist shots.

That night, we found out that another punk-rock tour was in town, starring New Jersey's The Bouncing Souls (a band I knew and loved from my youth) and Off With Their Heads (a new band to me, but one that I liked). They sent word to our bus that we were all invited to the show and would be on the guest list. However, sometimes on the road if you get a day off the last place you want to be is in a gig venue, back among the bustle and the noise. I decided to politely decline the invitation and spend the night watching DVDs in my bunk on the bus.

Just after 11 p.m., the door to the bus was flung open and an unfamiliar American voice roared down the gangway: 'Where the fuck is Frank Turner? You English son of a bitch!'

This turned out to be Ryan Young, singer with Off With Their Heads, a man who was a fan of my music and who'd been excited about me seeing his band. When he discovered that my name was not checked off on the guest list, he'd resolved to come and find me and demand some kind of restitution. I was, at this point, in whatever passes for pyjamas on tour (usually just T-shirt and underpants from the day), but nevertheless he dragged me from my repose.

On finding himself holding me up in my underwear, a little sleepy, in the gangway of an unfamiliar bus, I think Ryan realized that his plan lacked an endgame. After some consideration, he decided that we were going to have a *drink*, dammit. Resigned, I threw on some jeans and followed him out into the cold autumnal air. The nearest drinking establishment was across the road, a small dive bar called The Yellow Dog Tavern, so we decamped over there to get to know each other and take a chunk out of the house whisky supply.

As it turned out, with some kind of grim predictability, there was a tiny stage and PA in the corner of the bar, complete with an old guy playing traditional folk and country tunes on a battered old acoustic. After a few drinks Ryan demanded the stage and the guitar for me, but the old guy (quite understandably) refused to hand over his prized instrument. So before I could say 'This is my day off . . .' Ryan had run back to the bus, grabbed my guitar and brought it back to demand a show. The old guy finished his set and I set up at the corner of the bar, on a stool, with the faintly amused barman feeding me shots after each song that Ryan called out and I played. After a while the Gaslight and Bouncing Souls crew all gathered in the bar as well, so we had a genuine show on our hands.

I finally put my tired reticence behind me and started to enjoy myself. In the end it was a great evening. The owners of the bar couldn't quite believe that I was also playing with Gaslight across the way the next day and they took my offer of guest-list spots with a fair amount of cynicism. The following night, after my opening slot with Gaslight, they found me at the merch table and conceded that I hadn't been bullshitting.

Every time I swing back through Winnipeg, I make sure I have a drink at The Yellow Dog.

SHOW # 731
Berbati's Pan, Portland, OR, USA, 1 November 2009

I've spent a lot of time thinking about, and changing my mind about, whether or not what I do for a living can be described as a 'job'. On the one hand, obviously, I do something I'm passionate about, something I did for much less than a living for a long time, something most of my friends would give their eyeteeth to do. I'm not just working here for the fucking money. I'm also not doing something as meaningful or socially useful as, say, a nurse or a teacher. On the other hand, what I do isn't exactly easy – a lot of people try to get to this point and fail or can't take the physical and emotional strain. The amount of time I spend each day doing the fun, vocational part (making music) is much less than I spend travelling, waiting around, doing admin chores and so on. So in the end I suppose I subscribe to the old B. B. King* adage: 'I play for free; it's the rest of the shit I get paid for.' Some days, the rest of the shit can be almost overwhelming.

After the end of the Gaslight tour in North America, I headed home for a very quick turnaround before the official UK tour in support of *Poetry*. This tour was a real step up for me, moving

---

* I've heard this quote attributed to an awful lot of different people, but B. B. King is the oldest of them, so I'm sticking with him.

from the 500-capacity level up to around 1,000 – and sometimes more – people a show. We had Fake Problems and Beans On Toast out as the support acts. It was a solid run around the UK and Ireland, starting in Dublin, and a lot of the shows were starting to sell out before we hit the road.

It was a memorable run. In Glasgow, we crashed the open mic at the Student Union after the show (and got given lifetime honorary membership cards). In Nottingham, at the legendary Rock City, we had a transcendent moment. We'd booked into the big room there for the first time, which holds 1,800 people, but had been expecting to sell it without the balcony, roughly 1,000 tickets. On the day, we arrived to discover that the whole room had sold and there were still people queuing outside in the hope of getting a ticket. That was a real moment of knowing that things were starting to go crazy. We played the Winchester Guildhall – not usually a venue for rock 'n' roll shows, but the biggest room in the city that was available, so we booked into it and sold the place out. As a band we were playing better and better, coming together with new material and old, while also spending a fair amount of each night staring with barely disguised wonder at the crowd, which seemed to be forever growing, but never losing the feeling of togetherness, of connection, of dedication.

The London show was at Shepherd's Bush Empire, and it was a special one. Charlie, my manager, and I had jokingly made a deal many years before that if I were ever to sell out the Astoria, he'd do a stage dive during the set (not something usually in his nature). The Astoria had closed, but the capacity at the Empire was the same, so as far as I was concerned the deal still held. All 2,000 tickets for the show had sold. With a little encouragement, he kept up his end of the bargain, leaping into the audience at the triumphant end of 'Photosynthesis', performed with everyone from the tour on stage at the same time. The atmosphere was electric.

After the show we celebrated and I went back to Isabel's place to sleep. I had a grand total of one day off before I had to trudge my weary way back to Heathrow and get on a plane to the USA, to rejoin Chuck Ragan and the Revival Tour, in Portland, Oregon. The scheduling was pretty insane, a tight turnaround not conducive to my sanity or health, but I can't really place the blame on anyone else. I've always pushed my team – Joanna, Charlie and the rest – to get as much stuff in the diary as possible, to fill the gaps and deal with the consequences later. They have usually been the voice of restraint – not the way things habitually work in the music business.

This particular journey was very, very tough for me. I was absolutely not recovered from the UK tour (and arguably the Gaslight run before that) as I squeezed into my economy-class seat for the twelve-hour flight. I made it to Portland late and at night and crashed out in a cheap hotel room, completely exhausted, before predictably waking up a few hours later, frazzled by jet lag. I spent a weird and lonely day wandering around Portland, waiting for the venue to open and the rest of the tour to arrive in town.

When they finally did, it was lovely to see Chuck and friends, and to meet Austin Lucas, Audra Mae, Jim Ward and others, and indeed Casey Cress, the tour manager, a man who will feature heavily in the rest of this story. Even so, I was drained and fighting a losing battle against time zones. No matter how many times I do long-haul flights, there simply isn't a shortcut or trick to beat jet lag (regardless of what I may have said in a song), it's just a bitch. Somehow or other I ended up being given the last slot of the night, which meant I was due onstage for my solo performance at around 11.30 p.m. I vividly remember sitting on my own in the dressing room, clutching a pillar and a beer, desperately trying not to shut my eyes in case I fell asleep on the spot. I can't actually remember much of my set, it went by in an unsteady blur, albeit with a little help from my Revival friends. I collapsed into my bunk on the tour bus straight afterwards and slept like the dead.

That was one of the days when it felt more like a job.

SHOW # 745
Juanita's Cantina, Little Rock, AR, USA,
15 November 2009

My stint on the Revival Tour in 2008 was brief; this run was a much more substantial chunk of shows. We started in Portland, in the north-west of the USA, swept down the coast to San Diego, before trekking through the desert via Vegas and Texas, across the South and finishing up in Florida. With the exception of a brief pit stop in upstate California right at the start of the run, we had no days off at all. There were a lot of players on the bus, which, with the Revival format of an opening ensemble followed by individual sets, made for a long and booze-soaked show every night. At various points the run featured: me, Chuck, Audra Mae, Jim Ward (lately of At the Drive-In and Sparta), Austin Lucas, the Anderson Family Bluegrass Band and Jon Snodgrass and Chad Price of Drag the River. I made new friends, learned new songs night after night and was inspired to write new ones of my own during the day, putting together the first foundations of what would become *England Keep My Bones*.

I also covered a lot of new ground, in particular the American South. A friendly return to Birmingham, Alabama set the tone, but I loved being in Arkansas, Louisiana, Georgia and Tennessee. I have a real soft spot for that part of the world and the people there – it seems to me that they're so beaten down by the negative aspects of their recent history that they end up being more open, more relaxed, less uptight than other people (something I've found to be the case with people from Northern Ireland). They also have the best manners in the world – and that's a fact.

In all honesty, not every show on the run was the best organized or attended. Chuck's enthusiasm for the road occasionally outpaces his logistical planning. There were a few nights where the crowd was a little sparse, to say the least, if not actually outnumbered by the touring party. One such was Little Rock, Arkansas. Everyone – the venue staff and the crowd – was lovely, but at the end of the day you can't make fifteen people fill a venue built for 400. Thankfully, we're professionals and if thinking about Black Flag taught us anything, it's that you should throw the same passion and energy into a show for one person as for a thousand. By the end of the night we had a circle of chairs on the floor of the venue, with everyone sat around and hanging out. At one point Jim poured a shot of whisky for every single person in the room from one bottle. In the end it was one of the best gigs on the whole tour.

A few days later, in an alleyway behind the venue in Orlando, Florida, Jon Snodgrass and I decided to immortalize our time in Arkansas with a song, which we threw together in about ten minutes. 'Big Rock in Little Rock' is a fun song. It also gave rise to the idea of the two of us writing together, which gave the world 'Buddies', which we recorded in Colorado the following summer.

SHOW # 770
Union Chapel, London, UK, 19 December 2009

After the end of the Revival Tour, I hopped back across the Atlantic to rejoin the band and head out on my first proper headline tour in

Europe. Matt, Ben, Nigel, Tarrant and I loaded up in a van, along with Graham, Barbs and Sarah for three weeks' driving and playing across the Continent, relying mainly on the Gaslight shows I'd done in February to get the word out. They were small gigs but for the most part they were packed out, which felt great, like I was making some proper headway outside the safety of the UK, as well as being a welcome confidence booster after some of the sparser shows in America.

Organizationally, many things were shifting around this time. One part of it had to do with tour management and budgeting. In the past I'd done it all myself, as more often than not I was the only person on the road. Now that we had a full band and crew, I was keen to hand off that responsibility to Graham – it's pretty unusual, not to mention unworkable, to have the main person in the band running the tour logistics as well. Having the intention to do something, however, isn't the same as actually doing it and I found it hard to relinquish control at first. This led to something of a fuck-up on this tour.

I'd sort of assumed someone else was minding the budget, and so had Graham. I was also lulled into a false sense of security by the fact that the UK full-band tour in October had made a fair amount of cash. Basically, oversight was lacking. I remember realizing that something was awry and running a quick provisional tour budget in a hotel room in Sweden. To my horror I worked out that we were on course to lose a serious amount of money. Touring with a band and crew is expensive and even factoring in merch sales, it's hard to break even when you're playing to 200 people a night across hundreds of European miles.

After a mild heart attack and a panic-stations phone call with Charlie, we resigned ourselves to the facts – after all, we were now on the road, so there wasn't much to be done about it. It all came out in the wash in the end and this tour set a pattern for my business plans that, to some extent, endures today. The money I make touring in the UK (and these days Germany and some other parts of Europe) mostly goes towards funding my ability to take the full band and crew show on the road in other parts of the world. I'm not trying to garner sympathy – I make a decent living out of what I do now – but it's not quite as simple as some people think. Playing big shows in the UK doesn't automatically mean I'm rolling in cash. I'd be better off if I didn't bother touring quite a few of the places that I go to, but where's the fun in that?

The actual shows were a blast – small sweaty rooms in Germany and further afield packed to the rafters with people who knew the words. We also had the amazing Jaakko & Jay on the road with us, a perfectly bonkers Finnish folk-punk duo who kept everyone entertained with their bizarre broken English between-song banter. I had a mad and exhausting dash back to Manchester for a radio show in the middle of the run that nearly wiped me out and the whole touring party apart from me and Matt was laid low by a vicious bout of food poisoning in Vienna. The gig the next day in Graz went ahead as a duo show, but even then Matt played piano with a bucket next to him in case of disaster. We finished up by the calming waters of Lake Geneva in Lausanne, before winding our weary way back to the UK.

I spent a bunch of time in between tours in 2006 and 2007 hanging out in Paris, because I was dating a French girl at the time. We'd long since broken up, but I had (and still have) a fair few Parisian punk friends from that time and from the tour I did with Cham. So I'd arranged to jump ship from the touring party on the way home and play a solo show in Paris on a boat called *La Péniche Alternat*. Gigging in France is a logistical pain in the arse thanks to their arcane tax laws, which meant I could only really afford to play a solo show, rather than getting the whole band in town. It was also a chance for me to catch up with friends. The plan was that I'd play, stay at Cham's place and then get the Eurostar back to London to rejoin the others for a special end-of-year show at Union Chapel. UC is a beautiful old church in Islington where they have acoustic shows and we had a special set of alternative versions, covers, rarities and guest spots planned. The show was sold out.

The plan was going well – the Paris show was great and Cham and I relived our memories from 2006 by tearing across the city late into the night. Waking up slowly in the grey light of the following day was when the plan started to fall apart. Overnight there had been a massive blizzard, blanketing the city in a few feet of snow. Over coffee and painkillers for breakfast, it wandered across my mind that getting home might be problematic. Cham checked online and discovered that the whole cross-Channel train system had ground to a halt, all trains cancelled (and one caught in the tunnel itself) with no prospect of things getting back to normal. Oh shit.

Tour-managing (or disaster-response, call it what you will) instincts built up from years on the road kicked in, with a healthy dose of adrenalin and panic. Cham and I set up a battle station in his front room, complete with laptops, coffee and cigarettes. How to get one Englishman and a guitar from Paris to London before a show-time of 9 p.m., on one of the last travel days before Christmas, when the weather had paralysed everything? Secretly, moments like this make me feel alive. We tried everything. All train activity was dead. Flights seemed to be booked out and no one was certain if they were going to take off. We even, at one point, called a rich friend of Charlie's who might have had access to a helicopter (disappointingly, that option was ruled out, not least by the eye-watering cost).

Finally we managed to buy a ticket for a flight – I'm pretty sure we bought the last seat going that day – for over £500, which put the whole tour even further into the red. My troubles weren't over yet, however. On attempting to get to the airport I discovered that the French railway workers, lovingly living up to their stereotype, were on strike. Back to Cham's and into his car for a fraught drive to Charles de Gaulle. Having finally checked in, I settled into a moment of luxury in the departure lounge (the ticket I got was business class out of necessity; this was the first time I ever saw that side of the fence), only to be told that the weather was possibly going to ground my flight.

Throughout the whole ordeal I had, of course, been in regular phone contact with both Charlie and Graham, keeping them updated on my progress (or lack of it) and trying to work out if the show that night was going to go ahead. One of the additional problems was that all the special extra material we had planned for the show was as yet unrehearsed. The plan had been for us all to gather at the venue at 2 p.m. and have an extra-long sound check to make sure that the collaborations with Emily Barker, Adam Killip (of The Tailors) and others would go smoothly. That obviously wasn't going to happen now, so even if I did make it, what, precisely, would we be playing?

After sitting on the runway for some time in a stationary plane, we finally took off for London. Following a problem-free flight, it felt good to at last be in the country where I was meant to be playing. However, in keeping with the spirit of the day, they saw fit to leave us sat on that runway too, for an hour or so. I finally escaped the airport with my guitar at about 8 p.m. An hour until the show; this would be a race against the clock. I took a train into Paddington Station, where I met Charlie in his car. He drove from there to Islington like a man possessed – I actually thought we were going to die in the Euston underpass – and I ran in through the back door of the venue, greeted by cheers and high-fives from the band and crew, about five minutes after our scheduled stage time.

I took a breath, had a drink and handed Barbs my guitar to be tuned. I then sat down with the assembled musicians and the set list, as well as a thick marker pen, to try and work out what we could play in the time remaining. Some judicious editing and over-confident estimations of people's ability to wing it through various new arrangements later, we finally took the stage, to a massive round of applause from a patient and hopeful audience, who'd been kept posted about my whole adventure.

As is often the case, victory was snatched from the jaws of defeat. The show wasn't the carefully constructed, complex exploration of my songs that I'd been planning on; but the given circumstances, the exhaustion and panic combined with the relief and the camaraderie of everyone in the room, and indeed the beau-tifully resonant room itself, all combined to make for a magical evening of music. We finished with an under-rehearsed romp through Wham!'s 'Last Christmas' with all our friends on stage with us, thankful just to have made it to the end of the show and indeed to the end of a crazy year.

PART THREE

SHOW # 781
Emo's, Austin, TX, USA, 8 February 2010

Sometime in 2009, something changed. At the start of the year I was still spending time rolling around on trains, playing weird, chaotic shows. By the end of the year, we'd sold out Shepherd's Bush Empire and I had a tour bus and a proper touring band and crew (in the UK at least). That's a huge oversimplification, of course, but there was definitely a gear change in there somewhere. And I still didn't feel like I'd played *that* many shows; time flies when you're having fun, I suppose. I get asked a lot in interviews about when the change was – what was it that lifted me up into the next league? I always reply that it wasn't just one thing, it's been a series of little steps up – and that's the truth. Thinking back over everything that's happened for the purposes of writing this book, I'm not any clearer on what precisely switched. In the end I'm actually quite happy about that, it perhaps proves my glib soundbite true – there wasn't just one thing that happened, it was cumulative, a wave, a momentum.

We headed into 2010 and things moved on again. While retrospective categorization is, by design, teleological, I think it's fair to say that 2010 marked the start of the second phase of my career. A phase that is marked by longer, more gruelling but more regimented touring, especially in the USA. In some ways it's a less chaotic, more coherent phase, with less sleeping on the floor, waking up and playing in strange places and so on. But it also meant I was taking my music to a much, much wider audience, forging an unbreakable unit with the band and moving into new territory creatively. The new phase was emphatically marked by a new tour, which opened with a baptism of, well, maybe not fire, but certainly hot south-western sunshine.

I can't now remember how it was that we got offered the tour with Flogging Molly in the USA. It probably had something to do with Epitaph, something to do with the fine work of Caitlin (our then US agent) and hopefully some musical appreciation of my work, but I've asked a few people and checked some emails and the exact reasoning has been lost in time. Regardless, we got offered the main support slot for Flogging Molly (or the FloMos as we came to call them) at the start of 2010, playing full band, with a four-piece from Kansas City called the Architects opening. I'd done a few American tours before this, but this was the first time taking the band out with me.

I accepted the tour immediately – it was too good an opportunity to turn down – but I was also a little nervous about it. Taking five musicians with backline (amps, drums, guitars and so on) and a van and trailer on the road is a considerably more difficult thing to do than just borrowing a seat or a bunk from the headline band as a solo artist. We'd need equipment, transport, an American tour manager; probably start making enough money from shows and merch together to be liable for American taxes. It was a big undertaking and one that looked set to lose me a lot of money. But big picture it was clearly worth it as it would put us in front of a whole new audience over the pond, so Charlie and I set about making the numbers work.

Our first task was hiring an American to help out. I'd met Casey Cress on the second Revival Tour. Casey was hired as tour manager and sound guy for the run and a long and fruitful touring relationship was born. Together we managed to scrape together a van (borrowed from our friend Craig Jenkins in Santa Barbara, owner of the Velvet Jones club and future crew member) and a backline (mostly borrowed from Epitaph Records). Flights were booked, merch was ordered and the tour was set to go.

Before we got started, I spent a little time jetting around North America on my own doing some promotional work for *Poetry of the Deed*. I made a return to Canada for some shows and then went to Los Angeles for more (including a great house show in Riverside, about sixty miles east of LA). Having pleased the label bods, it was time to get on the road for the tour proper.

There was a slight logistical hurdle to be surmounted first. The van, Casey and the backline were in Santa Barbara, California. The first show with Flogging Molly was in Dallas, Texas. We had a warm-up headline show booked in Austin the night before so that the band and I could get to grips with our unfamiliar equipment and blow out the cobwebs built up over the festive-season break. A quick glance at a map will show you that Santa Barbara and Austin are, to put it mildly, fucking miles away from each other. But it was a journey that had to be made. So Casey and I loaded up at his house and set out on a journey that we conservatively estimated to consist of twenty-four hours' solid driving. (Our show in Austin was in thirty-six hours' time.) We planned a break in El Paso at Jim Ward's house for some sleep. I, as you might remember, don't drive, so I was on duty to play DJ and keep Casey awake and generally entertained. I don't think I'd ever even thought about driving that far in one go before and I was a little nervous about it.

The journey was unlike anything I'd done before. The first eight hours just flew by, but at the first pit stop we realized we were barely out of California. We left in the morning and planned to be with Jim by the evening, but as these things always go, we were running behind. In the end we pulled into his yard at about 1 a.m. Jim greeted us sleepily, accepted the gift we'd bought (a 3-D picture of a tiger from a gas station) and put us to bed. We slept for a few hours then got back on the road – we had to get to Austin Airport in time to pick up Ben, Nigel, Matt and Tarrant and then get to the venue for a sound check.

It was a race against time in the end. We bundled the exhausted band into the van after pulling up a few hours behind schedule, then hightailed it over to the venue – Emo's, a classic Austin punk venue that was, alas, closed down not long afterwards. We spent a frantic hour unpacking boxes, tuning drums, restringing guitars, counting T-shirts and generally trying to put a tour together. We just about succeeded and played our first ever full-band US show in front of a couple of hundred enthusiastic Texans. It was panicked, ramshackle, exhilarating and a taste of the tour to come.

SHOW # 807
Egyptian Room, Indianapolis, IN, USA, 8 March 2010

The Flogging Molly tour was a crucial experience for me and the guys in the band (we still hadn't decided on them being called The Sleeping Souls at this stage). It was a gruelling, draining, testing experience and there were times when we came close to not surviving as a unit. The fact that we did bonded us together. I often think back to that run and if we made it through that, we can make it through pretty much anything.

The pressures of the run were endless. The drives were long and boring and we were cramped together in the back of our Econoline van (Flogging Molly were in a bus), making infrequent pit stops at faceless gas stations to buy shitty food. When Subway sandwiches become miles and away the healthiest option and you're drinking beer and whisky every night before sleeping on the floor of a crowded motel room, you have to watch your health. Extra pressure came from financial and logistical factors. I didn't have enough money to pay the guys in the band very much, yet the tour was still costing me a fortune. We didn't have any crew to help out with loading in and out, to mind the stage or to sell merch – I was doing that part myself, counting in and out every day, selling from when doors opened right up until our set and then again until the end of the night. The whole thing was suicidally draining.

Of course, I don't want to complain too much about life on the road or about self-inflicted problems. We were touring the USA, playing to thousands of people a night and winning a lot of them over. We were making new friends, getting drunk, kissing pretty girls (those of us who were single, which I temporarily was – the road and relationships are not exactly conducive) and seeing parts of the world we'd only ever read about in books or seen in movies. America has a romance for rock 'n' roll kids from England that never quite wears off.

We sweated through Texas and the South; Matt got crazy drunk in Florida, put an 'Out of order' sign on the bathroom to keep it for himself and then got upset that the bathroom *was* out of order. We saw alligator farms in South Carolina and played sweaty punk-rock headline shows in Gainesville (Florida) and Richmond (Virginia) on Flogging Molly's off days to make ends meet (days off cost money). We drove through unbelievable blizzards in the north-east, argued with in-house merch sellers in New York and played our first ever show in Boston. We triumphantly headlined Asbury Lanes in New Jersey, the site of my first really exciting US show. I played a basement show in Pittsburgh on a day off and got really sick afterwards. It was never boring.

Towards the end of the run, everyone was starting to get pretty worn down by the whole thing. Due to the lurgy I'd picked up in Pennsylvania we had to cancel one of the shows to give my battered voice time to recover, so we spent a pretty miserable day laid up in some faceless highway motel. The following day we had a fill headline show booked at a dive bar called Mac's in Lansing, Michigan, a place where I'd played a solo show before with Fake Problems. After some hacking and coughing in the morning, I decided the show could go ahead – I had little option, financially – and we loaded in for the gig.

The gig was packed out, sweaty, fun and the Michigan crowd were forgiving of my rasping vocals, lending their voices where they could. Being a dive bar kind of show, there wasn't much in the way of a dressing room, so the promoter had given us tokens for the bar instead of a case of beers. This is where the trouble started.

The stress of living in a van with five other people, driving long distances, eating terrible food and being broke often decompresses through the medium of alcohol, but it's a dangerous situation at the end of a long tour. Tarrant was wiped out after the show but managed to make it to the bar with a fistful of tokens – pretty much all of them in fact – and exchanged them for almost an entire bottle's worth of vodka, which he put away efficiently while I sold merch and equipment was packed and loaded into the trailer. He was a little miffed to be told that it was time to drive the ten minutes back to the motel, but grabbed a few cans of beer for the journey.

In the state of Michigan they are very strict about drink-driving laws and even one open container of alcohol in a moving vehicle can result in a DUI for the driver. When Casey heard the telltale hiss of a can opening, he suspected, correctly, that Tarrant was continuing to drink. He immediately shouted for him to toss the beer out of the window, which Tarrant obstinately refused to do. A brief argument ensued, in which I made the fatal decision of weighing in on Casey's side. The beer was eventually tossed, but Tarrant's tour-strained mood quietly continued to blacken as we rolled up to the motel.

Our sleeping arrangement for the tour was to have two rooms – the most we could afford – with three people in each. The Oxford contingent – Ben, Tarrant and Nigel – took one, while Matt, Casey and I were in the other. Each night two people would get a bed (or share one) and one person would take the floor. That night I was in bed, in my pants and shirt, reading a book, while Matt slept next to me and Casey was on the floor. Suddenly the door to our room burst open and Tarrant stormed in, quaking with drunken rage.

'Fuck you, you fucking cunt, you think I need your money, the peanuts you pay to put up with this shit, you bastard?' he shouted in my face. Tarrant can be intimidating when he's riled up, but I did my best to just sit there and let the outpouring of frustration wash over me. Which it did, for some time – a spit-flecked tirade, all the tension of the tour spilling out over me and my bedspread.

He concluded his rant with a threat to head to the airport in the morning. 'I quit. Fuck you!' he shouted and marched out of the door. Two seconds later he burst back in, but apparently had forgotten what his postscript point was, so just shouted the (now immortal in our touring crew) line:

'And another thing . . . uh . . . Fuck you!'

And with that he was gone, the door slapping uselessly against its broken lock in his wake. We managed to get the door shut and then I spent an awful night tossing and turning, sleep out of reach thanks to my sickness, my tour stress and my anger and worry about everything Tarrant had said. Come 6 a.m. I gave up trying to sleep and walked to a nearby diner to try to gather my head and think about what I was going to say and do. If Tarrant was leaving the tour, we were a man down with a week of shows left to go; in the long run I would've lost an amazing bass player and a good friend. I was very shaken up.

Van call (that is, the time the van is set to leave for the next show) was set for 9 a.m. I wandered nervously and reluctantly back over to the motel for that time, dreading what might await me. In the end I found Tarrant by the van on his own, his hoodie pulled up over his head and the worst hangover face and eyes I've ever seen. He coolly looked me up and down, and then whispered:

'I forgive you.'

Like that the ice was broken. A whole slew of tension was released and the others all set about mocking both him and me for our falling-out as we drove on to Indianapolis to rejoin the Flogging Molly tour. Tarrant felt like shit all day, unsurprisingly. Word went around the whole touring camp about what had happened the night before and when Tarrant arrived on stage for our sound check he found a crowd of ten or more people around his bass rig, each holding a bass guitar, awaiting the open auditions.

The rest of the tour slipped by in a blur and before we knew it we were heading back to the UK for the next tour. We survived this run by the skin of our teeth, but in the end I feel like we came out of it stronger, tighter, more determined than ever to succeed.

SHOW # 820

Roundhouse, London, UK, 24 March 2010

Our journeys back to the UK were fragmented. Casey and I dropped the band off in Chicago (in the midst of an apocalyptic storm) to fly home a few days early in order to get the UK tour prepared. The two runs, American and British, had been booked with no daylight in between them. It's a common feature of life on tour – often the logistics are organized by someone sat in an office looking at flight schedules, which show that, on paper, everything is doable. When you're on the ground, it all gets a bit more hectic and there was a certain amount of preparation that needed doing. So it was that Casey and I rolled on to Milwaukee together, reprising the start of the tour, while Matt, Nigel, Tarrant and Ben flew to Newcastle to put together the show.

This was our first 'full production tour' of the UK – full production being a run where you take trucks with your own PA system, your own lights, sometimes even your own stage, often catering supplies and a lot more crew. You essentially become a self-contained unit. I remember the first time I saw one in action – Million Dead were the opening act on that run – and thinking it an extravagant waste, given that a lot of the venues had staging and lighting already. Now that I'm a little older and wiser, I know that often it's more economical to take your own system with you – and it's certainly much more reliable – and it makes for a better show. Bottom line, a full production tour was a much larger undertaking than just jumping in the back of a van. The fact that I'd reached the stage of being able to do this at all was both exciting and daunting. Usually a tour like this has a good week of prep work from the band and crew. The crew had stepped up, the band had flown in a few days early and, as per usual, I'd arrived on the morning of the first show, jet-lagged to hell but ready.

We started in Newcastle and wound our way around the main cities of the island for just over a week of sold-out shows. In tow we had Chuck Ragan and Crazy Arm, a band from Plymouth who'd recently stolen my heart and signed to Xtra Mile Recordings. As mentioned, we had our own sound system, our own lights and a light show to go with it. We had bigger backstages, bigger crowds, official tour merchandise – the whole nine yards. The crowds were great, the shows packed out and in the middle of it all, I felt a touch uncomfortable.

Reconciling the increasing levels of success I've enjoyed with the basic character of what I do has never been easy. It's still something that I spend a fair amount of time thinking about and trying to get right. There are two conflicting imperatives: on the one hand, I want to be successful and I want everyone who is into my music to be able to come to shows and enjoy them; on the other, I don't want to lose that sense of connection, of community, the egalitarianism between the stage and the floor that made me enjoy this and find it interesting in the first place. It's a difficult line to walk and I certainly have not always got it right. This tour is an example of that, for me.

It's important to stress that I'm not laying this on anyone in the crew, or the band, or indeed the crowd. The fault is entirely mine. Somewhere in the middle of the full production, I lost sight of the importance of the connection with the crowd. There were moments at these shows when I felt like I was starting to lose something that mattered, that I was starting to become just like the other acts at this level who flounce off in cars after the shows back to fancy hotels, who never meaningfully converse with the people standing in front of them, who regard their audience as so many interchangeable heads. It freaked me out quite a bit.

The London show was at the Roundhouse – a famous, 3,000-capacity venue in Camden. Somehow I felt disconnected from the show, even though it was rammed to the rafters, my friends and family were in attendance and on the surface everything went well. I almost feel bad writing this down, because I don't want to detract from the retrospective enjoyment of anyone who was there – by all accounts the show was a good one. But it set my mind whirring as to how to overcome this problem in the future. I'm not sure it had been so starkly presented to me before – standing on stage in front of thousands of people feeling like I wasn't quite part of the proceedings.

I'm pleased to say that I think that it's a problem I've largely overcome since this show, though it's not always been plain sailing. Maybe this gig was a wake-up call of sorts, a reminder that I needed to keep my eye on the ball if I was going to continue down this road and maintain my interest and integrity. I think what I'm doing is working.

SHOW # 835
Coachella Festival, Indio, CA, USA, 17 April 2010

After the UK tour was done, we'd made enough profit to be able to tour in Europe without totally breaking the bank. So we headed out on a short run around the northern half of the Continent, playing slightly bigger shows, feeling like we were making headway. After that, the next item on the agenda was a whistle-stop visit to the West Coast of the USA for a few shows around the Coachella Festival.

Coachella is a massive festival in the desert in southern California. It's one that people who work in the music industry generally regard as *Important*, with a capital I. In practice that means it's usually something of a pain in the arse, with a pretty hipstery crowd, but there's a significant media presence and a lot of glad-handing opportunities, so it is (allegedly) worth the effort. I've done a fair amount of stuff like this over the years and it does serve a purpose, but it can be pretty depressing all the same.

We flew out to San Francisco to meet Casey, the van and our American backline, and to play a warm-up headline show at the

Rickshaw Stop (the show was opened, incidentally, by Franz Nicolay, who we'll meet again later). I remember sitting on the metal stairs that led up to the dressing room feeling utterly desperate in my jet-lag fug, wondering if I'd be able to keep my eyes open until showtime, let alone do an actual show. In the end we made it – but barely. After that I flew north for a solo stop in Vancouver while the others went south to Los Angeles. We reunited the following day and prepared for our sojourn in the desert.

If there's one thing the British do well, it's festivals. I feel like it's a cultural innovation we can happily lay claim to and, unlike cricket and football, we're still the best at it. Our American cousins, bless them, are still getting to grips with the format and despite their best efforts, there's always something slightly off about the whole thing. Coachella is a case in point. Everyone is *very* good-looking; everything is very clean and tidy. The festival site is carpeted with fake grass – I actually saw some people walking around in bare feet – and there are misting guns all over the place that make you feel cool, damp and terribly LA. In other words, it's totally against the grain of what I, personally, feel a festival should be – dirty, chaotic, exciting, unpredictable and weird. Imagine walking around barefoot at Glastonbury – you'd probably do yourself a mischief, and a good thing too. I'll take that over AstroTurf any day of the week.

So we arrived at the site in the burning desert heat, but with confusingly cool feet, and wandered aimlessly around, getting our bearings. We were the first band on the smallest stage, which in itself can be a little demoralizing when you've flown 6,000 miles to be there. In the event the show was great fun, with a decent-sized crowd coming out of the woodwork for our set. Afterwards I pressed some media flesh and we got 'gifted' some free sunglasses and jeans (Tarrant immediately cut his off into shorts in front of the horrified 'gifting' rep). We then had some time to hang around, as we were staying in a condo nearby.

The whole thing felt too sterile, too safe, too predictable for my taste. So it was that Casey and I decided to set about making things more interesting. We had a ferret around the assorted people we knew in the guest area and managed to locate an afterparty that seemed like more fun than standing in the designated drinking area watching Muse's light show. Off we went into the night. From here on in the details get pretty hazy, but I do remember seeing in the dawn with Casey, both of us in swimming shorts sat on a green of a golf course with a bottle of gin, talking absolute bollocks. When the van, with the rest of the band rested and sober, came to pick up the sleepless pair of idiots, we declared ourselves winners of the festival and passed out on the journey back into the city.

SHOW # 843
Brisbane Hotel, Hobart, Tasmania, 1 May 2010

Australia. Down Under. Land of soap operas, convicts, retirees, emigrant surfers and other clichés. Home of two of the original members of Million Dead. About as far away from where I come from as it's possible to get while remaining in the terrestrial atmosphere. Not a place I ever thought I'd get to, least of all through the medium of playing guitar and singing.

And yet there I was, in the departure lounge at LAX, preparing to board a plane to Brisbane with Chuck Ragan, Tim Barry, Ben Nichols and other assorted touring people (Todd Beene, Jon Gaunt, Jill Ragan et al.). We were headed Down Under for the first Australian Revival Tour. I was beyond flattered to have been asked to go by Chuck – although it was partly a case of him putting his money where his mouth was. He'd spent many hours on the road telling me that this was the promised land of touring and now he was going to prove it, apparently.

Regardless of which way you come at the place, flying to Australia is going to fuck up your body clock. I was still a little stuck on UK time, having only been in California for a week, so by the time we landed in Brisbane I was thoroughly bamboozled. We were met at the airport by the wonderful Mel Kraljevic – she would be our tour manager, merch person and general guide for the next week or so. My first taste of the truth of Chuck's assertion was the hotel in Brisbane; it was, by the standards of hotels I've stayed in on the road, luxurious. We had a day to acclimatize (not nearly enough, but nice all the same), so Ben and I headed to the bar to settle in.

We were booked in for eight shows and, as usual in a country I'd never visited before, I had no real idea what to expect. I imagined that no one would know who I was. After a surreal day wandering around the hotel desperately trying to convince myself that my watch wasn't lying, we loaded into the van to drive over to the venue. Given the collaborative nature of the Revival Tour, the first show is always a little ramshackle, so we spent a long sound check trying to remember each other's songs and learn new ones in time for the show. It was all made more difficult by the dazed state we were in. By the time the doors opened we had a set of sorts together and we'd also found out that the show was pretty much sold out, which was a pleasant surprise for me. I wandered into the street to find some food before things kicked off and got waylaid by a group of guys coming to the show. They excitedly showed me their tattoos of some of my lyrics and told me how much they were looking forward to the show. I almost thought I was being pranked – how on earth did these people on the other side of the world know who I was?

In the end, a lot of people were excited to see me and I had an infinitesimally small nugget of Beatlemania as I garnered a sing-along or two at my first ever Australian show. The rest of the run passed in much the same way, something of a dream, to be on the other side of the world meeting people who'd been listening to my records for a long while. It gave me an undying love of that continent and I've been back as much as the road has allowed since. We rolled through Sydney, Newcastle, Perth and Adelaide. It meant early morning starts and flights every day but the schedule didn't get to me, I was so into the place. We played two shows in Melbourne, including one at the legendary Arthouse (the CBGB of Australia).

The maddest show of the run was easily the one in Hobart, Tasmania. Hobart is a cute but remote little town, a place where a lot of tours don't go but that nevertheless has a sizeable community of music fans waiting for shows. Places like that often make for magical evenings and that was very much the case here. We flew in in the morning and settled briefly into our hotel, before heading over to the venue for sound check. There was a small bunch of kids hanging around as we got there, waiting for the show, and they were friendly enough, so we said hello and hung out while strings were changed and mics were arranged. They ended up singing along with pretty much every song we played in check, which was cool but a little bit weird.

The crowd filled out for showtime and we had ourselves a time on stage – a classic Revival show, old songs and new, playing together and alone, sinking whiskies and losing ourselves in songs. The audience as a whole was great, though our friends from earlier were a notably hardcore presence down at the front. We finished, as ever, with Chuck's anthem 'Revival Road', before retiring en masse to the bar to drink the night away. Our new friends joined us, but they had, during the course of the show, managed to hit a new level of weirdness.

They were now dressed in Mexican wrestling masks and declaring loudly that they were 'The Suicide Crew'. Apparently membership of said crew involved two things: undying loyalty and dedication to the musicians who'd just played the show; and a willingness to do some seriously dangerous and stupid shit. A girl I was talking to at the bar pierced her own cheek with a pin badge apropos of pretty much nothing halfway through a conversation, while Chuck stood bemused as kids smashed heavy duty shot glasses on their foreheads after downing the contents. Even Ben Nichols, ladies' man *par excellence*, was seen backing away in some confusion and heading for the hotel earlier than he normally would.

I come from a small town myself so I don't want to indulge in too many clichés, but yes, the people of Hobart were, shall we say, intense.

SHOW # 853
D-22, Beijing, China, 15 May 2010

As if touring in Australia and New Zealand (where I'd done a couple of shows) hadn't been wild enough, my itinerary now took me from Auckland to Hong Kong, for my first shows in Asia. The idea had come about thanks to Justin Sweeting, a Hong Kong native who'd spent time in Oxford and had become a good friend of Ben, Tarrant and Nigel's. A live-music enthusiast, he'd suggested that I could play a show in Hong Kong on my way back to Europe. Not only that, he'd then put me in touch with a company called S-Plit Promotions, a booking agency in mainland China run by a Scotsman (Archie) and an American (Nathaniel). After much slightly shady back-and-forth emailing, we ended up with a run of shows starting in Hong Kong and finishing in Beijing.

Being born and raised in the West, where I have done the vast majority of my touring, it's debatable whether or not the music I make and the themes I address can really translate into other cultural and social zones. That's a debate I was keen to have, so I was excited about the prospect of the shows, if also a little nervous about them. All things considered, however, I just felt lucky to be able to go to new places, all on the back of me playing my acoustic guitar.

The Hong Kong leg of the trip was actually pretty easy. Justin met me from the airport and I spent a few days falling desperately in love with the place. Since the British officially left in 1997, the city has acquired its own identity and pride – it's no longer just a playground for arsehole rich kids on holiday from Chelsea – it has its own distinct feel and culture, a mix of European and Chinese. I stayed in a fancy hotel and got taken to weird parties and generally soaked in the post-colonial atmosphere. The place reminded me of a Graham Greene novel somehow – everyone seemed to be a character with a story to tell. The show, at Rockschool, was good fun if a little amateur – the live-music scene was very much a new thing there, especially on the underground level. But there were a couple of hundred people in the room, ex-pats rubbing shoulders with Taiwanese punks, American military personnel and plenty of locals. A lot of people knew words to my songs, which remains a thing of wonder for me, regardless of where in the world I'm playing.

The day after the Hong Kong show, Justin put me on a train towards the Chinese border, where the tracks stop. I was then due to walk across into Shenzhen and meet Ciga, my tour manager and guide for the next ten days, on the other side. I was a little concerned about the border crossing – I had a visa in my passport, but my name was down as Francis rather than Frank, I was on my own, and those situations make me nervous at the best of times.

Thankfully, I successfully sweated my way through the checkpoint (partly because of the humidity) and made it smoothly into China.

I had some reservations about playing in the country. Nominally, the place is still a Communist state and the regime that massacred the students in Tiananmen Square in 1989 (to say nothing of the famines and depravity of earlier years) remains in power. That said, I'm interested in music as a force for engagement and I suspect that the social liberalization of Chinese youth will have unavoidable long-term implications for the country and its government, for the better. I also think it's important to differentiate between people and their state – I don't want to be associated with many of the things 'my' government has done in my lifetime. Archie, Nathaniel and indeed Ciga told me that the tour would be fun, interesting and worthwhile, both for me and for the Chinese who decided to come to the shows.

The first show was in Shenzhen – a startlingly new city built in twenty years or so from a fishing village, the result of Deng Xiaoping's economic liberalization policies in the 1980s. That gig was a little weird – I was more like the piano player in the corner of the restaurant entertaining the diners than a performing head-line act. I was also shattered from the journey and taking time to adjust to the Chinese food, so I went to bed early feeling a little out of sorts.

Thankfully everything picked up from there. The show in Guangzhou was great and we had a few days off there to explore and for me to get to know Ciga, who I found fascinating. A vivacious, entrepreneurial and sassy woman around the same age as me, she was a fashion blogger and live-music promoter with a love of Western style that was in no way culturally slavish – she makes everything her own. Discussing politics with her was wild – she was proud to live in a Communist country but had never heard of Marx, condemned Mao as a murderer but was unaware that anything of note had happened in Tiananmen Square in 1989 and so on. I felt like I was having my eyes opened to a whole new side of human existence. Plus she's loads of fun to go drinking with.

We took a frankly insane internal flight to Wuhan – the plane would be flattered by the description 'junk bucket' and it seemed like the pilot was new to the concept of 'landing' – where we played a proper punk-style venue, an old air-raid bunker converted into a grafitti-covered squat. The promoter, Dostav, was from Kathmandu originally and talked up a wild plan for me to cross the border for a show there – a plan that has never yet come to fruition. We took an incomprehensibly packed train to Wuxi, where I played another dinner-style show and then made our way to Ciga's home city, Shanghai. There I played to a sold-out house at Yuyintang and got to meet Archie. Archie is a remarkable soul, a mad Scotsman living in China, fighting to bring live music to the locals. We had quite the night out before and after the show, which itself was one of my favourites that I've ever played – locals, ex-pats, a birthday boy, sing-alongs, new songs and old. Life affirmed in all its glory.

I bade Ciga a fond farewell the following morning and flew north to Beijing for the last stop on my whirlwind Antipodean-Asian trip. In the capital I was met by my friend Qiang. Qiang was in a band with me when I was at school with Chris Lucas and Ben Dawson, but he disappeared after a while. His father was a Chinese diplomat but he had an Australian passport and so was able to travel more freely. I hadn't seen him in a decade (Chris, Ben and I had gone on to form Kneejerk and with Ben I progressed to Million Dead) but he'd surfaced when he heard about the shows, as he was a friend of Nathaniel's, the other half of S-Plit Promotions (with Archie). We had a fond reunion, during which he told me mad stories about time in Chinese jails and other unprintable things. We met Nathaniel, had a final excellent Chinese meal and got ready for the show.

The venue for the evening was another punker bunker called D-22. There were a bunch of other Chinese bands playing on the bill with me, ranging from Libertines-esque punk bands to weird folk-rock fiddle-based hybrids. I had a little time to reflect on the whole scene. Live music of any kind is such a recently tolerated phenomenon for young Chinese, everything is so new for them and so there is an electric atmosphere in the air. It's like New York in the mid-1970s combined with Elvis on TV and Beatlemania all at the same time. But it's also weirdly iconoclastic – it's not based around any one band, it's a decentralized, organic thing, that takes much from Western music but makes it defiantly its own. It was a privilege to witness, in a way. It also made me think hard about the music that I make, the cultural world that I inhabit – rock 'n' roll is my life, my passion, but it's also culturally ubiquitous, blaring from restaurants and endlessly co-opted by advertising campaigns. Somehow, standing in the middle of all those Chinese kids who were so brimming with life and enthusiasm and passion for this new-found voice, I almost felt ashamed at taking the music I love for granted.

Over the course of this run of shows, a new song had been taking shape in my head, an attempt to right that sense of dereliction of duty. 'I Still Believe' got its first, very tentative outing at the Shanghai show. After a hasty rewrite or two on the plane to Beijing I played it in its (mostly) final form at D-22 and knew instantly that I had a serious song on my hands, one that said something strident and important and personal all at once. I flew back to the UK feeling confident about the next record.

I wrote another song on that run. During the layover at Sydney Airport, heading for Hong Kong, I was so battered by time zones and lack of sleep that I made a weird phone call to Isabel, who I was separated from at the time. I probably shouldn't have made it and I had no idea what time it was for either of us when I did, but it rekindled something. In the hotel room in Guangzhou I demoed a rough outline of a song called 'The Way I Tend to Be'. At the time it felt too raw, too personal, so it got shelved for quite some time, until I felt like it had a home on a record and I was ready to share it. But it was born there, in China.

SHOW # 862
Sublime, Tel Aviv, Israel, 4 June 2010

My summer of exotic touring locations wasn't quite over. I had one more place to visit, and a controversial one at that. Many years ago, my friend Nadav worked in London at a record store, but after a while he moved back to his home country, Israel. He's a punk guy and a live-music promoter. We had vaguely stayed in touch and earlier in the year he asked me if I'd be interested in playing some shows in Israel. As per usual, I said yes, keen to get to new places, meet new people and experience new things. I was aware, of course, that playing in Israel was not a choice without some ramifications, but I had thought them through and it seemed like the right thing to do.

The temperature of the political debate was raised enormously right before my trip was due to happen, thanks to the Israeli government forces choosing to storm an aid flotilla bound for Gaza. At the time there was a huge international outcry and a lot of other artists, including Elvis Costello, cancelled upcoming shows in the country. I think a lot of people looked to me to do the same thing. In the event, I thought even harder about my choices and stuck to my guns.

I've rehearsed this argument to a degree in talking about China, but once again, I feel it's important to make a distinction between a people and their government. In the case of Israel, with the complications of Jewish identity and the lurking spectre of anti-Semitism, it seems even more important to me to be very careful who you condemn for a political action and why. The events around the flotilla did not change my initial decision to go and play. I'd been asked by a punk collective – about the most anti-establishment group you could find in the country – to go play shows that were in no way endorsed or sponsored by the state. Bands have kept coming to the UK despite the Iraq War (which, as I've already written, I proudly marched against in 2003) and I'm glad they have. To change my schedule and not visit Israel in this instance seemed to me to be, at best, grandstanding. Israel is a small country and no international touring acts make their full living there – boycotting the place is kind of cheap, in other words. The same logic would dictate boycotting tours of the USA as a result of the actions of their government, but bands don't do that because that's where they make their money. That seems pretty lame to me, so I stuck to my principles to go and see the place for myself, meet the people and try to understand what was happening.

At the same time it seemed important to me to see if I could find the time and the means to play in the West Bank. I have some friends who are activists who have been there and I have heard of shows there as well. My Israeli friends had no problem with me following that lead, though they were sceptical about whether or not I'd be successful. In the event, I managed to email a promoter there, but he told me that as I was playing shows in Israel, I was not welcome to play in the West Bank as well. I completely under-stood and accepted his point, but at the same time my plans and obligations had already been made so I decided to go ahead with the original itinerary.

Flying to Israel from London is unlike any other journey I've ever taken. The security vetting starts before you even check in for the flight, which you have to do in a totally separate part of Heathrow Airport. They fired questions at me in Arabic (I think) and grilled me on my reasons for going, trying to ascertain if I had ulterior motives for my visit. At one point they were even suggesting that they might have to dismantle my guitar to check for bombs – thankfully that didn't actually happen. It was an intense experience all in all, but it gave me an impression of how seriously they take their security.

My time in Israel was absolutely fascinating. Nadav picked me up from the airport and showed me around for a few days. I played shows in Haifa and Tel Aviv and spent some time hanging out, as well as visiting Jerusalem. The entire time I kept my eyes open and my mouth mostly shut, trying to learn as much as I could. It was pretty crazy seeing things from the ground. The people I was hanging out with, Israeli punks, are fucking serious. It's not an easy social choice to make, as it is in the UK, and everyone has had to serve in the Israel Defence Forces to some extent. They were all pretty radically opposed to their own government and had some crazy, crazy stories to tell. The shows themselves had an electric atmosphere. Because of the recent events and cancellations, everyone was very effusive in their thanks to me for coming to play and for making the distinction between them and their leaders.

Tel Aviv in particular was a wonderful show for me. Again, people knew some of the words and they listened intently to the rest of it. I tried out new songs, as the material for my next album was starting to come together. We had sing-alongs, we smoked weed after the show, talked politics and I revelled in the Mediterranean atmosphere and (to be honest) the sublimely beautiful women. In the end I left feeling like I knew even less about the world than I did before I went, though perhaps I was a little more informed about that part of the world. I haven't had a chance to go back as of yet but it is something I would very much like to do.

SHOW # 869

Southside Festival, Neuhausen ob Eck, Germany,
20 June 2010

Playing live, over and above radio play or press coverage, has been
the main motor driving my career forwards. Within that, headline
shows are a kind of consolidation, but the main work of spreading
the word happens at festivals and with support slots for larger
bands. The summer of 2010 saw that lesson writ large in what
remains one of the most logistically insane few days of my life.

Hurricane and Southside are two large German festivals, kind
of like Reading and Leeds in the UK. They are massive, rock-
oriented affairs, with a revolving bill between the two events, one
in the north of the country and one in the south. We'd played the
year before but had been invited back for a bigger and better slot
in 2010. We got ready to drive out there in a bus with the band and
our live crew. So far, so simple. Then we got the phone call.

Joanna, my agent, had been doing some serious behind-the-
scenes work while I was away in Australasia and China. While I
was on the train to Shanghai, she called me and told me the news.
Green Day had asked me to open their two UK summer shows,
one at the Lancashire County Cricket Ground and one at Wembley
Stadium. In total we'd be playing to 150,000 people at two shows.
It was an amazing opportunity, a fantastic piece of news and I
jumped up and punched the air, terrifying my fellow train
passengers.

There was, however, one small, well, actually quite major, logistical snag. The two shows fell on either side of the Hurricane
Festival. That meant we'd have to play in Manchester, drive to
northern Germany, then drive back to London and finally back
again to Germany for Southside in Baden-Württemberg. Or else

we'd have to look at flying, with our equipment. Otherwise we'd have to choose between the two opportunities.

Never one to turn down a challenge, I decided that we couldn't possibly cancel the German festivals – we'd already been announced, after all. And there was no way that I was turning down the Green Day shows. So it was that we set about trying to work out how to do all the shows without anyone dying. The main credit here has to go to Graham, as tour manager, who put together a schedule that really might have killed lesser bands.

The first stop was easy – at least as far as driving schedules go. We trekked up to Manchester and loaded into the largest venue we'd ever been anywhere near, the Lancashire County Cricket Ground, an open space set to hold around 60,000 Green Day fans. We were playing first, before Joan Jett and the headliners. There was a crazy amount of production, endless tour buses, frantic crew members shouting at us for being in the wrong place, fluorescent taped lines on the floor explaining that things would be exploding on one or other side of said line at some point. It was all quite overwhelming. Our backstage area was a box in the stands and we were hermetically sealed off from meeting Green Day – we might as well have been at a different gig.

That said, their crew were nothing but helpful to us, showing us where to be, what to do when and helping us to get our equipment in and out for the show. Once we were set up and completed sound check, we retired to the front balcony of our box, overlooking the empty field, and waited for the gates to open. As they did, a veritable sea of humanity flooded across the grass up to the barrier and I remember being genuinely intimidated by the scale of the occasion. Our set time rolled around and there were an awful lot of people waiting out front, mostly dressed in Green Day T-shirts and making a point of looking thoroughly apathetic about any opening bands that might be standing between them and their heroes.

The set went ... OK. In all honesty I was very nervous and didn't really settle into a rhythm until about halfway through the gig. I don't usually get nervous unless I'm in an unfamiliar setting – and this was very much one of those. My sense of tempo goes very awry when I'm out of my comfort zone and I suspect I played the songs too fast. I noticed at one point that the guys from Green Day were watching the show from the wings, which gave my confidence a boost. That, however, was quickly shot down by a prime piece of onstage idiocy from me. There was a little ramp running from the centre of the stage out into the audience. It was clearly part of the headline show, but no one had told me I wasn't allowed out there. As we played 'Photosynthesis' to finish our set, I decided to stride boldly down the ramp towards the crowd during the solo section. Alas, we were not at a stage where we could afford wireless connections for our guitars, so I was tethered by a long guitar lead plugged into my tuner pedal at my microphone centre stage. As I walked down on to the ramp, the lead neatly and effi-ciently unplugged itself, leaving me holding a guitar not making any amplified sound in front of 60,000 people, most of whom were still deciding whether or not to give me and my band the time of day. Not, perhaps, my finest hour.

After the show we had time to relax, calm down and watch the other bands. Joan Jett & the Blackhearts were great and we met them afterwards – lovely people all. Green Day's show was a reve-lation of how to work a massive crowd. I think most musicians who watch other bands play are secretly taking notes on the stage-craft and I was certainly learning a lot about how to engage and connect with that many people all at the same time. Once they were done, with the smoke and reverberations from the pyrotech-nics ringing in our ears, we boarded our tour bus and headed south, towards Germany.

We had a whole travel day in which to make it to Scheeßel in northern Germany, so by the standards of the weekend it was an easy ride. We drove down to Dover, boarded the ferry and arrived in good time on the Friday morning at the festival site, seventeen or so hours after setting off. We had band, crew and a host of drivers aboard – restrictions on the amount of time any one person can spend driving a bus in Europe being such that we needed at least three to complete our mission. Hurricane Festival went off without a hitch. It was a fun show and almost relaxing after the pressure of the Manchester one. It was once we were done there that the real madness began.

We finished our set and band and crew as one packed our equipment down as fast as possible for the return journey to London. We had to be at Wembley Stadium the following lunchtime to load in and get ready for the second Green Day show. We drove hell for leather, made the ferry and arrived in the northwest of the capital in good enough time. Wembley stadium is pretty much the biggest gig in the country – 90,000 people were set to come and watch the show that night. Despite the fact that it's a new stadium, it's also *kind of* where Queen played in the 1980s, which is a huge deal for me. We were excited and nervous, but the fact that we had Manchester under our belts made it all a little easier to handle.

Sound check went fine and we then hunkered down in our dressing room deep in the bowels of the stadium to await stage time. As is standard practice, just before we were due to go on, Barbs, our guitar tech, wandered on to the stage to run a line check with Graham at the sound desk. That essentially just means playing each instrument briefly to check that everything is still plugged into the place where it should be. Line checking in front of a restless stadium crowd is a weird job. On this occasion Barbs was busy doing his job and didn't see that the crowd were lackadaisically knocking a beachball around the floor of the venue. The ball rolled on to the stage behind him and when he noticed it he casually kicked it to the side of the stage to get it out of his way. The assembled bored masses booed in unison, thinking him a spoilsport. When he returned to the dressing room we asked him how everything was looking, he told us the crowd was hostile. The tension ratcheted up again.

In the event the Wembley show was fine. Actually, scratch that ludicrous understatement – it was an amazing experience; to play that stage to that many people. It helped my career no end, it was a massive tick on my bucket list, it was an honour and a privilege. Unfortunately it was not one we had much time to savour. Once we were offstage it was time for another manic pack-down of our equipment, back on to the bus (after a very quick Wembley tattoo for me backstage and a quick hello with the Green Day guys in a backstage corridor) and off towards Germany, yet again.

By this time, the people working in the canteen on the ferry had started recognizing us and gave us a friendly, if slightly bemused, hello as we collapsed once more into the uncomfortable plastic seating. The drive from Calais down to Neuhausen ob Eck, home of the Southside Festival, is considerably longer than the one to Hurricane and all the accumulated time on the tour bus – close to fifty hours by now – was starting to take its toll on everyone's mood and morale. This was compounded, on our eventual arrival at the festival, by the fact that the weather had taken a turn for the frightful and the whole site was ankle-deep in mud. In all the excitement of the Green Day shows, no one had really thought to bring any suitable footwear.

We dragged our exhausted selves on to the stage for the last show of the weekend. As ever in these situations, the mere fact of being onstage in front of a willing crowd always pulls the last reserves of energy out of me and the actual gig was great. Once we were done, however, we collectively collapsed in a heap in the dressing room. We had utterly spent all the possible driving hours that we had, so we were legally bound to sit tight at the festival for at least twelve hours. It so happened that Biffy Clyro were in a similar situation with their tour-bus driver (though for slightly less insane reasons). So there we were, two happy but totally drained bands, old friends reunited by an enforced sojourn in a backstage with nothing to do but drink Jägermeister and beer. I *cannot* tell you how extreme the carnage got that night. Literally, I *can't* tell you. I blacked out after about half an hour in a room with the Scots. The final journey back to the UK was pretty awful as a result.

SHOW # 879

2000trees Festival, Withington, near Cheltenham, UK, 16 July 2010

In the midst of the madness that summer – China, Israel, Wembley, Tennessee (for the Bonnaroo Festival, where I broke more strings than I didn't and basically did a spoken-word set), Ireland, Glastonbury, Finland and more – there was a lovely moment of respite. I've already written about the time I played at the first 2000trees Festival back in 2008 and what a great experience it was. That summer festival organiser James Scarlett asked me to return to play again, but this time for me and the band to headline the main stage. This was the first time I'd ever been asked to headline a festival, but it was one I felt extremely comfortable at, so it was a great fit. James also let me help pick the bill for the show, so I had a lot of friends on site.

I spent the rain-tinged afternoon wandering around the site and ended up guesting on perhaps one too many sets. Still, it was great to play with Emily Barker and Chris T-T, to beatbox for Beans On Toast and so on. The evening rolled around, the machine creaked into gear and we had a fantastic set, just over an hour of sing-alongs, dancing and joy. I remember coming offstage and feeling like I was at home; but also like I had, perhaps, graduated in some way to a higher level. I felt comfortable headlining the show. This feeling was immediately followed by a fear that I was becoming too big for my boots, losing my grip on reality. But in the end I think it's possible to strike a balance. It would be disingenuous to constantly shrink like a violet away from the obvious fact of my success. But I hope I can handle it in a way that remains true to the personality and character that I started out with. In the end it's not for me to judge, but on this occasion, as 'The Ballad of Me and My Friends', a song written to be played in empty bars, rang out over a few thousand people in a field, I felt like I was getting something right.

SHOW # 886

Calgary Folk Music Festival, Calgary, Canada,
25 July 2010

I've written about Ian Dury giving the world his unholy trinity – sex, drugs and rock 'n' roll. Obviously, his tongue was firmly in his cheek, but a lot of people have taken it more seriously and that end of the industry I work in has always made me feel a little uncomfortable. The thing that really gets me is the exclusivity, the clique; the idea that there is a secret club, a rarified caste of models and musicians, who are allowed not only to enjoy these devious pleasures, but also to avoid any consequences of their actions while doing so. It's a huge cultural façade that simply disguises bad manners as far as I can see and I don't want to be part of that cliché.

Having said all of that, you can take the three elements individually and find good things to say about them – I like rock 'n' roll music, I've had fun taking drugs in my time and who doesn't like getting laid? On a few occasions in my life I've had a party that captures all of these things in a beautifully crazy way, without damaging or hurting or excluding anyone, and I've lived to tell a happy tale afterwards. One is the Calgary Folk Music Festival in 2010.

Not long after 2000trees, I got on a plane to Calgary. I'd been through once before on the tour with Gaslight Anthem in 2009. On that occasion I'd played my regular set, then at the merch table I'd met a guy called Jey who said he'd come to see me and had missed my show. After a bit of negotiating, we cleared a space in a bar downstairs from the main venue and I played a fun second set for Jey and his friends, among whom I soon counted myself. The Canadian Folk Music Festival scene is well-established and can be a lot of fun, but it's usually quite expensive, quite serious and involves quite a lot of chins getting stroked. When I'd announced this weekend of shows (you generally have one main set and a bunch of workshops over the weekend), Jey had got in touch. He didn't have the money to get to the festival, and anyhow I was the only act he wanted to catch, so he asked if I'd be up for a house show. Of course, I said yes.

I met up with Casey in the airport after a long flight. We were doing the weekend as a duo, him working as sound guy and tour manager and general partner in crime. You get well looked after at the folk festivals and we were pleased to check into a pretty nice hotel in the centre of the city. We had the first evening off to acclimatize, which was spent in the predictable battle against jet lag, sat at the bar drinking beers and trying to pretend we weren't feeling tired. I woke up early the next morning and spent a few hours wandering around the city waiting for Casey to join the living. Eventually we headed over to the festival and got set up for the show. Everything went smoothly – I played a forty-five-minute solo set to a polite and appreciative audience, perhaps swinging my song choices more in the traditional direction. It was a beautiful summer's evening in Canada and all was well with the world.

Once we were done with the main set, I hung out and said hello to a few people for a while, leaving Casey to contact Jey and figure out the second half of our evening. We got the address, jumped in a taxi and headed into the oncoming night and the suburbs. The party was due to happen, for reasons that now escape me, at a friend of Jey's house. We arrived in good time, said hello to old friends and new and settled in to wait a while for the full contingent of the audience to show up. Beers and jokes were cracked in equal measure.

After a time, and before I'd played my set, Jey nervously told me that someone had provided some weed for me and Casey. I've never been much of a weed smoker, so while I was grateful, I was also a little confused as I hadn't asked for the supplies to be provided. After some enquiries I worked out that the locals were a little nervous about having an itinerant English musician and his tour manager showing up and weren't sure whether we'd be totally satisfied with just beer and whisky. I laughed heartily, gave Jey a hug, told him to chill out and declined the weed. I was then asked if I wanted to get hold of anything else; something stronger perhaps. I hesitated, considering the matter, but in the end decided to just let it lie and let the evening take its natural course.

The guitar came out and I ended up playing for a good couple of hours. I have a soft spot for shows like this – conversational, collaborative, unplanned, nothing so crass as a set list, just making it up as I go. There were probably forty people there, some of I'd met the year before, some were new to me. I slightly got the impression that Jey had invited all of his female friends, perhaps for the same reason that he'd provided the weed. Regardless, it was a lot of fun and eventually I decided to put the guitar away and just enjoy the party, to stop trying to be the focus of attention and let things take their course.

And take their course they certainly did. By the end of my set I was a few beers and a few more whiskies down, as was Casey. My memory gets a little hazy around now, but at some point someone else arrived with some different party supplies; it turns out my hesitation in the kitchen had been liberally interpreted. Since it had arrived, it seemed rude not to get involved, so I set about sharing the wealth with the assembled company. Everything sped up, everyone got loose and, well, let's just say it was a wild evening for everyone involved. Once dawn rolled around, the surviving partygoers were laid up in the garden, damp with the dew and I was strumming soft country songs on my guitar and wondering if we'd ever get to sleep.

A cab eventually arrived and took Casey and I back to the hotel for a few hours' recuperation before I was due back at the festival for some workshop shows. The site felt grey and grimy to my exhausted eyes and part of me longed to be back playing another house show or, better yet, sleeping.

Once the dust settled on this episode I was able to look back and laugh pretty hard. Jey is a great guy, we are friends to this day, and I still gently rib him about his party nerves. We certainly did tick off all three of Ian Dury's boxes. The Californian and the Englishman taught some Calgary kids how to enjoy themselves that night.

SHOW # 904

Area 4 Festival, Lüdinghausen, Germany,
21 August 2010

I spent the rest of the summer of 2010 on aeroplanes, or so it seems to me. After Calgary I flew back to the UK for a couple of days to attend the Kerrang! Awards, where I was given a gong for my 'spirit of independence', which was nice. Almost immediately I was back over the Atlantic playing a festival in Minneapolis (where I met Koo Koo Kanga Roo, one of my favourite live bands), before heading to Montreal for the Osheaga Festival. I spent a magical evening there swapping war stories with my old Revival comrade Tim Barry on the edge of a lake as the sun went down. Next up was a short run of headline shows on the East Coast with the band. We were also accompanied by the wonderful singer William Elliott Whitmore, who opened the shows with heart and character unlike any I'd seen before or since. These shows were, at least in theory, a warm-up (and financial crutch) for an appearance at the Lollapalooza festival in Chicago – a show at midday in the rain that was witnessed by approximately fifty people.

Tarrant, Ben, Matt and Nigel headed home and I went off to visit my older sister in Colorado. I also found the time to meet up with Jon Snodgrass and write and record an album in twenty-four hours, which was later released as *Buddies*. I also snuck in a show at Jon's bar in Fort Collins, Surfside 7, before dragging my weary bones over to Ottawa for another folk-festival weekend with Casey. Once that was done I gratefully settled into a cramped economy seat for my final journey across the pond that summer. We were due to do a short run of festivals around Europe before finishing up at Reading and Leeds, our fourth appearance in a row.

It had been an exhausting summer. The number of shows on my calendar was not significantly higher than it had been in previous years, but the geographical range had increased exponentially and the promotional schedule was keeping pace. I was also a year older, predictably enough, and it was all beginning to take something of a toll on my constitution. I had yet to learn fully about taking care of myself on the road with that kind of schedule – eating better, drinking less and getting early nights. So there were days when my mood and my voice could be a little off.

Area 4 is a perfectly pleasant, mid-level rock festival in north-western Germany. We had a slot in the middle of the bill on the Saturday, all standard-issue stuff. But I was a little out of sorts on the day – my voice was strained and scratchy and I was generally not in the best of moods. The show went OK – we had forty minutes or so, as I remember. Festival changeovers between bands can be brutally short, which often means that the onstage sound isn't particularly clear; that in turn can lead to singers blowing their voices out as they strain to be heard. Towards the end of our set I was increasingly frustrated by not being able to hear myself (despite the best efforts of Johnny, our monitor engineer) and by the fact that I was starting to sound more like a honking angry goose than a professional singer.

As we kicked into 'Photosynthesis', our reliable set closer for many years, I was looking forward to the show being over so I could retire to my bunk and just sleep off the fatigue, the sore throat, the bad mood. Ben ripped out his solo on his electric mandolin and we then brought everything right down, as usual, for me to introduce the band to the crowd. As I did so, I noticed that people in the crowd were starting to sit down on the floor. It was just a few at first, but by the time I'd got round everyone and called out Nigel's name, almost the entire audience was seated. I had no idea what was going on, but the first thought that entered my tired brain was that this was some kind of protest. The next band were due onstage in about fifteen minutes and I thought that maybe their fans had arrived early, en masse, and were encouraging us to hurry up and fuck off. That didn't exactly do wonders for my mood and my usually effervescent speech about community that preceded the final denouement of the song and the set was noticeably colder that day.

In the event, when Nigel brought the drums back in and we kicked into the finale, the whole crowd jumped as one on to their feet and started dancing like people possessed. I was so surprised by this spontaneous, self-organized piece of crowd participation that I pretty much totally forgot the words to the last section of the song. No matter. They were screaming them back at me. It turns out that the whole thing was a display of enthusiasm and loyalty, performed in an inimitable German style. I stumbled down the ramp after the gig, sweating hard in the summer heat, hoarse, confused but ultimately bowled over by the warmth of the reception we had been afforded. Since then the whole 'sit down jump up' thing has become almost standard issue during that song at my shows; I've taught the technique to many a crowd across the world. But it will forever remain a German innovation. *Danke schön!*

SHOW # 921
Meskalina, Poznań, Poland, 3 October 2010

The summer finished off with the Reading and Leeds festivals again, as was becoming customary. We played to a huge crowd on the second stage and my feelings of establishment as an artist came on apace, though not without their attendant doubts, as per usual. That triumphant weekend was followed by a quick early-

Above: Onstage in Austin, SXSW 2009, with Steve Soto.

Below: Playing solo at Plush in Austin; another shot from this set got used on the *Poetry Of The Deed* liner notes.

Below: Union Chapel, December 2009, the show I made by the skin of my teeth!

Above: Revival Tour USA 2009; onstage with Chuck Ragan, Auda Mae and the Anderson Family Bluegrass Band, somewhere in North America.

Left: *Poetry* on tour: in the dressing room with the Sleeping Souls, including new boy Matt; **(below)** onstage at Shepherds Bush with Fake Problems, total chaos!

Toasting my Gaslight Anthem friends at the end of the tour in Dublin.

Right: The last show of 24 on 'The Road' video shoot, with director Adam Powell, at the Flowerpot.

Below: Nervous in an empty Wembley Stadium, pre-Green Day show.

Above: Walking up the ramp to the stage for my first festival headline at 2000 Trees, 2010.

Left: German Photomat selfies!

Left: Onstage at 2000 Trees.

Below: Casey Cress and I at the end of a not-very-sensible Canadian Folk Festival weekend.

Bottom: Cooling off in a fountain after a very hot festival show in Switzerland.

Left: Getting tattooed by Matt Hunt on the set of the 'I Still Believe' video.

Below: Playing at Inside 8 Seconds at The Fest in 2010 with Fat Mike…

…And outside in the parking lot (right).

Below: The Leftfield stage, Glastonbury 2010, with Beans on Toast and Billy Bragg.

Above: Selling
my own merch
on the road
with Social D in
Florida, 2010.

Right: With the
late great Josh
Burdette.

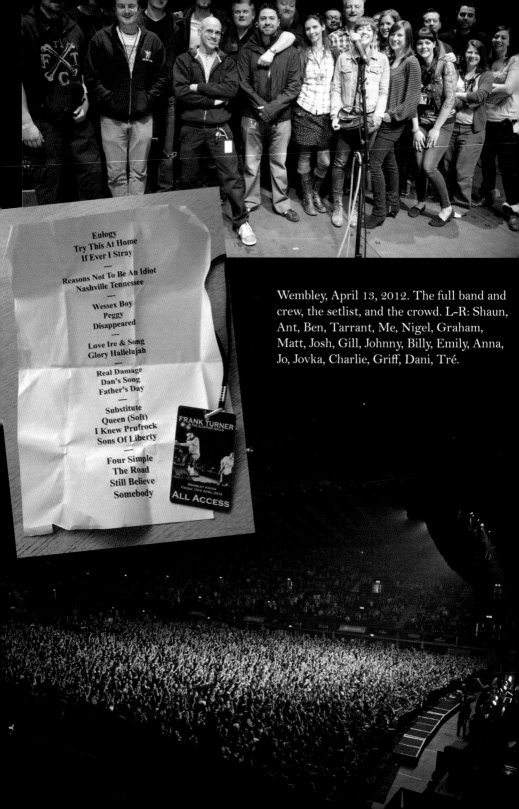

Eulogy
Try This At Home
If Ever I Stray

Reasons Not To Be An Idiot
Nashville Tennessee

Wessex Boy
Peggy
Disappeared

Love Ire & Song
Glory Hallelujah

Real Damage
Dan's Song
Father's Day

Substitute
Queen (Soft)
I Knew Prufrock
Sons Of Liberty

Four Simple
The Road
Still Believe
Somebody

FRANK TURNER

WEMBLEY ARENA
FRIDAY 13TH APRIL 2012
ALL ACCESS

Wembley, April 13, 2012. The full band and crew, the setlist, and the crowd. L–R: Shaun, Ant, Ben, Tarrant, Me, Nigel, Graham, Matt, Josh, Gill, Johnny, Billy, Emily, Anna, Jo, Jovka, Charlie, Griff, Dani, Tré.

autumn trip back to the USA for some showcase solo shows with Casey and a small (and slightly weird) festival in the bustling metropolis of DeKalb, Illinois, where I was lucky enough to catch up with the guys and gal from Murder By Death.

On my return, the band and I headed into the studio in north London with Tristan Ivemy, the friend with whom I'd recorded early demos and who had mixed *Love Ire & Song*. Ideas for the next full album were slowly coalescing, but I had the idea of doing an EP first. This was partly to mirror the *Campfire Punkrock* EP back in the early days and partly to give me, the band and Tristan a trial run at working together. We hammered out five songs in a short period of time, including my new song written in China, 'I Still Believe'. I left them to be mixed and set off for Germany for a run of solo shows.

Over there, things were bubbling nicely. Graham, Barbs, Sarah and I headed out in a people carrier, which had just enough room to carry all of us, the equipment (such as it was – a pair of acoustic guitars) and the merchandise. It felt liberating to be cruising the autobahns in something other than a van or a bus and we made good time between the gigs. The run was set up around a festival in Hamburg on the Reeperbahn (the famously debauched red-light district where the Beatles cut their teeth), after which we were set to swing south and then east, catching some fairly obscure towns, before ending up in Berlin.

The run was great. Travelling in a smaller group with less technical baggage usually feels more like a holiday than the full-production, full-crew, full-band runs that I was starting to get used to. Hamburg was fun. In Trier we had a welcome return to the ExHaus – a venue I'd played with Polar Bear Club on the Gaslight tour more than a year before – a weird, gutted, old building that's now covered in graffiti and run by punks, but gives the impression that it was once used for something grander, more imperial. In Karlsruhe I tried out a new song I'd been working on about my hometown, Winchester, called 'Wessex Boy'. It had originally had a totally different musical arrangement that hadn't been working out for me. A chance stumble on a simple but catchy descending melody turned it around. It was a strange place to try out a song about a small city in southern England, but it went over well and I even got people singing along with the end section. A promising sign.

Erfurt was a different experience. This was one of my first shows in the former East Germany and the ravages of half a century of economic madness are still clearly visible in the landscape, architecture and the looks on people's faces. The show was a weird one – maybe 100 people in an upstairs bar. A group of cantankerous English guys were kind of ruining things for everyone by being aggressive drunks, picking fights and pawing at the local women. I was geared up for a confrontation, but discovered after the show that they'd just returned from Afghanistan, where their unit had sustained an almost unbearably high casualty rate. That gave me some pause for thought and some sympathy, so in the end I left them be.

The Berlin show was at a fancy, plush venue called Roter Salon, where I played to a room that was full, but half-stocked by industry types, which never makes for the best of atmospheres. After we were done, Sarah and Graham loaded the car and prepared to head back west and home. Meanwhile Barbs and I had some post-show drinks before heading to a hotel near the train station, our faces turned to the east.

I'd played in Berlin a handful of times prior to this show and at each one I had met, in the post-show throng of signing and photographs, a guy called Maciej. Maciej is from Poznań in Poland and had travelled by train west across the border on each occasion to catch the gig. I'd always been amazed by his dedication and willingness to travel. I studied Central and Eastern European history at university and had attempted to maintain an amateur interest in the subject, yet had never been to Poland. So I was intrigued. After discussing this a few times, both in person and on email, Maciej had offered to put together a show for me in his town, at the local music bar Meskalina. It had worked out that, if only Barbs and I were to travel, we could take the train after the Berlin show, play the bar, stay the night and fly back to England the following morning.

The early-morning train journey was blighted by hangovers and bad weather. I was also filled with a sense of foreboding. The history of the movement of people, trains, arms and more across that part of the world is long and depressing. The level of economic development seemed to drop with each passing mile as well, the roads getting narrower and falling into a state of disrepair, with abandoned vehicles and machinery by the side of the tracks.

When we arrived in Poznań we were met by Maciej and his girlfriend Natalie. Almost immediately my earlier reservations about Poland melted away; I actually felt a little bad about them. The centre of the city is beautiful and has been completely restored to its former glories after the destruction of the war. Everyone we met was helpful, friendly and enthusiastic and, dare I say it, there was a positive, almost entrepreneurial spirit to the country. We walked down to the bar and met Benek, the mad proprietor, whose excitement for the show was in direct negative correlation with his ability to speak comprehensible English (not that it stopped him from trying). We checked into a hotel, had a wander around to see the sights, attempted to learn a few words of Polish and ate some local food.

The show was a delight and gave me an everlasting love for this small city in Poland. There was a great crowd in, appreciative, attentive and not shy of getting involved. I was, as ever, concerned about the language barrier, but, as ever, I shouldn't have been. My ragged attempts to speak Polish were greeted with friendly laughter (really, it's the fucking hardest language to speak I know of), but people sang along with the songs and by the end of the show people were literally dancing on the tables and the bar. Benek got insanely drunk on vodka and a variety of other spirits I couldn't identify, even when he was making me take shots with him onstage. After the gig I had to speak to him about payment for the show. He took me into a small cupboard and cried with happiness and appreciation (at least I think he did, like I say, his English wasn't great) while pushing handfuls of euros and Polish currency into my pockets and down my shirt. A generous man.

Barbs and I did not get enough sleep that night. Why would you? When you're in a bar in Poland surrounded by friendly locals plying you with booze? The journey to the airport and the flight home was a painful blur, but a well-earned one.

SHOW # 956
Jannus Landing, St Petersburg, FL, USA,
12 November 2010

My second major stint on the road in the USA with the full band took place in the second half of 2010 in the fall, to use the American term – mostly opening for Social Distortion. That was something I was pretty excited about – *White Light, White Heat, White Trash* was one of the first punk albums I ever bought. Apparently frontman Mike Ness's son turned him on to my stuff and he became a fan. He then discovered we were on the same record label (Epitaph) and offered me the tour.

The Flogging Molly run earlier in the year had been pretty

tough on all of us, so this time around we wanted a slightly more comfortable mode of transport. We ended up with a vehicle called the Bandwagon – essentially a box truck converted into a semi-tour bus. It had a handful of bunks, a small lounge and even a little shower at the back, which didn't see much use on account of the small size of the attached water tank. We had Casey with us, as ever, but we also had our friend Craig Jenkins, from Santa Barbara's Velvet Jones club, onboard as a driver and extra pair of hands. All this was easier, logistically, than the previous American run, but it was still pretty rough and ready. In particular, the suspension on the Bandwagon left a lot to be desired and there were many nights where sleep was impossible, bouncing around in our bunks in the back of the truck.

The run opened with a slot at the Austin City Limits Festival in Texas. We had a mid-afternoon slot and played a slightly jet-lagged set to a medium-sized and appreciative crowd. From there we tore across the inescapable void that is West Texas, heading for Albuquerque, New Mexico. We arrived the night before our show and some of us may have got a little worse for wear in the local bars. The show the next night – a headline fill-show-cum-warm-up – was at a bar appropriately called Low Spirits. The turnout was minuscule and my voice was a train wreck. Not perhaps my fondest memory from the road.

The next day we drove to Salt Lake City to meet up with Social Distortion and begin the tour proper. The venue we were playing was a bizarre emporium that looked like the Brighton Dome – all faux-oriental towers – situated in the middle of the desert, by the end of the actual Great Salt Lake. We spent the early afternoon wading ankle deep out into the mirrored emptiness of the water, where I felt like I could have walked out and touched the horizon itself – a completely surreal and unforgettable experience.

Back at the venue, we met up with Social Distortion and their crew and with the guys in Lucero, who were the main support for the tour (we had the first-on slot). This motley bunch comprised some of my closest road friends and are people to whom I owe a great debt of gratitude. Social D were welcoming – Mike is a touch off in his own world, but Brent, David, Jonny and Danny couldn't have been friendlier. I was a big fan of Lucero and of course I knew Ben and Todd already from the Revival tours. They and their tour manager, Jimmy Perlman, quickly became partners in mischief.

We were prepared to be the young, hungry unknowns on the tour, without much in the way of a sound check and that's how it was, running the show by the seat of our pants. I was on the merch booth again for this tour, so my days were a frenzy of activity – counting in shirts, restringing guitars (we had no techs), setting up for the gig, checking, scoffing down some food, selling from when the doors opened, rushing to the stage to play for half an hour, then running back to the merch to sell shirts to surprised Americans for the rest of the night, sinking friendly whiskies, before finishing up with a count out, an argument with the in-house merch guy about how much you owe the house in commission followed by a well-deserved crash-out in the Bandwagon.

Playing as a support act, and one almost totally unknown at that, is something that The Sleeping Souls and I have become pretty good at over the years and this tour is probably the one, more than any other, where we honed our skill. It was immensely satisfying, heading out every night in front of Social D's notoriously 'difficult' crowd – ageing punks, for the most part, not overly interested in discovering new bands – and smashing expectations, walking off soaked in sweat and applause. We made a lot of new fans on this run and the fact that I sold most of them a shirt or a CD afterwards cemented their new-found loyalty.

From Salt Lake City (where I played another impromptu car-park show for some folks who'd travelled far to see my set but had missed it), we headed east through the mountains, stopping in Denver for a few nights, where I saw my sister and played a side-show at Illegal Pete's, a Mexican restaurant run by punk friends. From there we went through Kansas City, up to Minneapolis and the legendary First Avenue venue and through Chicago, where I had an altercation with some of Social D's rather more skinhead fans, who seemed to take exception to English accents and acoustic guitars. Thankfully it didn't turn into a fight at the merch table after our set, though I was nervous for the rest of the evening. In Detroit I got shitfaced with the Flogging Molly guys, delaying our border crossing into Canada and pissing Casey off no end (sorry man). In Toronto we played a triumphant headline set at the Horseshoe Tavern – one of my favourite shows ever. Some nights everything comes together and suddenly you're in the eye of a punk-rock storm – bodies flying, music exploding, sweat dripping from the walls, the atmosphere tangibly life-affirming. The next night we rejoined the main tour.

Heading back into the USA, we ground through the miles on the East Coast, filling in off days with headline shows. We made our first stop at the famous 9:30 club in DC, where we met the legendary head of security Josh Burdette for the first time; we played Philly, Boston, Atlantic City and New York; Casey and I flew south and back again for a manic twenty-four hours and three shows at The Fest in Gainesville, Florida; and we played an awesome headline show at Asbury Lanes, a place fast starting to feel like home. Social D had to cancel in Baltimore, so Lucero and I ended up playing a free show to a thinned-out but grateful crowd. As we headed south through Virginia, North Carolina, Tennessee and Georgia, the tour really started to tire us out. In the end, with fill shows and impromptu extra gigs, I played forty-five times in just north of six weeks. At one point I did sixteen days in a row without a break.

The warm weather in the South buoyed everyone's spirits. The show in St Petersburg, Florida was at an outside spot called Jannus Landing. It was blissful to wander around in shorts and T-shirts during the day and play in the cool evening air. We ended up with a little more time to sound check that day, so while Nigel and Casey were running through the drums, I was mucking around with some country-style riff ideas on my guitar quietly in the corner of the stage. Suddenly everything pulled into focus and I found myself playing that rarest of things – a riff that is distinct, characterful and unique, but which also sounds old, timeless, maybe even obvious. I kept at it and the whole song just unfolded into my lap in the space of about twenty minutes. I even started getting words for it, right there. I'm not a superstitious or religious person, but I really felt like I was channelling something that shouldn't be interrupted. By the time sound check was done, I had about 75 per cent of a song called 'If Ever I Stray' completed.

It felt slightly incongruous to be writing songs about England while charging around a different continent, but in some ways being away gave me time to think about home. Every night, the five of us were the only English people in a crowded room. It highlights the cultural and national differences between you; not in a chauvinistic or hateful way at all, I just find it curious to see how something as vague as national identity can affect your individual character. All of these thoughts were coming together at around this time in new material that felt stronger and more coherent than the previous batch. I have a lot of affection for *Poetry of the Deed*, but in retrospect it was an album made in a hurry by a band who were still finding their feet as a collective. This time around my writing was stronger and more focused and we had gelled as a musical unit after months of punishing road. It was an exciting time.

The Florida run went smoothly enough, even if Brian from Lucero, a vegan, did get a tattoo of a strip of bacon done late one night. In Orlando I did the first of many in-store performances at Park Ave CDs, a great record store and good friends. We crossed the South again to hit Texas, feeling like we'd lapped ourselves. In Dallas I met Oliver Peck, the tattooist, for the first time and got some work done on my leg in a dingy backstage room. On our second drive through West Texas in as many months, we stopped off at Jim Ward's studio in El Paso and demoed about fifteen new songs in one day, as the next album continued to take shape.

Finally we made it to Arizona for the last shows of the run. Once again we had a crazily tight turnaround between tours, so we were jumping off a few days early in order to prepare for the UK leg. After a wild night in Tempe, complete with a second show in a bar with Lucero's brass section backing me up, we boarded a long flight home.

SHOW # 972
Guildhall, Southampton, UK, 7 December 2010

Our next run around the UK was another step up. As I've mentioned, the London venue is often a good watermark for the size of the tour; this time around we were booked to play Brixton Academy, another fabled spot to cross off my bucket list. When we booked the tour, Joanna had been openly laughed at by her boss. In the event we sold the room out. I guess I was still flying under the radar at this point, working from word of mouth and the support of a few rogue DJs and journalists. I like to think her boss was pleasantly surprised.

We were breaking in some new songs on this run, in preparation for our time in the studio, which was booked for January. In particular we had started playing 'Glory Hallelujah', a controversial song to say the least. I'd written the chorus a while back and had casually played it to Jay Beans on the back of a bus some time. He immediately announced that the song had to be finished, that the statement in question was too strong to be left on the scrapheap; so I dutifully complied. In the event I spent a really long time working through the words, trying to make sure that the tone was right. I grew up in a religious household – my grandfather was a priest and if I'm honest, subconsciously I may have delayed finishing the song until his passing – and I'm not really interested in castigating the beliefs of others. I merely wanted to state mine for the record and to do so in a joyous fashion. Of course the song still raised some hackles here and there – even with a lengthy justification appended as an introduction – and I received some heated emails on the subject. But I felt strongly that I had a right to state my case and have continued to do so to this day.

There were a few new things in the works for this tour. One small difference was this was the first time as a band that we started wearing the white stage shirts that we keep to this day (not the same actual shirts of course, that'd be disgusting). We sweat so hard onstage that having a separate set of clothes makes hygienic sense; once I'd got used to that, it was easier to overcome my initial reluctance to have any kind of official 'stage wear'. After a brief stint of wearing checked plaid shirts we settled on the white ones. I think it gives us a visual impact and coherence onstage that subtly adds to the show. I also can't think of anything better so we're sticking with them until I do.

The other difference for this tour was that it was the first we did without Barbs on our crew. This episode remains pretty much the hardest, most heartbreaking thing I've had to do on tour. We'd been having a few issues with some technical and professional things for a while and it had eventually ended up in a situation where there was a lot of hostility between various people in the touring party as a result. We reached a point where the only way to move forwards was for us to part ways. Barbs was (and is) one of my best friends. The decision was made while we were in the USA with Social Distortion. I took an afternoon to go for a long walk and called Barbs to let him know he wouldn't be on the next UK run with us. It was a horrible thing to have to do, Barbs was understandably upset and it took us many years to patch our friendship up. I felt awful about the whole thing and once the deed was done I walked through the streets of New York on my own for a long time, desperately double-checking with myself that I'd done the right thing. When I finally got back to the bus, I was touched to see that the boys in the band had bought me a present (a book of Siegfried Sassoon poetry) to cheer me up. Even writing this stuff down is making me feel sad. Jimmy Pearlman, Lucero's tour manager, consoled me by saying that every band that rises above a certain level has to make a call like this at some point, a choice between friendship and professionalism, but that knowledge didn't (and doesn't) seem like much of a balm against the pain of the separation.

So it was that we were travelling without Barbs. In his place we had the wonderful Dougie Murphy, a delightful Scouse lad who has been on my crew here and there for years, and Dave Samwell, who we borrowed from The Wombats' crew. Also aboard was Jamie Stuart, the other member of Dive Dive, who were opening the shows, meaning that Ben, Tarrant and Nigel were on double duty for this run. It felt good to give those guys the time on stage. I'm often gripped by a feeling of embarrassment around Jamie as I slightly stole the rest of his band off him!

The middle slot on the tour was occupied by the one and only Mr Ed Harcourt. These days Ed's a multitalented singer and songwriter, and I was excited to have him on the tour with us and riding on our bus. He's an ebullient, larger-than-life character who kept us all entertained.

The first show of the tour was booked to be in Aberdeen, but in the event a massive snowfall meant that the bus and the equipment truck were unable to make the drive up there and we had to postpone the show. That was a demoralizing start to the tour, so after the show in Glasgow, which became the first stop, we headed out into the snow-covered streets to drink the night away. After the gig I offered Ed a shot of Jameson whisky, my drink of choice; he said no, on the grounds that he couldn't drink whisky, it did bad things to him. I told him to man up and he agreed to one small one. The night then rapidly took a turn for the demented. We were drinking quietly in a small venue-cum-bar that I'd played before, Nice N Sleazy, when Ed swept the table clear of glassware, smashing everything on the floor, declaring loudly, 'You people are all cunts!' He then charged into the night, bit Tarrant on the chest (a difficult thing to do, Tarrant is very skinny) and threw himself down the tour-bus stairs. I guess I shouldn't have given him whisky.

One of the later stops on the tour was at the Southampton Guildhall. I was excited for this show because I used to go there as a kid to see bigger touring bands and daydream about one day taking the stage myself. I'd opened up for the Levellers there in 2008 but this was my first headline slot. As the day drew near, the winter weather had started to affect my health and I was coming down with a nasty cold. The show the night before in Cambridge had seen me struggle through the high notes by the skin of my larynx. In the morning in Southampton, I knew in my gut that I wasn't really in shape for the gig. Cancelling any gig for health reasons is almost indescribably painful for me; it makes me feel like a useless sack of shit, an albatross around the necks of my band, my crew and the disappointed punters, a dog who should be taken out back and put out of its misery. Added to this was the fact that we were at the Guildhall. I *really* didn't want to cancel, but in sound check I sounded like a dying giraffe. After some discussion we decided to detune our instruments a little to help me with the high notes and soldier on.

I spent the evening mainlining hot honey and lemon, Throat Coat tea, Vocalzone throat pastilles and anything else that might possibly help my poor battered throat through the night. My mum was on hand to offer sympathy and tutting, but nothing really helped. In the event, the show went OK – the thrill of being in front of a sell-out crowd on that stage, plus said crowd's enthusiasm and help in the singing department, meant that I struggled on to the finish line. Once we were done, I stumbled offstage and pretty much straight into my mum's car. She took me home for some rest and recuperation and we postponed the following day's show in Exeter, which made me feel shitty, though there was no question that it had to be done.

Two days' bed rest and maternal care did wonders for me and we picked up in Leicester before finishing triumphantly at Brixton.

I promised Ed I'd never make him drink whisky again.

SHOWS # 988 # 989
Trof, Manchester, UK, 4 March 2011

By this stage in my career, as far as the UK was concerned, my regular tour shows had decisively moved up above the toilet-circuit level, into theatres and other larger rooms. In some ways that was great, a reflection of hard work paying off, of success. In others it was a shame, to leave behind the rooms I know so well, where I cut my teeth. I was increasingly playing rooms that Million Dead had never been anywhere near, unless as a support act. At the end of the day, my choice of venue to play is governed by one factor above all others – trying to make sure that everyone who wants to come to the show is able to get in. I don't like the idea of my shows being exclusive, panic-driven affairs, where people have to be in the know somehow to get into the gig. I was never in the know when I was younger and I feel like I'd be excluding people like me from the shows. So if a lot of people want to come to the show, we'll play a bigger place. Even so, it was sad to think that the days of Barflys and bunker squats might be behind me (unless everything goes really badly at some point in the future).

We spent January in the Church Studios in north London. The record was tracked in twelve days, which was less time than we'd actually allowed. Everything went smoothly, working with Tristan Ivemy again was a blast and there were no major musical arguments, confrontations or conundrums. The record just kind of fell into place, which was great. Towards the end of the session, I was panicking about the album's title. My friend Ben Morse, who'd shot a few videos for me in the past and has gone on to become my official documentarian, was chatting through some ideas with me over a beer in the studio kitchen one evening. The album had a definite English theme to it, underpinned by a sense of mortality. Ben was a drama teacher at the time and a man well-versed in English literature. He mentioned a Shakespeare quote that I was unfamiliar with and everything pulled sharply into focus – *England Keep My Bones*.

After recording the album we fulfilled our obligations in Aberdeen and Exeter, filling in the yawning gap between the two cities with extra shows, taking our friends Jim Lockey & the Solemn Sun along for the ride. After that there was a gap in the official tour schedule to allow time for promotional work to prepare for the release of the new record, which was scheduled for the start of June. In the midst of all this I got a fortuitous email from a lady named Laura Scott.

Laura was a name and a face I knew from shows – an acquaintance, shall we say, rather than a friend. She told me a story about how a friend of hers called Spencer had recently lost his battle with blood cancer and that she was keen to raise money for some relevant charities as a way of commemorating her friend. She titled her email 'A long shot'. I guess it was, but for whatever reason it caught my imagination. Among other things, this was a way for me to play in a small room again. My stipulations about trying not to make things exclusive felt satisfyingly overruled, when both charity and the last-minute nature of the show were taken into account. We agreed that I'd drop some hints about the show on Twitter and only announce it properly a few hours before. All things considered, it was shaping up to be an exciting and worthwhile evening.

I took the train up to Manchester by myself and wandered in the direction of the venue. Laura had secured a tiny place called Trof in Fallowfield, a student area. I'd been tweeting various hints as to the location of the show and word had started to spread. By the time I showed up, there were already a handful of people waiting around. I'd been rumbled. I did a quick sound check in the tiny upstairs room – I'd say you could squeeze maybe 100 people in there, at a push – and stepped outside to find some food.

By the time I actually officially announced the show, there was already a queue down the street and when I got back from eating it had got properly out of hand. There were clearly way too many people to get into the show standing outside. I had a quick chat with Laura and the people running Trof. We decided to split the evening into two, in order that everyone could come to the show and we'd raise more money for charity. The gig room had a small balcony that overlooked the street and the ever-growing line. I stood on the balcony and announced the new idea, feeling a little bit like a tinpot dictator. Everyone seemed to agree that it was a good idea and the evening got underway.

The shows were a total blast in the end. I played old songs, new songs, songs from the as-yet-unreleased album and pretty much anything anyone in the crowd wanted to hear – as long as they were prepared to throw some extra cash in the bucket for the privilege. After playing for an hour or so, we shuffled everyone out of the room and brought in the fresh blood, trying to make sure that no one sneakily hid and stayed for both. By the end of the second set I was exhausted, drenched in sweat and my throat was pretty ragged. But it felt great to be that close to the crowd again, that involved. It reminded me of some things I'd forgotten about stagecraft; switching up the size and types of venue that I play helps a lot with that. In the end I did another secret show the following day in Leeds at Bar Santiago. Across the three gigs we raised over £2,000 for the charity Lymphoma Research. It felt like a good way to spend my downtime.

SHOW # 1000
Strummerville Spring Sessions, London, UK,
21 April 2011

After a short break to gather my breath before the coming onslaught, the ground campaign to prepare the world for *England Keep My Bones* began in earnest. More so than ever before, this was to be an international release, so predictably my schedule was hectic. After a quick pit stop for a benefit at White Rabbit down in Plymouth (a great little venue that was threatened with closure at the time; alas it has since gone) and a video shoot in Bristol for new single 'Peggy Sang the Blues', I headed for Germany for some press days and shows.

German press schedules are legendary for their intensity. I was set up in the wonderful Ramones Museum in Berlin, a great punk-rock hangout in the city run by my friend Flo. I had two solid days of interviews – more than fifteen each day – followed by a gig each night at White Trash, a cool punk-rock venue with a restaurant and tattoo parlour attached. Being interviewed that much in such a short space of time is a surreal experience. Your head starts to spin by the end of it and it's very rough on the voice, but you also get a chance to work out, in detail, what you think about the art that you're promoting and your station in life. So in a weird way it can actually be educational, as you iron out the kinks in your philosophy.

After great shows in Berlin, I headed to Cologne for another similar day of blathering, plus a show at Blue Shell. A few hours' kip later I was boarding a plane from Cologne Airport to fly (via several other places) to Sydney, Australia. I was happy to be heading back Down Under, this time for some headline shows of my own (albeit playing solo). However, the strains of a twenty-four-hour flight and a ten-hour time-zone change on the back of the schedule of the last few days meant that I was feeling like a total alien by the time I arrived. I remember taking a cab through the deserted dawn streets, at once so familiar and yet weird in their Australian character, and wondering where on earth I had landed. It was many hours before the city awoke and I sat on my hotel balcony drinking coffee and wondering if I should be sleepy or not.

I had five shows booked in the big cities – Sydney, Melbourne, Brisbane, Adelaide and Perth. Before that, I had a pair of press days in the first two cities, with yet more talking through the new record and the motivations behind it. It was reassuring to find that most of the journalists I was talking to seemed to be enthusiastic about the new material. After three records, it's easy to feel that you're Wile E. Coyote, suspended in midair, the solid cliff far behind, waiting for reality to kick in and the fall to begin. It was nice, a relief even, to hear that the general consensus was that my fourth record might be my best to date.

The press days went OK, despite my propensity for falling asleep at weird times. The shows were busy or sold out and great fun. In Melbourne I made a return to the Arthouse and did a sold-out show. It was one of the last shows there, as the building had been condemned, which felt like an honour. I also had the totally gobsmacking surprise of meeting Dennis and David from Refused in the dressing room shortly before my set (they were on tour with another band of theirs). The Refused reunion hadn't yet happened; when I was drunk I told them both to get to it, so I'll take some credit for it (haha).

After the Arthouse show there was a free day in the diary before my return to the UK, which Chris from Blue Murder (who promotes my Australian tours) had been planning to fill with a second Melbourne show. This, however, presented a problem. It had come to my attention that I was coming up to my 1,000th show. I'd always kept a show list, a slightly OCD tic of mine, but one I'm glad I've kept up with as it's helped me remember where I've been (and to write this book!). At first I hadn't thought much about the numbers rolling over – it seemed slightly trivial to me – but after a time I changed my mind and decided it was something worth commemorating.

So I booked a gig with my friends at Strummerville, a great organization that runs some shows at Glastonbury and in London and tries to help disadvantaged kids get musical instruments. They'd been keen to do a London show with me for a while and after I suggested a date for my 1,000th show, everything had been arranged. Unfortunately, this meant that I really had to watch how many gigs I was doing in the run-up to the big rollover. When Chris suggested a second night at the Arthouse, probably the last ever show on that hallowed ground, I had to sadly decline as it would have thrown the numbers out. He was initially slightly incredulous but in the end came to understand my reasoning.

My journey home, after bidding Australia a fond farewell, was pretty nightmarish. I left Perth and flew to Sydney, from Sydney to Kuala Lumpur, from Kuala Lumpur to Munich and from Munich to London (the German dogleg was necessary because it's where I'd started my Australian adventure from). By the time I arrived at City Airport, more than thirty hours later, I was so confused that I thought the guy at baggage claim asking for an autograph was trying to rob me.

I arrived in the morning and had the rest of that day to recover. Thankfully I hadn't been in Australia long enough to adjust to the time zones fully, so I felt weirdly more in sync with the world than I had for the previous week. The following day was another press day in the UK and then there was the Strummerville show. They'd sorted an underground car park in Shoreditch, east London, for the occasion. We had two different stages and a bunch of tickets sold. I arrived for sound check and was immediately glad to be in the company of Trish and Jamie, the two main operators at Strummerville at the time. They had drafted in some help to promote the show from Dave Danger and Jay (Beans On Toast) and in the end the event turned into something of a Nambucca reunion, bringing together a bunch of people who hadn't all been in the same room at the same time since before the fire. It made the evening even more special.

What to say about playing 1,000 shows? Reading back through the list that I keep (which is now, at the time of writing, closer to 2,000), it seems surreal, confusing even, to scroll down, thinking of the number of times I've introduced myself to a room mostly full of strangers. I lose the ability to process the information after a while and have to take a step back. But at the same time, this has been my adulthood, it's where I've been and what

I've done. I'm not claiming to have achieved much in this life, my calling isn't nearly as important as most, but I can look at that list with some degree of pride. This is my trade, my craft, I set out to do it, however cautiously at first, and I did it. That night, as I sang 'The Road', after one line in particular – 'The nights, a thousand nights I've played' – I paused for breath and effect, and the crowd cheered, before I sang the next line – 'A thousand more to go . . . before I take a breath and steel myself for the next one thousand shows'.

I'm not someone who is often comfortable in my own skin, but there and then, with the crowd and my old friends around me, singing my exhausted throat raw in a run-down car park in London, I felt like I was in the right place.

After the show was done I managed to rein in my party spirit, because the following day I had to take a train south, back to the Hampshire hills, to see my mum getting remarried. I figured that showing up hungover and sleep deprived wouldn't be the best look. Actually, while at White Trash in Berlin, I had my first finger tattoos done (an alpha and omega on my pinkies) and that probably wasn't a good look for my mum's wedding either. Thankfully I think Mum was too wrapped up in the day to notice them.

After that I got on a plane heading for Toronto, for a solo, promotional North American run. When I got to the hotel and met up with Jimmy Perlman (who was tour managing this run), the exhaustion of the insane schedule hit me pretty hard – England, Germany, Australia, England, Canada. I was twenty-nine then and could just about hack it; I doubt I could now.

After a cheeky extra show in a punk-rock art gallery the night before my official appearance in town, Jimmy and I sat in my hotel room, overlooking the city, and he hand-poked a new piece of ink on my chest: 1001. It seemed to me that commemorating the show after the milestone made more sense. Making 1,000 shows was great, but it wasn't the end of anything. I wanted to mark the start of the next phase.

SHOW # 1028
St George's, Bristol, UK, 24 May 2011

The campaign to promote *England Keep My Bones* continued to gather pace like a runaway train, yet the record was still some way from being released to the world at large. Looking back through the tour and promotional schedule they had me on, it's exhausting just to read. But I was fired up and hungry and younger than I am now and while I was often tired, I was never sick of the road, always keen to get up in the morning, wash the sleep and hangover from my eyes and get back into the van or car or bus or plane.

Jimmy Perlman and I flitted across the North American landmass, doing fly-in dates, picking up cars at the airport and driving to faceless hotels for long days of interviews and longer nights of packed rooms, sing-alongs and whisky. We played a parking-lot festival in New Jersey, nearly got into a fight with an interviewer in Chicago (there's a limit to my patience with people who set out to be rude), had our (well, my) hearts broken by pretty girls in San Francisco and finished up with a crazy night in Craig's bar in Santa Barbara, Velvet Jones. I then bade Jimmy a fond farewell and headed back to England for the pre-album release tour.

The album was set to be unveiled at the start of June. In the run-up to the big day, Joanna had put together a pretty far-reaching UK tour. For this run I'd opted to go back to playing solo, something I hadn't done on my home turf for some time. It felt like a cool way to introduce people to the new material and just a nice change-up from what had become the usual set. I was also very happy to have two great friends along for the ride. Firstly, there was Franz Nicolay. Franz used to play for The Hold Steady (one of my very favourite bands) but now does his own unique brand of punk-rock-vaudevillian songwriting. As well as being a nice guy, he's a great songwriter and performer and a fount of knowledge on everything to do with the history of entertainment. Ben Marwood was also on the bill, a guy from Reading who I'd known since 2006 or so. Completing the bus line-up were Sarah (on merch), Graham (on sound and tour managing) and Ben and Nigel from the band (stage teching and generally hanging out).

The route took in twenty-three towns and cities up and down the UK. We started in Stockton and finished in Winchester, hitting some pretty obscure towns in between. It was great to play in some slightly different rooms. There are places that can take a solo acoustic show that couldn't handle a full rock band with drum kit sonically. We played the library in Lancaster, a warehouse in Chester, a festival in Norfolk, a record store in Brighton and no less than three churches.

St George's Church in the Clifton area of Bristol is a beautiful Greek Revival-style building that has recently been renovated to accommodate live shows by jazz, classical and folk artists. It was slightly bizarre to see the usual ragtag collection of people who come to my shows filtering in through the tiny box office – punk kids, indie kids, folk enthusiasts, older people and a whole lot of just normal, unclassifiable souls. It was a seated show and the acoustics in the room were pretty much perfect. Most of the shows on this run had a special feel to them, but I remember this one in particular for having a near magical atmosphere. Ben and Franz had great sets, which I watched from the wings. The sound in the room spiralled into the high ceiling before falling gently back on to the rapt audience, watching in pin-drop silence. When my turn to play came around I felt gripped by a sense of wonder and had one of those rare shows where every song courses through me like it did when I first came up with the whisperings of an idea.

At the end of the show, I finished with 'The Ballad of Me and My Friends'. As was customary at the time I told the crowd that they had to carry the vocal as I was ditching the microphone. It's a trick that closes proceedings with a communal feel, but in the surroundings of an old church it took on a particularly intense vibe. After a few lines, the crowd started to rise to their feet to sing and the voices in chorus filled the room. I looked behind me to check my guitar lead would take the strain and then started to walk out over the pews until I was stood in the middle of the room. I love it when shows become something more than a lecture delivered from a stage to an audience, when they are more a dialogue than a monologue, when the performer's identity gets subsumed and becomes unimportant. At that moment I wasn't playing a show for those people, I was leading them in song.

SHOW # 1075
JK Zomaar, Itterbeek, Belgium, 20 August 2011

England Keep My Bones was finally released on 6 June. I was already ankle-deep in another mad festival summer, so on the day itself I found myself flying in from Germany – where we'd just played the Rock im Park and Rock am Ring festivals – for a quick launch-party set at the Barfly in Camden. It was a relief to finally have the damn thing out there. People seemed to be getting into the new songs, the reviews were generally positive and life was good. On top of all that, Ben, Nigel, Matt, Tarrant and I had finally solved an old problem – what to call the band. After much discussion over the years and many rejected suggestions (The 1970s, The 161

Band, The Contraband, Lazerchild . . .) we finally all agreed on a name. Taken from the lyrics to 'I Am Disappeared', a song from the new album, the band was officially christened The Sleeping Souls.

My summer was arranged around a series of shows opening for our old touring buddies Social Distortion. They had invited me and the boys to join them in France, the Netherlands, Denmark and Germany, where they were playing a series of multiple nights in Berlin and Hamburg. It was nice to see them again, this time on my side of the Atlantic. In between those stops I was rushing around playing various European festivals and headline shows. I returned to Poznań, this time with the band, though we did have to leave Johnny, our monitor engineer, in the parked, unpowered bus in a German lay-by for eighteen hours as there weren't enough seats in the Polish van (which we had to take to the show as the bus was not licensed to drive on Polish roads). We hung out with Converge in Switzerland and incongruously headlined a stage amid the mud and metallers at the Download Festival, Donington Park. We played with an Austrian band in Graz who had a person with dwarfism in a spacesuit dancing for them. Graham drank himself to pieces afterwards, perhaps to cope with the insanity of it all. I don't think I've ever seen a man so broken.

We played a four-night stand in Hamburg with Social D, which was an interesting experience. A tour is usually defined by leaving, being spirited away in the night and finding yourself in a new town, the wreckage of the previous evening a distant smudge in the rear-view mirror. Returning to the venue you played the night before often feels like coming back to the scene of a crime. On the other hand, it was great to be able to spend some time in the city, to see more of Hamburg than just the bars on the Reeperbahn. I lost myself in an antiques flea market for most of a day, walked around old churches and practised my pidgin German. On the last night of the stand I was drinking with Brent from Social D and talking about songs, when I had the idea for a punk-rock song with a vaudevillian opening, a song about dancing . . .

Back in England we headlined Blissfields Festival near Winchester, a homecoming of sorts, though I confess to losing my temper with the house sound guys – my monitor mix onstage so terrible that even Johnny couldn't save it. I felt pretty bad about it afterwards. We made our first visit to the island of Guernsey, which was a little surreal, like a British fifties time warp, and to Croatia, which was blissful, sunning ourselves in a beach resort on the Dalmatian coast. Next up was a triumphant return to Fonofest in Latvia and then a festival in Italy where the local punks offered to swap a pizza for our massive (and very expensive) stage backdrop. Another highlight was the Cambridge Folk Festival, which was a delightful contrast to Download and where I successfully fooled some of the local purists into thinking that 'English Curse' was a traditional song. We played a last-minute show at the Newcastle Academy after the festival we had been supposed to play at got cancelled – I think the locals appreciated the effort – and we made our first appearance on the main stages at the Reading and Leeds festivals, thereby fulfilling a childhood dream born at Reading 1995 when I saw Beck play that very same stage and slot.

I'm rushing through talking about a lot of these shows, which in a way feels appropriate. The pace of our live schedule, especially in the summer, had reached a feverish pitch. We were a well-oiled touring machine – me and the band, Graham and Johnny, Shaun Moore on lights, various guitar techs (though in the end we settled on Cahir from Fighting With Wire, who works with us to this day). We were used to living in buses, eating in catering tents, doing laundry when we could, sleeping in bunks, spending our mornings trying to find everything in the chaos of festival backstages. It's a strange existence, a weird bubble. You run into a lot of the same faces over the festival months; geography almost melts away as the circus rolls on from field to field, country to country.

In the midst of it all, though, we're still doing things the way we started out, trying our best to play rock 'n' roll shows, to bring a room of strangers together and lift the weight of the world for a few hazy hours. Occasionally a show will give you a stark reminder of that. Towards the end of the summer we were due to play at Pukkelpop in Belgium. We'd had a few days' rest at home, so were feeling refreshed as we rolled out on the bus the night before our appearance. We crossed over on the ferry from Dover to Calais, drove into Belgium and parked up in yet another faceless Euro coach stop. As we tucked into a few beers to soften the evening, word started to filter through that there had been some kind of incident at the festival. Through the confused chatter on the internet a picture gradually emerged – a freak storm had hit the festival site, a stage had collapsed and people had been hurt. We then heard that the festival was cancelled and that five people had died.

It was terrible news, every musician and music fan's nightmare. We sat dejectedly in the car park and talked about how lucky we were not to have been there ourselves. We were due to be at the Lowlands festival in the neighbouring Netherlands the day after Pukkelpop, so we started thinking about when we would head over in that direction. As we were sitting there, I received an email from some Belgian punks. They'd been at the festival, they knew people who had been hurt or killed, but they still wanted the show to go on – would I be interested in a last-minute show the following day?

It was a heavy decision to take – I wanted to be absolutely sure that it didn't in any way come across like I was profiting from disaster. But the people I talked to online were unanimous. A show would be a fitting tribute; it would be what the departed would have wanted. So it was that a venue was found – a small punk bar, JK Zomaar, in a suburb of Brussels, not far from where we were parked up – and a free show was put together. Word spread and come the evening I took a cab across town, with a few of the band and crew in tow, to a small but packed-out room. Everyone seemed grateful that I'd decided to play, but I was still cautious to be considerate of the emotions that were running high.

It was a special evening. There was a weird energy in the air that thankfully turned into something positive. There were plenty of people who knew my stuff, but also a fair few who didn't, who'd just come down to be with other people and commemorate. I played, we sang, we all drank to the dead and I felt humbled to be part of this makeshift ceremony with strangers in a foreign country. It reminded me of the soul of what I do, and of how, from time to time, it can be important.

SHOW # 1130

Theatre of Living Arts, Philadelphia, PA, USA,
4 November 2011

After the release of the album in June, preceded by months of promotional work and followed by a heavy summer of festivals, it was time to get on the road and tour *England Keep My Bones* properly around the world. I'd reached the stage where I could realistically look at a schedule and call it a World Tour with capital letters. In some ways it was daunting, in other ways exciting, but I think the main thing for me was that we were finally able to have one of those tour shirts with the cities listed on the back in small writing and it made for one hell of an impressive list.

I started out with a handful of low-key but fun solo shows in the Republic of Ireland and Northern Ireland, topped off with The Sleeping Souls joining me for Dublin and Belfast. We then boarded a plane for the USA and Canada, where we had forty-two shows scheduled, taking in pretty much every corner of the continent. We had a proper tour bus this time around, which made life considerably easier. We also had two awesome support acts, who were riding with us, making the vehicle one big party bus. Andrew Jackson Jihad are a folk-punk band from Arizona who I had long loved, and for this run we had Sean and Ben coming out to play as a duo. The other act, who would play first, was Into It. Over It. – also known as Evan, an emo-influenced folk singer. It made for a great and varied bill and most of the shows were sold out.

The tour was topped and tailed with performances at The Bowery Ballroom in New York, which made for an interesting dynamic. Over the course of a tour, set lists and songs evolve slowly, shifting around each night as you figure out better ways to run songs together, better opening and closing numbers, better ways of engaging the crowd with different tricks. By the time we got to the second show at The Bowery, just over a month after the first, we put on a completely different show. That was gratifying, as I often worry about repeating myself when playing night after night. It was good to see that we had grown and changed in the interim.

We tore down the East Coast, playing sweaty shows to lively crowds; on one infamous occasion we were so hot and drenched after the show in South Carolina that we lined up against the fence out the back of the venue to be hosed down by Casey, as the venue didn't have a shower. We swung through Florida and then back up through Texas, into Oklahoma for the first time, and to Kansas City, where we won the pub quiz taking place at the venue between sound check and the show. We crossed over into the

West, unfortunately having to lose the Albuquerque show due to my voice being shot, although we did meet Jerry Only from the Misfits in a car park there who sweetly tried to give me some medicine from a plastic shopping bag to make me feel better. Onwards we went, into California, where we played live on *Jimmy Kimmel* before tearing east to Pomona, arriving at the venue three minutes before we were due on stage.

From there we headed north, up the West Coast and into Canada, making the long drive across the north-western prairies through Alberta. I was constantly amazed at the number of people coming out to the shows, people who knew the words to all the songs. As much as I'd done a bunch of work playing in those parts of the world before, they still seemed (and seem) impossibly remote to me, so having the locals onside was a constant source of wonder. In Winnipeg I got to hang out with John K. Samson from The Weakerthans and indeed covered 'One Great City!', his ode to his hometown, with John looking on approvingly from the wings.

Dipping back into the USA, I finally got to play a show in Minneapolis's legendary Triple Rock Social Club, before heading on to Milwaukee, Chicago and Detroit. Around this time, due to the troubles I was having with my voice, I finally tried out in-ear monitors. This essentially means that instead of relying on the speakers on the front of the stage, which can be pretty fucking awful in some venues, especially on a tour of this size, you get a wireless feed to a pair of high-end headphones. It can initially be a little discomforting, as it kind of removes you from the room, but once you get used to it, it's a musician's dream, as you can hear everything you're doing much more clearly and thus just play better. The extra control meant I didn't have to strain so much and so it saved my voice on this run. I continue to use them religiously to this day.

Back up to Canada, we played Toronto and then into Quebec,

where I got to practise some of my French. Finally we headed south into the USA for the last few days on the upper East Coast, returning to our starting point. After the second Bowery show we had one more stop, in Philadelphia, at the Theatre of Living Arts (or TLA). Coincidentally, this was also the largest show on the tour and it was sold out. It was a fitting end – we seamlessly burned through a well-oiled set list and brought the packed-out house down. There was the usual end-of-tour mixture of sadness and elation, goodbyes and excitement about going home. Dave Hause came out to the show to hang out and ended up getting so wasted that he lost his car. But other than that, we finished the show, packed up and sat quietly in the front lounge of the bus, slightly dazed by what we had just achieved. The Sleeping Souls and I were now a bona fide successful touring act in North America; that's not something that's easy to achieve or that many people can say. It was a good feeling.

SHOW # 1131
AIM Awards, London, UK, 10 November 2011

After the punishing North American run, we had a few days off before heading to Europe to continue the world tour. During this downtime I attended the Association of Independent Music Awards (AIM) in London, both to receive an award and to play a song or two. It was a brand-new venture, their first year and it seemed like a cool way to spend an evening.

Awards and the associated ceremonies are a weird one for me. On the one hand, it's very flattering to be nominated or indeed to win, to be recognized by some (at least theoretically) higher power. There's a strong feeling of validation. On the other hand, as a kid

I was never much enamoured with stuff like the BRIT Awards or the NMEs – the bands that won were usually ones I didn't like – so such accolades can feel like a mixed blessing. The pompous pageantry of the ceremonies themselves can be a little cloying – I'm not really one for dressing up for an evening. On this occasion though it seemed like it would be fun, partly because it was a new venture (and being centred on independent music, one that I could fully get behind) and partly because I'd been asked to play, not just to show up in a tux. Matt, Nigel and I put together a couple of trio versions of some songs and brushed our hair a little (well, not Nige) in preparation.

I'd been told in advance that I was winning the award for Hardest Working Artist. Again, I have mixed feelings about this. The methodology of measuring something as abstract as that is necessarily pretty obscure and subjective. I know a lot of bands that work as hard as I do who have yet to win a trophy recognizing their efforts. And also, the work that I do is vocational – I love touring and playing guitar. Most of my friends work hard at jobs they hate, or at the most tolerate because they need the money. No one gives them any awards. Nevertheless, it was pretty cool to have all those years slogging away on the road recognized in some sort of official category.

Nigel, Matt and I played a song or two and I wandered awkwardly towards the podium to accept the award at the appointed hour. I had a short speech prepared saying thanks to the powers that be, but more importantly to Charlie, Joanna and The Sleeping Souls for being as much a part of the achievement as I was. Afterwards I posed for some official photos and returned to our table to get thoroughly and deservedly pissed.

Unfortunately, there was a surprise in the works. I had also been nominated for Best Live Act, but had assumed that I wasn't going to win it; after all, I'd been warned in advance about the other title and no one had said anything about this one. As it was, when that category rolled around, I had to be tapped on the shoulder and alerted to the fact that I had won again. This was slightly problematic as I was pretty soused by this point in the evening and had already said everything I had to say to the assembled company. I also felt even more strongly that this was an award for me *and* The Sleeping Souls, who were not officially namechecked. Charlie looked a little apprehensive as I stumbled back up on to the stage. Personally, I have very little memory of my second oration, but I'm reliably informed that what it lacked in coherence, it made up for in entertainment value. I guess I'm not cut out for the glitz and glamour of such occasions.

SHOW # 1162
Karlstorbahnhof, Heidelberg, Germany, 20 December 2011

After the brief pit stop, the tour resumed with a vengeance, this time through Europe and the UK, with Xtra Mile label mates The Xcerts (on the mainland) and Against Me! and Emily Barker (on home turf) in tow. We opened with a quick sally into the Netherlands and Germany, before traipsing over to Bournemouth to prepare for the UK leg of the tour.

By this point in time, my UK shows had become a full production affair. We had our own lights and PA system, mixing desks and other equipment rolling with us in a large truck. We even had our own catering, courtesy of the lovely Dylan Barnes, who still tours with me keeping me fed to this day. Having that many people around for a tour gets a little daunting after a while. Some members of the crew are people I don't know beforehand and often never see because their working hours are the inverse of mine. Nevertheless, it's great to have a family feel to the crew and I'm happy that we still have Cahir, Shaun, Graham, Tré and others on the team. For this run we actually booked out the first venue – the Bournemouth Academy – for a couple of days before the first show so that we could set up all the gear and check everything worked properly, run the set a few times, tweak the light show, that kind of thing. It felt immensely luxuriant to be able to play music with a full show and crew for a couple of days and then spend a quiet evening in a hotel nearby. Certainly it was a big change from playing the Portman Hotel to thirty people back in 2006.

Against Me! are a long-standing favourite band of mine, so it was fantastic to have them aboard. Unfortunately they had to pull the show in Newport as Tom (now Laura Jane) was having voice trouble, but fortuitously, Franz Nicolay happened to be in town and happily jumped on the bill. The rest of the UK shows went smoothly enough. We discovered that Emily's four petite folk-singing ladies could happily outdrink the Florida punks. We had a nasty run-in with some of the house security at the Manchester Apollo – an unpleasant throwback to the problems of venue security that I thought had been consigned to the dustbin of history. It all got sorted in the end though and the show itself was great. Hammersmith Apollo was a real moment of triumph – a huge and legendary venue, sold out to the rafters. The last time I'd been there had been to see Neil Young, so the stage felt like hallowed ground.

Leaving London behind, we returned to Germany for some solid touring. Germany was fast becoming my second-best country to play, in terms of the size of the shows. In Cologne we drew 2,000 people and the rest of the shows were comparably huge and packed. We made it out further east than before, hitting Rostock and Dresden. We made a return to Poland and this time managed to bring the whole crew (including Johnny) with us, getting as far as Warsaw. After that show we had a mad drive down to Ravenna in Italy, a mammoth 930-mile journey through five countries that took us about twenty-four hours. The cabin fever and boredom on the bus was intense, so I ended up scripting and filming a very silly short called *Murder on the Tour Bus Express* to pass the time. I'm pretty sure it's still on the internet somewhere.

The end of the tour took us through Austria and Switzerland. Everywhere we went on this run we caught up with old friends but also made new ones at the shows. Joanna and I have always tried to be loyal to the promoters that we use for my shows and it was great to see Silvio Huber in Austria, Martin Schrader in Switzerland and Silke Westera and Alex Kranz in Germany, all people who'd put me on in tiny bars as an act of faith in previous years; but this time around we got to enjoy the sight of a thousand people or more streaming through the doors. There was one sad event on the run, which was that Sarah, merch girl extraordinaire since the very early days, let me know that she was hanging up her touring shoes once we were done with this tour. It made total sense for her, but I know that the band, the crew and I all still miss her unique, crazy personality.

We wrapped up the tour, and indeed the year, in a frosty Heidelberg on 20 December. We were all so toured out by this point that the details of the show itself are a little hazy for me – not because of alcohol, but because of exhaustion. I do remember that we played a new song that night, one that had been coming together piecemeal over the tour. It was a song about dancing, which had started brewing in my brain in Hamburg, tentatively entitled 'Four Simple Words'. The crowd loved it. Heidelberg is a beautiful medieval city with a hint of the fairy tale about it and standing outside signing autographs in the cold winter air, with the wooded hills and the castle towering above me, I felt totally surreal, unmoored, a little disconnected from everything, but excited to be going home for Christmas. The year 2011 had been mammoth, but events in 2012 were shaping up to be even more momentous.

SHOW # 1174
Thee Parkside, San Francisco, CA, USA, 8 February 2012

I spent the festive period catching up with my family and friends, reminding my nearest and dearest what I actually look like. It was a much-needed break as the new year was already shaping up to be a big one. The main thing on the horizon was the fact that, at the start of the US run in 2011, we had announced and put on sale a show at Wembley Arena – my first arena headline show. Whatever else was going on in the months leading up to 13 April, there was a Wembley-shaped shadow hanging over pretty much everything else that I, The Sleeping Souls and my crew got up to.

We kicked off the year with some more support-slot shows in the USA. We had some shows lined up opening for Boston Celtic punk legends the Dropkick Murphys, but we were kicking off with another run with our old friends Social Distortion. This time around we'd be out west, in a part of the country we hadn't covered the last time we played with them stateside, back in 2010. The tour included a few pretty obscure stops in Nevada, New Mexico and Arizona and many obscure stops in California, Social D's home state. California is a state that is overshadowed by its two most famous cities, Los Angeles and San Francisco, but there's actually a whole lot more to it – some pretty weird, suburban, out-of-the-way places – as we were about to find out.

The tour started in Vegas and we flew into that city of sin a day or two early in order to acclimatize and get over our jet lag. Staying up late is usually the key to beating the time zones, but you can take it too far. Casey and I spent a wild evening drinking whisky and losing money at Blackjack, before gently dismantling half the furniture in our hotel room. This led to a hurried and scurried exit the following morning as we headed over to the venue for the usual first-day chaos and nerves.

I was down to sell my own merch on this run again; it's something I enjoyed doing a lot for those US support runs. It saves money on an extra crew member, of course, but it's also a kind of statement of ideological intent, to come straight off the stage and get back to slinging shirts, meeting people at the show. It demonstrates that you're not too self-involved to say hello and to get your hands dirty. These days it's not something that's really practicable for me to do, given the size of the shows I usually play now, and in retrospect I marvel at the amount of energy I had, running straight from the backstage to the merch table; but it was a lot of fun at the time.

The first day, from a merch perspective, is always a pain, because you get a ton of boxes shipped in from the merch company, which all have to be opened, counted and organized into new boxes, leaving the bulk in the trailer and only taking into the venue what you need for that night's show. I remember Casey and I sat on the floor in the corridor outside the main gig room, sweating and complaining about our hangovers, hurriedly counting shirts. Some young kids in identikit 'punk-rock' outfits (Clash T-shirts, wallet chains, dinky bondage trousers, spiked hair) wandered over to try and listen to Social D's sound check through the closed door. When they saw the two of us, lowly crew members toiling away, they gave us a flashed glance of contempt. I was sorely tempted to leap to my feet and explain that this, right here, was much more the substance of rock 'n' roll dreams made real than the clichés of limos, jets, groupies and louche, pampered comfort. In the end I decided to leave their preconceptions intact for another year or two – or maybe I was just too hanging to do anything about it.

The shows with Social D were fun, but perhaps not as momentous as the previous occasion that we had shared the American road with them. I'm not sure if that's because, after three tours with them and with the best will in the world, we were a little over opening for them, or if it's down to the fact that the crowds in some of these towns were a little more, shall we say, set in their ways. The average Social D fans of Chico, Modesto, Oakland and Albuquerque were a little colder towards us, I think, than some of the folks we'd met back in 2010. In Modesto, we even had a problem with some racist idiots shouting abuse at Matt (who has Pakistani heritage) while we were onstage. Social D's frontman Mike Ness, of course, gave them short shrift and had them thrown out of the show. Afterwards they tried to bum a smoke off Matt in the alleyway out the back of the venue. Not the sharpest knives in the drawer.

We had some fill shows here and there on Social D's days off – we nipped up to Eugene, Oregon, for a weird but cool bar show and we played in San Luis Obispo, California, where I twisted my ankle getting off the bus and then made the genius decision to go walk up a big hill, by the end of which I was pretty much incapable of standing up and had to do the show on a bar-stool, much to the hilarity of The Souls. In Pomona we were down for a two-night stand but my voice totally gave up on me thanks to a nasty tour cold and we had to cancel the second show. That was a little awkward, as Charlie and I had just finished negotiating a new songwriting publishing deal with BMG Chrysalis. They'd flown out to sign the deal and celebrate by catching a show, which now wasn't happening. Thankfully Ben and Hugo from BMG were confident enough in their judgement to go ahead anyway.

In the middle of the run we had a mishap in Reno, Nevada, a city that I had never been to before. As we were rolling through the mountains to the city, Greg Walker, our indefatigable tour-bus driver, told us that something in the bus was shot and needed fixing – we'd be up on blocks as soon as we arrived. Fortunately, we had a two-night stand booked in town, followed by a day off, so there was time enough for us to hole up at a hotel while the bus got taken care of. We arrived at the venue, parked up and started loading in and setting up our equipment as Social D geared up for a sound check.

Half an hour later, word came through that both shows had been pulled because Mike was feeling under the weather. I know better than anyone how shitty it is when you feel ill on tour, especially as a singer, so my intention here is not to impugn Mike at all. That said though, the situation looked pretty calamitous for us. We were on low fees for the tour and were plugging holes in the budget with merch income. Now that the shows weren't happening, not only would we not get paid but we'd also not sell anything. The tour budget was holed below the waterline. For headliners, this is an easier situation because you're generally in the black anyway and are likely to have pretty comprehensive cancellation insurance. Not so the lowly openers. And to top it all, I live to play, that's why we were there, thousands of miles from home. It was a pretty bad situation.

Naturally, my first instinct was to try to put together some last-minute make-up shows to plug the hole in the diary (and the budget). For reasons I can't quite remember now, Reno itself seemed to be a no-go, but I took a quick look at a map and saw that we were in the general vicinity of some cities I knew in Northern California. Casey is from that part of the world originally, so he was also keenly on the scent of possible gigs. After some frantic phone calls, we had ourselves two shows – one at the Blue Lamp in Sacramento (where I'd played on the Revival Tour three years earlier) and one at Thee Parkside in San Francisco, a city that we'd sadly noticed was not on the original tour schedule. Unfortunately, the bus was still fucked, so both shows would have to be solo – Casey and I put the band up in a hilariously cheap motel, rented a car and set off through the mountains.

Our departure time turned out to be fortunate. As we drove it started snowing and by the time we rolled out into California, Reno was pretty much snowed in. I felt bad leaving The Souls there, but there was nothing to be done about it. The Sacramento show was a lot of fun, with a reasonably large crowd showing up (for a last-minute gig on a weeknight). The next day we drove to San Francisco. The show was set up by the wonderful Audra, who runs Thee Parkside, a classic little punk-rock dive bar. During the day we got news from Greg that the bus had been fixed and the band made it over in time to turn it into a full-band affair. Many locals showed up, including Fat Mike from NOFX, who had become a good friend by this point. NOFX had even started covering 'Glory Hallelujah' in their set, so for this show he came up and sang the song with us in his own inimitable style.

It was a life-affirming night, a sold-out show on the other side of the world, with friends and peers in tow. We just about managed to plug the hole in the tour budget and get the show back on the road.

I've still never played a show in Reno.

SHOW # 1207
Tsongas Center, Lowell, MA, USA, 17 March 2012

We said goodbye to Social D, their crew and the west and hunkered down for a mammoth cross-country drive. In a few days we made it from California to Columbus, Ohio, stopping off for a show in St. Louis, Missouri. After my sickness in Pomona the journey felt oddly cleansing. There's something about the American road that is different from the UK and Europe. It feels fresher, more open. When we drove from Poland to Italy I felt trapped, claustrophobic and dirty when I arrived. On this run the huge drive gave me time to regroup. I remember sitting by the window watching the faceless states roll by and feeling peaceful.

For the next leg of the tour, we were set to open for the Dropkick Murphys, a band I knew by reputation, of course, but who we hadn't crossed paths with before. We had some experience of the American Celtic punk thing, but this time we were going to end up in and around Boston itself on St Patrick's Day – a daunting prospect for some lily-livered Englishmen.

I'm happy to report that of all the bands I've had the privilege to open for on the road over the years, the Dropkicks are probably my favourite. It's not just that they're excellent at what they do – we all know that – it's also that the guys in the band and, in particular, their crew, constitute some of the nicest, soundest, most reliable folk I know. From the very first show with these guys – in Indianapolis, as it goes – we became really close and have remained so ever since. The tour took us through Minneapolis, then down to Texas, across the South to Florida and then up the East Coast towards New England. All this was familiar territory for me now and we played many venues we'd visited before, but we were still picking up steam and new friends as we went.

I made a brief, utterly manic solo trip (with Casey and Greg Nolan, a photographer buddy from the Nambucca days who was with us on this run, documenting the chaos) down to Austin, Texas, for the annual chaos of SXSW, during which I managed to lose my passport (complete with US work visa) in the back of the seat in front of me on the plane. In my defence, I was exhausted after a New York show the night before and I'd only had a couple of hours' sleep at most. I reported the loss immediately, but the turnaround time of US domestic flight schedules is such that I never saw it again. This presented something of a problem; not just getting out of the country and home at the end of the tour, but also getting from Austin *back* to Boston for the last shows with the Dropkicks. In the end I successfully identified myself at the airport using the SXSW official programme and my credit card. The woman rolled her eyes but eventually let me through, which was a relief.

Being proud Boston Irish boys, the Dropkick Murphys traditionally celebrate St Patrick's Day in their hometown with some raucous shows, usually a string of headline dates at the House Of Blues, a 2,800-capacity room across from Fenway Park. This year that had extended to a run of four shows (we were down to play the last two), followed by a two-shows-in-one-day extravaganza on St Paddy's Day itself at the Tsongas Center in nearby Lowell. Funnily enough, I'd actually played that cavernous, 12,000-capacity ice-hockey rink with The Offspring back in 2009. This time around I was down to play a solo set at the matinee show and then we would resume our usual full-band set for the evening's performance.

I knew it was going to be a long day, not least because I was still selling my own merch on this run. Given the size of the venue, the Dropkicks merch team had several stands with extra people drafted in to help out. I was still working on my own at the one table, plus I had to play the two shows. But I like a challenge, so I prepared for the ordeal by . . . getting very drunk in Boston the night before. I spent the morning of the seventeenth lugging in all the remaining merch boxes from the trailer, sweating hard alcohol and feeling a little daunted.

As is usually the case with these situations, before my set I had a trickle of traffic at my table, mostly curious people asking when 'that Frank Turner guy' was going to be on, interspersed with a few folk who already knew who I was, who would ask for photos, thus confusing the hell out of the first group of people, who thought I was the merch guy. After a few hours I headed down to the stage, leaving Ben from The Sleeping Souls to tend shop while I played a solo set. I had got used to playing full band and the switch-up to playing alone can be disconcerting, particularly in the context of being the support act, so I think that first set was a little uncertain. But after I was done I hiked back up to my merch spot and sold a ton of shirts and records, making new friends and laughing with some of the people who'd come past earlier, wondering who I was.

When the Dropkicks had finished their first set, it was time to empty out the venue and then start the whole rigmarole over again. That took a while and in the end the time I had to relax, eat some food and count my merch takings and my remaining shirts was precariously short. In no time at all the gates were open again and another horde of Murphys fans were streaming into the venue. There were a few repeat customers, but it was mostly a fresh set of punters and the whole 'Who the hell is that?' dance started over again.

For the second time, I tore downstairs to get my tired arse onstage, this time with the welcome backup of The Souls. We had a storming set. Playing out in an arena like that, even as the opener, felt like welcome practice for the upcoming Wembley stop. Drenched in sweat and throwing on a clean shirt, I made the final return journey up the stairs to the merch table. Fatigue was definitely setting in by this point, which was combined with the typical St Paddy's fare of endless shots of Jameson whisky. When the show was over, the Dropkick's efficient team managed to get through all their customers within half an hour of the music ending. On my side of the aisle, however, there was a huge queue of people still waiting to pick up some swag and maybe get a photo. I was at my post, with help from The Souls, for a good hour after that, endlessly slinging shirts, collecting cash, posing for photos and signing records. By the time the line was finally done, ushered away by the weary and slightly irritated security team, I was totally and utterly beat. I genuinely don't think I've ever worked that hard on any other day of my life – which maybe is telling of my soft, middle-class upbringing, but whatever; I felt exhausted, empty and elated.

When the onslaught finally ended, Ben came over to ask if I was OK and, in a Pavlovian physical gesture, I threw my arm over his shoulder and span round for the photo op that my tired brain assumed was coming. He punched me in the ribs and laughed, calling me an idiot. We'd sold pretty much every scrap of cloth and every record that we had with us. A good day.

SHOW # 1214
Rockhal, Esch-sur-Alzette, Luxembourg, 4 April 2012

On returning, once again, from the USA, we had a ten-day gap in the touring diary. This was time for last-minute promotional and preparatory work for the Wembley show and also for a breather after a pretty fierce start to the year. Graham and my crew were in overdrive working on putting together our first ever arena head-line show and I was busy chatting to all and sundry in the press about the upcoming gig. We were doing pretty well on ticket sales, edging ever closer to the sold-out finish line. I took a few days off to disappear up country, but have to admit that I was still checking daily sales updates like a demented stockbroker.

After many interviews and a few rehearsals, we headed over to the Continent for just over a week of shows that were acting as a kind of warm-up run for the big day. We took Emily Barker and The Red Clay Halo girls (Anna, Gill and Jo) with us, partly because they're great, but also because I had planned on incorporating them and their extra instrumentation into parts of my set at the Wembley show. At these shows we were running the set list that we planned to play at the big show in order to see if it worked properly and then to get comfortable with it.

I remember this run as being a little weird, a little tense. In some ways I felt bad because so much of my attention was focused on the big event that perhaps I wasn't giving the European crowds we were playing to their full due. We were also playing some pretty off-the-map places – this run, including Wembley, consti-tuted the final push for the *England Keep My Bones* world tour, in a way. As well as playing through the set, I was working on new songs and The Souls and I were running them in sound check. I was, arguably, a little distracted.

The penultimate show of the run was my first ever show in Luxembourg, at what seemed to be about the only venue in the tiny city-state, Rockhal, an imposing warehouse-like place. Though we'd never actually played there before, the promoters, Joanna and I all thought that the fact that I had toured extensively around it meant that the show made sense and the turnout would be good. Alas, we were mistaken. The room holds over 1,000 people when it's full, but we arrived on the day to discover that we had sold just under 100 tickets.

The promoters and the people running the venue had that typical mixture of apology and accusation in their eyes that every band knows well from a situation like this. They did a reasonable job of making the room look and feel smaller, bringing in curtains to rope off some of the cavernous emptiness. There was also the requisite assertion-cum-prayer that there might be 'a good walk-up'. In the event I seem to remember us just about making it into triple digits. As I've said, I always try to live by the Henry Rollins maxim, that you give your best regardless of the number of people in front of you and The Souls and I certainly threw ourselves into the show, giving it our all and thinking of the big day looming in the diary. But in all honesty, it was a surreal and slightly disheart-ening appearance, to see our sounds and our gestures floating aimlessly into the rafters in front of the small and not overly enthu-siastic assembly. I'm not sure it helped my simmering nerves much.

SHOW # 1216
Wembley Arena, London, UK, 13 April 2012

Wembley. The word rings out in English, British and interna-tional culture. For most people the first association is football, not something I've ever been a fan of. But there's more to it than that; it's also part of the rock 'n' roll world. Live Aid in 1985 is the most famous and obvious example, though for me personally it's beaten by Queen's utterly sublime headline show there from the following year. If you include the arena as well as the stadium, the list of bands that have triumphed and made their mark in north-west London is endless, but no less daunting for it.

Booking an arena headline show was a strange experience for me. It made logical and professional sense after we had sold out Hammersmith Apollo a few months in advance. That hall holds 5,000 people, so the next step up is to either go to Alexandra Palace in the north of the city or to go to Wembley Arena, both of which hold around 12,000 people. When given the choice, I unhesitatingly chose the latter, partly because of its cultural resonance and partly because we had played the stadium there with Green Day in 2010, a show that had been something of a turning point in my career.

Nevertheless, it was a weird one. I realized that I had never actually been to an arena show before playing one. We had done a few opening slots here and there in larger rooms, so it wasn't totally virgin territory, but growing up I used to go see bands at the Astoria, or Brixton at a push. It's not necessarily elitism – it's just that the bands I liked played those venues. I'd never really thought about how a show works in a room that size, with that much distance between the stage and the last member of the audience; about how the sound reverberates around the room, about how little gestures, nods and winks would get lost in the cavernous space.

So it was with some trepidation that I had given Charlie and Joanna the OK to book the room and to announce the show and get it on sale back in October 2011. I was worried not just about how the show itself would be received, but also how the announcement would go down. My career was reaching that tipping point where, regardless of what you do, a certain demographic is going to start rejecting you. Being polite about it, I guess I can see that some people only enjoy music in a certain underground context; I suppose you can imagine what the less polite response would be. But I felt confident in myself that I had got where I was without compromising my principles, so I was comfortable about it.

In the event, most people seemed to take the announcement and the show itself in the spirit it was intended – as something inherently slightly ridiculous, because I was still an independent artist, working hard and with people still coming to hear about me mostly through word of mouth and yet here I was, here we were, in a room that is usually reserved for mammoth rock acts or hyped-up pop 'artists'. There was a slightly anarchic vibe to the show, the idea that we'd somehow stolen the keys to the staff-room at school.

The logistical side of the show was a huge consideration in itself. Graham, leading my production crew, had a massive task ahead of him. Even though it was only the one show, a mere two hours on stage, there was a world of technical hassle to get into, new hoops to jump through, staging and PA to hire, backstage to organize, all that kind of thing. The people at the arena were helpful, friendly and mindful of the fact that we were beginners in this world. But it was still a ton of work and I remain eternally in awe of Graham, Tré, Joanna and the rest of the crew for putting it together. At one point I wanted to have a kind of all-day show, with bands starting in the afternoon; however, that proved totally impracticable, as the cost of opening the venue earlier increased astronomically by the hour. I was determined to keep the ticket price down (£20), so that was not an option. I also spent some time looking at trying to do a pop-up solo section of the set at the back of the room, but that too turned into a logistical nightmare, so to save Graham's sanity we dropped that as well.

Planning the set was something I also spent a crazy amount of time and mental energy on. Initially, I had it in my head that, for the new context, we needed a totally new show, a different approach. But it quickly became apparent that that would have been a grave error. The whole reason I got to the point of being able to play that stage was that I got up and did what I do, with The Sleeping Souls – honest rock 'n' roll shows. To have changed it then would have been a betrayal of sorts, I think. In the end I settled on including some extra instrumentation – The Red Clay Halo girls – and a few other little tricks. But for the most part, it was to be a regular show.

Once we got back from Europe, final preparation for the big day began in earnest. We had a rehearsal room in London booked for a couple of days to run the set a few more times just to check that everything was in place. Billy Bragg came over to rehearse a couple of songs as well. I'd been amazed when he had happily agreed to be the main support for the show, but knowing him better now it's typical Bill. He's not one for airs and graces and he's an avid supporter of younger musicians. I am but one of many lucky people who have benefited from his advice and kindness. The rest of the bill for the show was made up by the excellent Dan le Sac Vs Scroobius Pip, an electro-spoken-word duo from London that I love, and Beans On Toast. Jay was the only person I could imagine opening the show. It was partly a way of saying thanks to him for all his friendship and advice over the years and partly a way of getting the crowd to relax about the arena environment. Jay doing what he does always breaks the ice.

The presence of two special people added the icing to the Wembley cake for me. Firstly, we had Greg Nolan. He'd been riding with us for the past six months, documenting life on the road and the chaos of the build-up to the big show. Now that we were finally there, Greg was in his element and I'm glad he was along for the ride – I think the film he made, *The Road to Wembley*, is fantastic. Secondly, we had Josh Burdette. Josh, as previously mentioned, ran security at Washington DC's legendary punk club, 9:30. We had become friends over the years and he'd expressed an interest in visiting London (he'd never been before) and catching the show. After some discussion with Graham, I found a way to run him through the budget as my 'personal security'. Now obviously I don't actually need a security guard, but it was an efficient and fun way to get Josh over.

The day before the show itself, I was in Camden Town running some errands (making some presents for The Sleeping Souls – little Wembley trophies, since you ask). I happened to run into my old friend Lil. Lil runs Household Name Records, the hardcore label that ran the UK scene when I first started going to punk shows in the late 1990s. He'd helped school me in the workings of the underground and we had remained friends. During times when many of the people I knew from that DIY scene were declaring me a sell-out because of my success, he had remained stubbornly loyal, appreciating all the hard work I had put in. I asked him if he was coming to the show the following day. As it happened, he didn't know about it. I immediately called Tré and arranged for him and his wife, Kath, to have the best seats in the house. It felt good to know he'd be there.

The big day finally lumbered over the horizon. There's a hotel in the Wembley complex that usually hosts the artists and footballers passing through. We had rooms booked for everyone, so I actually woke up next door to the arena. I knew it was going to be a nerve-racking day, so I had set myself a task to keep myself busy. I was planning to make a companion piece for Greg's film, to be entitled *Beans on Toast's Road to Wembley*. In practice this meant that Josh and I went over to Camden to drag Jay out of bed and get him ready for the big day. The resulting cinematic masterpiece is about ten minutes long, but it's a lot of fun and it kept me out of the way of my crew, who had a lot to get through and didn't need me hovering on the sidelines.

I did manage, however, to get a bit of hovering in when Josh, Jay and I made it back to the venue. The first of my production crew (run, I should mention, by the great Nitelites company, who I continue to work with today) had loaded in at 8 a.m. By the early afternoon the stage, lights and PA were starting to come together. Tré was busy running around finalizing the titanic guest list, Charlie and Joanna were generally supervising things, The Sleeping Souls were wandering in and out with their significant others, nervously tapping feet and gazing open-mouthed around the echoing enormity of the room. I started asking pointless questions of everyone, trying to occupy my mind – exactly the thing I'd been trying to avoid. Josh walked over and pretty much hoisted me out of the building back to the hotel, where he unceremoniously dumped me in the hot tub and ordered me to relax.

People had been gathering around the front doors of the venue since first thing in the morning. In fact, I'd caught wind (on social media and through Greg) of people travelling from all around the world to catch the show. In the afternoon, Joanna triumphantly announced the news we had all been waiting for – the show was sold out. Once the doors opened at around 6 p.m., a tidal wave of people swarmed into the room and filled out the barrier. From then on, time seemed to speed up and the day went by in a blur. Jay was sublime, leading the crowd in Mexican waves, group smiles, playing his new song 'Hello Wembley' for the occasion, overrunning his set and finishing up by crowd surfing all the way to the back door. Dan and Scroob got the room bouncing, but I had to bow out of my side-of-stage vantage point to start preparing for my set. That meant I also missed most of Billy's turn, which was a great shame, but needs must and I'm told he brought the house down.

The warren of backstage rooms was filled with old friends, family, people I work with, crew and band members. There was a spark of excitement and nervous tension in the air. Gradually, the crowd in my dressing room thinned down to just me and The Souls. We changed into our white shirts, warmed up arms, wrists and voices, stretched our nervous bodies out and tried to just relax and remember that – on many levels – this was just another show.

Finally showtime rolled around. As had become customary, everyone high-fived everyone else in the wings over the rumble of 12,000 people on the other side of the curtain. When the intro tape – the horn arrangement from the recording of 'Eulogy' – kicked in as the lights dimmed, a tidal wave of a roar rose up, deafening us all even through our snug in-ear monitors. Adrenalin surged and before I knew it we were skipping across the stage to take up our instruments and our positions. The sea of humanity in front of me was something difficult to take in, but the faces I could see were all smiling and cheering. And so the show began.

The actual gig itself slipped by in what felt like minutes. In fact, I actually don't have a very clear memory of all of it, though of course I have watched the footage back (filmed by Jack Lilley, a guy I met as a university film student, who now has his own production company, Sea Legs Productions, who were documenting the occasion). There were some obvious highlights, of course. I'd arranged to have Josh go fetch my mum from her seat in the guest area and bring her to the side of the stage in preparation for 'Dan's Song'. I'd got into the habit of pulling an audience member out of the crowd and teaching them to play harmonica for this song, but that didn't seem like the right call for Wembley. I'd racked my brains trying to think of musician friends to come out and do the turn, but in the end the only person who could fill the role was my mother. She was not aware that this was about to happen, but, with forty years of primary-school teaching under her belt, she rose to the occasion without missing a beat. She was amazing and was briefly trending on Twitter afterwards. I later had to explain to her what Twitter is.

Having Emily, Gill, Jo and Anna onstage for the middle section of the set was a delight and the fact that everyone sang every song back at us (with the exception of new song 'Four Simple Words', which got everyone dancing instead) made the show all the easier to get through. By the time The Souls and I reassembled side-stage in the brief breather between the main set and the encore, after finishing with a Queen cover ('Somebody to Love'), we were drenched in sweat, exhausted and happy. I wandered over to my tattooist friend Matt Hunt, who had his works set up behind the stage, to get the date of the show added to my existing Wembley tattoo, before heading back to the limelight.

The final part of the set started with Billy and I playing a Dylan cover, 'The Times They Are A-Changin''. We'd spent a fair amount of time trying to choose the right song to play together, but in the end there was no escaping old Bob. We did an OK job, though for the record Bill is the one who got the verses in the wrong order! After that, I announced that I was going to play 'The Ballad of Me and My Friends' for the last time. Nigel had suggested the idea and at the time it made sense – a fitting place to put a song about being the underdog to rest. Actually, I've since realized that this was perhaps a little hasty; at the time I guess I was just bored of always playing the song right at the end of every show. These days it makes an occasional appearance on special occasions.

Finally, The Souls and the ladies rejoined me for a rousing rendition of 'Photosynthesis', complete with a long (perhaps overly so) speech in which I tried to sum up the occasion. I'd been thinking about what I was going to say and the key line for me was that it wasn't *me* headlining Wembley, it was *all of us* – the community of people who had supported me, come to the shows, bought records and shirts and continued to believe in me and my music. On the final chord of the song, the tongue-in-cheek confetti cannons we had hidden at the side of the stage blasted the assembled company with a snowstorm of pink paper and I finally had a moment to stand at the lip of the stage, look around and take the whole thing in. It's a moment I won't forget.

After the show, there was a torrent of well-wishing, some glass award-like statuettes from the venue and a framed poster from Will Blake at SJM, the man who had promoted the show. We had a couple of afterparty rooms set up for our guests and I wandered in to say hello to friends and family. Quickly, though, it all became a bit much. The aftershow had been thoroughly infiltrated by people I didn't really know and standing around having photos taken and being patted on the back felt artificial and inappropriate. Isabel was with me and after half an hour or so we bowed out and went over to the hotel where the guys in my band and crew were having a more private drink at the bar. That was much more the atmosphere I was looking for, so we settled in and drank until dawn.

POSTSCRIPT

SHOW # 1217
MacEwan Ballroom, Calgary, AB, Canada,
18 April 2012

In the run-up to the Wembley show, there had come a moment when the monumental nature of the event (for me) had started to get a little uncomfortable. People were talking about it almost like it was my farewell show, like there was no life after Wembley. I was also cautious not to disappear up my own backside in the wake of my first arena headline show. With all that in mind, Charlie and I had been giving a fair amount of thought as to what came next.

Nick Storch, my North American booking agent, came up with the goods. He sent through an offer of a support slot on a tour in Canada in mid-April, opening for a guy called Joel Plaskett. I'd never heard of Joel at the time and initially I was a little sceptical, but the timing and the venue sizes made sense, so I agreed to head out there a day or two after the big gig.

Casey and Nick had both been at Wembley. After a day's recuperation, Casey and I boarded a flight from Heathrow to Calgary, leaving the dust of London swirling in our wake. We had given ourselves a couple of days off in Alberta to adjust to the time zone and to readjust our mind-sets to something a little more normal, in my scale of events. I was due to be the only opener, playing solo. The shows were at prestigious, often seated venues, to crowds who largely had no idea who I was. It felt like the perfect antidote to the arena lights. I also soon discovered that Joel is an amazing songwriter, singer and guitarist, and a lovely chap to boot.

The day of the first show rolled around and Casey and I made our way to the venue. It felt restorative, almost purifying, to carry my guitar case into the venue, along with a box of shirts; to set up shop in a backstage cupboard and get busy restringing my guitar while Casey counted merch; to run a quick sound check, my mic stand and tuner pedal set up in front of Joel's band's equipment, a few minutes before doors.

When showtime rolled around, I stepped out into the spotlight, on my own, with just a battered old acoustic guitar and some songs I wrote on the road, in front of a sea of quizzical faces. I tuned my guitar, positioned my capo, took a deep breath, and said:

'Good evening, my name is Frank Turner.'

ENDNOTE

Time and memory are strange beasts.

Time is strangely elastic. Looking back through all these entries, on top of all the reading and remembering that was involved in writing them, made me feel distinctly weird. Some bits seem to have flown by; others have crept. Some parts seem longer ago than others, often leaving me with a jumbled and instinctively incorrect chronology. For instance, the Million Dead years, which I haven't covered here, seem somehow to not be as long ago as the early years of solo touring by train. It doesn't make much sense, but there it is.

Taken as a whole, the years covered by this book also feel slightly unmoored from any objective, rational measure of time. In some ways it feels like an eternity since I took the train home from Southampton in 2005. The vast majority of what I normally consider the notable bits of my life have happened since; it's certainly the time in which I've defined myself as an adult, made my way in the world and encountered most of the people reading this. But then again, there are times when I think that seven years isn't much, all told. If you take the number of shows covered herein and compare it to the number of days in seven years, there's a serious shortfall. Some of those show-less days were spent travelling, sleeping, recording or whatever. But there were plenty of days off – there must have been. What was I doing? Could I have done more?

This is where memory starts to get odd. There are a fair few shows on the list that I really can't remember anything about, despite grilling my friends and tour mates, and I generally have a pretty encyclopedic memory for gigs. Some of these stories I remember in the repeated telling, but the actual mental image of the events themselves has become lost in time. And some of them stand out crystal clear in the murk.

There are days when the collected whole of my miles on the road weighs down on me and I feel like an old pair of shoes, or an old tyre, the tread worn down into faint Nazca lines, vestigial memories of the person I was when I started out. Some days it feels like the vast majority of this stuff happened to someone else and I have trouble identifying with the me that stood on stage in Latvia or Southend back in 2006.

Sometimes I wonder about how I've changed, worrying about what happened to the guy who set out at the beginning; but that's a fool's errand. As people we are defined by our experiences and I've now spent more of my life on the road than off. The hypothetical homebound 'me' doesn't exist any more, if he ever really did. I've made my choices, decided on the kind of person I want to be and the kind of life I want to live and I've followed through as best I can.

Some people get agitated about musicians or artists they like changing over time. I've always found this slightly presumptuous to glance at someone's entire life and their choices and pass judgement over it almost instantaneously. Having had some success in what I do it's with tedious inevitability that some people have carelessly thrown words like sell-out at me at various times. I'm obviously not saying I haven't changed – of course I have, I'd hope to change over such a time period, through such experiences – and I'm also not saying that there aren't bands who have made questionable career decisions. I'm far from perfect and there are business decisions I've made that haven't been flawless, but then I'm not very good at business, I'm a musician. Overall, though, I like to think that, having read this, you, the reader, might have sympathy for my choices in life and might understand how it's possible to go from playing basements and bars to arenas while keeping your integrity intact. I believe I've just about managed that.

What have I learned? What does any of it mean, for me or for anyone else? Everything and nothing much, respectively, I suspect. I started out trying not to write an autobiography and I haven't – it's not even a full overview of my career, just the touring side of it. But I do think I've given a pretty comprehensive overview of who I am and what I do, to the extent that that's interesting to other people. I hope you've enjoyed it; I certainly enjoyed writing it. But I'm happy to know that most people won't care.

My final comment is this: I'm not a fan of endings. After the Wembley show I went straight to Canada to tour at ground level, partly to keep my head together and partly to keep the wheels moving. The last shows I've written about here happened a few years ago now and I haven't been idle in the interim. I'm not saying this specifically to threaten a second volume (though I might be talked into it someday), I'm just saying that writing this book isn't the end of anything.

Ben Franklin, a hero of mine, never got round to finishing his autobiography because he was too busy. That's about the best epitaph for a life well-lived that I can think of.

I'm off to get busy. See you on the road.

ACKNOWLEDGEMENTS

No man is an island and this man certainly didn't write this book without a lot of help.

First and foremost, thanks are due to the people who made the book happen. Dan Bruton is the man who planted the seed and was encouraging with my early writing. Richard Roper and the crew at Headline Publishing then got the project out of my head, beat it into submission and printed the thing. I was nervous about being edited and scrutinized, but I shouldn't have been – it's now a much better book than I would have been able to do on my own.

Katie Dunne and the folks at PledgeMusic have been wonderful at getting the fan edition out into the world, for which I am eternally thankful.

This is a book about touring and on that level the people to thank next are the people who have come with me along the way. They're mentioned in the text, for the most part, but it's worth shouting them out here as well. Ben Lloyd, Nigel Powell, Tarrant Anderson and Matt Nasir, The Sleeping Souls (with honorary mentions for Ciara Haidar, Chris T-T, Ben Dawson and Steve Soto and friends) have had my back for many years and shared the joys and hardships. Thanks guys. Then there's the crew, all of whom work harder than me: Jamie Grime, Graham Kay, Tom 'Barbs' Barber, Sarah Crowder, Tré Stead, Ant Fail, Cahir O'Doherty, Johnny Stephenson, Casey Cress, Shaun Moore, Jovka de Boer, the whole Nitelites crew and all the various bus drivers we've had over the years.

I've shared miles, stages, vans and hotel-room floors with many bands. They're generally mentioned in here. The bands that took me on tour as an opening act gave me my career. Noodles, from The Offspring, once told me that the only thanks required was to take out bands that I liked when my turn came and I've stuck to that principle. I've been lucky enough to tour with many singers and players who are better than me.

Next up, the other side of the industry I work in. Dani Cotter, Anthea Thomas, Dan Griffiths and everyone who works or has worked at Xtra Mile are like family to me. Epitaph Records took good care of me outside of the UK. Mick Shiner at Pure Groove was a rock in my storm. Nick Storch and Joanna Ashmore (with an honourable mention for Caitlin Roffman) have booked my shows and kept the machine running over the years.

Over and above all of these, thanks and love to Charlie Caplowe, my manager since day one and still the unsung hero of everything I do. Here's to another decade.

I love my friends. Many of them are mentioned in this book. The ones who aren't should feel equally valued and then make me buy them a drink for failing to mention them. Particular shoutouts go to Dave Danger and Jay Beans, and everyone who was part of Nambucca; to Evan Cotter; and to Lexie, rest her soul. My mum and my two sisters, Jo and Gilly, have put up with me (and put me up) since I was a kid. Nice work!

Finally, it's a well-worn cliché at this point to thank 'the fans', but I don't want to start sounding like Mötley fucking Crüe now. That said, I think that my trajectory through the music business has been supported and enabled to an unusual degree by the people who listen to records and go to shows. I've shared drinks with, sold T-shirts to, slept on the floors of and talked the ears off a large percentage of the people who will read this. I think that's fucking cool. Really, thank you for giving a shit, it's appreciated more than I know how to say.

INDEX

PICTURE CREDITS

All photos © Frank Turner except for:

SECTION 1

Page 1, top: © David Nicol; bottom: © Ricky Bates

Page 2, top and Page 3: © Daniel Chamorro

Page 4, top: © Rachel Brook; bottom: © Laura Marling

Page 5, top-left: © Michaela Waddell; bottom-left: © Marina Fedoseeva

Page 6, top: © Evan Cotter; left: © Rachel Brook; right: © Casey Lee; bottom-left: © Jamie Grime; bottom-right: © Sarah Kay

Page 7, left: © dangriffiths.com; bottom: © Evan Cotter

Page 8, top: © Ben Morse; bottom: © Jason Smith

SECTION 2

Page 1, top and bottom: © Graham Smith

Page 2, left: © Scott Toepfer; right: © Ben Morse

Page 3, top and middle: © Ben Morse; bottom: © Lenka Liebichová

Page 4, top-left: © Ben Morse; top: © dangriffiths.com; middle: © Jack Lilley

Page 5, top-left: © Jack Lilley

Page 6, top-left: © Ben Morse; centre and left: © Nicole Kibert; bottom: © Peter Dunwell

Page 7, top ©: Nicole Kibert; bottom: © Greg Nolan

Page 8, top and bottom: © Greg Nolan

SHOW LIST

23 September 2005 The Joiners Arms, Southampton, UK (Million Dead)

2004

18 September 93 Feet East, Brick Lane, London, UK

2005

30 January Chinnerys, Southend-on-Sea, UK

3 April Bread & Roses, Clapham, London, UK

7 April The Luminaire, Kilburn, London, UK

8 June The Underworld, Camden, London, UK

5 September The Spitz, Spitalfields, London, UK

13 September ICA, The Mall, London, UK

6 October Utopia Cafe, Southend-on-Sea, UK

7 October Curzon Soho, Soho, London, UK

14 October Love Apple Cafe, Bradford, UK

28 October Club Fandango, Plymouth, UK

30 October The Bull and Gate, Kentish Town, London, UK

4 November Tunbridge Wells Forum, Tunbridge Wells, UK

5 November The Cellar Bar, Cambridge, UK

6 November Chinnerys, Southend-on-Sea, UK

14 November The Star, Guildford, UK

16 November Junktion 7, Nottingham, UK

17 November The Fenton, Leeds, UK

18 November The Fighting Cocks, Kingston upon Thames, London, UK

20 November The Retro Bar, Manchester, UK

24 November Silks Bar, Basingstoke, UK

25 November F-Bar, Leicester, UK

26 November The Glebe, Stoke-on-Trent, UK

1 December The Marquee, Norwich, UK

7 December Kiss Bar, Oxford, UK

8 December Phatz Bar, Maidenhead, UK

11 December The Elbow Room, Islington, London, UK

13 December The Hub, Cheltenham, UK

17 December Nambucca, Holloway, London, UK

2006

8 January ICA, The Mall, London, UK

11 January The Depo, Riga, Latvia
13 January Fontaine Palace, Liepāja, Latvia
15 January New Riga Theatre, Riga, Latvia
19 January Barbican Theatre, Plymouth, UK
20 January The Peel, Kingston upon Thames, London, UK
22 January Mad Hatters, Inverness, UK
23 January 13th Note, Glasgow, UK
24 January The Rep Theatre, Dundee, UK
25 January The Tunnels, Aberdeen, UK
26 January Parkers, Kilmarnock, UK
31 January The Cellar Bar, Oxford, UK
1 February Bar Pure, Sunderland, UK
2 February Jax Bar, Hartlepool, UK
3 February Rachel's House, Newcastle, UK
4 February Bangor University, Bangor, UK
5 February Keele University, Keele, UK
6 February Chris's House, Wigan, UK
7 February Bar Fresa, Liverpool, UK
8 February The Glebe, Stoke-on-Trent, UK
9 February Monkey Chews, Camden, London, UK
11 February Terry's, Trowbridge, UK
14 February Steamboat Tavern, Ipswich, UK
19 February Nambucca, Holloway, London, UK
21 February The Railway Inn, Winchester, UK
23 February The Registry, Portsmouth, UK

25 February The Windmill, Brixton, London, UK
26 February Bush Hall, Shepherd's Bush, London, UK
28 February Baby Love, Oxford, UK
3 March The Marquee, Hertford, UK
4 March The Square, Harlow, UK
5 March Quicksilver Mail, Yeovil, UK
6 March The Globe, Brighton, UK
10 March The Roundabout, High Wycombe, UK
16 March Chinnerys, Southend, UK
17 March The Angel, Bedford, UK
18 March The Spread Eagle, Shoreditch, London, UK
19 March Nambucca, Holloway, London, UK
25 March Tunbridge Wells Forum, Tunbridge Wells, UK
26 March Junktion 7, Nottingham, UK
2 April The Vic Inn, Swindon, UK
3 April The Bell by the Green, Devizes, UK
4 April Mr Kyps, Poole, UK
5 April The Dove Inn, Winchester, UK
6 April Gander on the Green, Bournemouth, UK
7 April The Plantation Cafe, Guildford, UK
8 April The Corner Room, Oxford, UK
10 April The Joogleberry Playhouse, Brighton, UK
11 April The Bedford, Balham, London, UK
12 April The Snooty Fox, Canonbury, London, UK
13 April The Archway Tavern, Archway, London, UK
14 April Meesh's House, Newbury, UK

15 April The Wheatsheaf, Oxford, UK

16 April The Wheatsheaf, Oxford, UK

17 April Dingwalls, Camden, London, UK

18 April The Vine, Leeds, UK

19 April Whistlebinkies, Edinburgh, UK

22 April Cafe Drummond, Aberdeen, UK

23 April Magnet, Liverpool, UK

24 April The Jailhouse, Coventry, UK

25 April The Shed, Dudley, UK

26 April The Retro Bar, Manchester, UK

27 April Bar Tantra, Cardiff, UK

30 April The Louisiana, Bristol, UK

1 May The Watering Hole, Perranporth, UK

2 May The Student's Union, Plymouth, UK

3 May The Student's Union, Exmouth, UK

4 May The Loft Bar, Cambridge, UK

5 May Riffs Bar, Swindon, UK

13 May L'Empreinte, Savigny-le-Temple, France

14 May Le Baiser Sale, Paris, France

15 May Le Nouveau Casino, Paris, France

16 May Le Va Zen, Lille, France

17 May Le Mécanisme Dubitatif, Lille, France

18 May Le Bouchon, Tournai, Belgium

19 May La Cave à Bière, Mouscron, Belgium

20 May Saphir 21, Paris, France

20 May Le Nouveau Casino, Paris, France

23 May Le Munich, Annecy, France

24 May L'Ile aux Trésors, Limoges, France

25 May Le Fiacre, Bordeaux, France

26 May Blagnac Festival, Toulouse, France

27 May Festival YaKha Vivre Libre, Panissières, France

28 May Nambucca, Holloway, London, UK

29 May Coleford Music Festival, Coleford, Somerset, UK

3 June The Barge, Battersea, London, UK

4 June The Lock Tavern, Camden, London, UK

4 June The Buffalo Bar, Islington, London, UK

5 June The Hangar, Scunthorpe, UK

6 June Brudenell Social Club, Leeds, UK

8 June Sandinos, Derry, UK

8 June Dicey Riley's, Strabane, UK

9 June Nerve Centre, Derry, UK

10 June Iveagh Gardens, Dublin, Republic of Ireland

11 June Auntie Annie's, Belfast, UK

14 June Banquet Records, Kingston upon Thames, London, UK

14 June The Peel, Kingston upon Thames, London, UK

17 June Lexapalooza, GJ's, Colliers Wood, London, UK

23 June Glastoshot, West End Centre, Aldershot, UK

27 June The Portman Hotel, Bournemouth, UK

29 June Unit 22, Southampton, UK

30 June Camberley Town Football Club, Camberley, UK

1 July The Barn, Salisbury, UK

2 July The Cellar Bar, Bracknell, UK

3 July Fibbers, York, UK

4 July The Old Angel Inn, Nottingham, UK

5 July The Star and Garter, Manchester, UK

6 July The Dog and Parrot, Newcastle upon Tyne, UK

7 July Firebug, Leicester, UK

8 July The Ski Lodge, Yeovil, UK

9 July The Recreation Centre, Bridgend, UK

10 July Scruffy Murphys, Birmingham, UK

11 July Barfly, Glasgow, UK

12 July The West, Huddersfield, UK

13 July The Cavern, Exeter, UK

15 July Latitude Festival, Suffolk, UK

16 July The Railway Inn, Winchester, UK

21 July Fonofest, Cēsis, Latvia

22 July Tuntuma Festival, Lohja, Finland

24 July Platforma, St Petersburg, Russia

26 July Tabula Rasa, Moscow, Russia

27 July Club j'Est, Moscow, Russia

30 July Cafe de Paris, Vilnius, Lithuania

1 August The Depo, Riga, Latvia

2 August Reggae Bar, Tallinn, Estonia

4 August Fontaine Palace, Liepāja, Latvia

5 August Ramybe, Palanga, Lithuania

6 August New Riga Theatre, Riga, Latvia

8 August Barfly, Camden, London, UK

9 August Adam's House, Northampton, UK

10 August Central Station, Wrexham, UK

11 August Wasted Festival, Blackpool, UK

22 August Barfly, Camden, London, UK

3 September The Lock Tavern, Camden, London, UK

16 September 93 Feet East, Brick Lane, London, UK

16 September Farmageddon Festival, Cambridgeshire, UK

23 September West End Centre, Aldershot, UK

28 September The Works, Kingston upon Thames, London, UK

4 October The Windmill, Brixton, London, UK

9 October The Hub, Exeter, UK

14 October The Tap n Tin, Chatham, UK

19 October London Astoria, Soho, London, UK

19 October Proud Galleries, Camden, London, UK

20 October The Leadmill, Sheffield, UK

21 October The Horwood Bar, Keele University, Keele, UK

22 October Bristol Academy, Bristol, UK

23 October Cardiff University, Cardiff, UK

24 October The Dome, Brighton, UK

25 October The Night Owl, Cheltenham, UK

26 October Brookes University, Oxford, UK

27 October The Old Fire Station, Bournemouth, UK

28 October The Lamb Inn, Devizes, UK

29 October The Fighting Cocks, Kingston upon Thames, London, UK

30 October The Market Hall, Brecon, UK

31 October Warwick University, Warwick, UK

1 November Aberystwyth University, Aberystwyth, UK

2 November The Hobgoblin, Bath, UK

3 November The Forum, Kentish Town, London, UK

10 November The Furnace, Swindon, UK

12 November Mad Hatters, Inverness, UK

13 November The Tunnels, Aberdeen, UK

14 November The Warehouse Theatre, Lossiemouth, UK

15 November Satchmos, Dundee, UK

16 November Bar Bloc, Glasgow, UK

20 November The Jericho Tavern, Oxford, UK

24 November The Sun Inn, Dunsfold, UK

25 November The Windmill, Brixton, London, UK

26 November Vibe Bar, Shoreditch, London, UK

26 November The Square, Harlow, UK

16 December The Peel, Kingston upon Thames, London, UK

19 December Meonstoke C of E School, Meonstoke, near Winchester, UK

31 December Club j'Est, Moscow, Russia

2007

1 January Bilingua, Moscow, Russia

2 January Krisis Zhanra, Moscow, Russia

9 January Tomus' Birthday, Pop, London, UK

15 January Fopp Records, Westbourne Grove, London, UK

15 January Fopp Records, Camden, London, UK

15 January Fopp Records, Covent Garden, London, UK

15 January Fopp Records, Tottenham Court Road, London, UK

15 January Nambucca, Holloway, London, UK

16 January Pure Groove Records, Holloway, London, UK

17 January Banquet Records, Kingston upon Thames, London, UK

20 January Port Mahon, Oxford, UK

24 January Joseph's Well, Leeds, UK

25 January 53 Degrees, Preston, UK

26 January The Brickyard, Carlisle, UK

27 January XFM All-Dayer, Camden Barfly, London, UK

28 January The Social, Nottingham, UK

29 January Night and Day Café, Manchester, UK

30 January One Up Records, Aberdeen, UK

30 January The Tunnels, Aberdeen, UK

31 January Academy 2, Newcastle upon Tyne, UK

1 February Avalanche Records, Glasgow, UK

1 February Nice N Sleazy, Glasgow, UK

2 February Korova, Liverpool, UK

3 February The Horwood Bar, Keele University, Keele, UK

5 February Clwb Ifor Bach, Cardiff, UK

6 February Thekla, Bristol, UK

7 February The Loft, Cambridge, UK

8 February Moles, Bath, UK

9 February Plug N Play, Reading, UK

10 February The Colosseum, Coventry, UK

11 February Fibbers, York, UK

12 February The Bar Academy, Birmingham, UK

13 February The Borderline, Soho, London, UK

14 February The Joiners Arms, Southampton, UK

15 February The Zodiac, Oxford, UK

16 February The Great White Horse, Ipswich, UK

17 February Bar Lojo, Lohja, Finland

18 February Bar Mary, Porvoo, Finland

24 February Whelan's, Dublin, Republic of Ireland

25 February Queen's University, Belfast, UK

26 February McHughs Basement, Belfast, UK

27 February The Lower Deck, Dublin, Republic of Ireland

28 February Masons Bar, Derry, UK

2 March Side Cinema, Newcastle, UK

9 March The Borderline, Soho, London, UK

14 March The Sanctuary, San Antonio, TX, USA

15 March Fadó Irish Pub, Austin, TX, USA

15 March Plush, Austin, TX, USA

16 March Epoch Coffee, Austin, TX, USA

18 March Modified/Arts, Phoenix, AZ, USA

19 March Knitting Factory, Los Angeles, CA, USA

20 March Bottom of the Hill, San Francisco, CA, USA

21 March The Delta of Venus, Davis, CA, USA

22 March The Old Ironsides, Sacramento, CA, USA

23 March Sacred Grounds Coffee, Arcata, CA, USA

24 March Mississippi Pizza, Portland, OR, USA

25 March Fantasia, Bellingham, WA, USA

26 March The High Dive, Seattle, WA, USA

27 March Le Voyeur, Olympia, WA, USA

3 April The Boileroom, Guildford, UK

4 April The Globe, Brighton, UK

5 April Unit 22, Southampton, UK

6 April The Vic Inn, Swindon, UK

7 April The Lamb, Devizes, UK

8 April The Railway Inn, Winchester, UK

14 April Frog, Mean Fiddler, London, UK

20 April The Camden Crawl, Oh! Bar, Camden, London, UK

22 April Night and Day Café, Manchester, UK

23 April The Globe Café, Newcastle University, Newcastle, UK

24 April Cabaret Voltaire, Edinburgh, UK

25 April HMV in-store, Inverness, UK

25 April The Ironworks, Inverness, UK

26 April Nice N Sleazy, Glasgow, UK

27 April Korova, Liverpool, UK

28 April The Charlotte, Leicester, UK

29 April The Sugarmill, Stoke-on-Trent, UK

30 April The Plug, Sheffield, UK

1 May Cambridge Junction, Cambridge, UK

2 May Bush Hall, Shepherd's Bush, London, UK

4 May The Social, Nottingham, UK

5 May The Soundhaus, Northampton, UK

6 May The Bar Academy, Birmingham, UK

7 May Thekla, Bristol, UK

8 May The Cavern, Exeter, UK

9 May The Cuckoo, Truro, UK

11 May Tunbridge Wells Forum, Tunbridge Wells, UK

12 May The Zodiac, Oxford, UK

13 May The Arts Centre, Norwich, UK

16 May The Green Room, Portman Hotel, Bournemouth, UK

17 May The Great Escape Festival, Brighton, UK

20 May The Pyramids Centre, Portsmouth, UK

21 May Brookes University, Oxford, UK

22 May The Roundhouse, Camden, London, UK

23 May Wulfrun Hall, Wolverhampton, UK

24 May Cambridge Junction, Cambridge, UK

26 May Leeds Metropolitan University, UK

27 May Newcastle University, UK

28 May Academy 2, Manchester, UK

3 June Town Hall, Middlesbrough, UK

3 June The Central, Middlesbrough, UK

4 June Scala, London, UK

7 June Fopp Records, Gloucester, UK

7 June The Porter Cellar Bar, Bath, UK

8 June The Bridge House, Copsale, UK

9 June The Hayward Gallery, South Bank, London, UK

9 June Royal Festival Hall, South Bank, London, UK

10 June Nambucca, Holloway, London, UK

14 June The Works, Kingston upon Thames, London, UK

15 June Wireless Festival, Hyde Park, London, UK

6 July Rooz Studios, Hackney, London, UK

13 July 2000trees Festival, Cheltenham, UK

15 July World's Smallest Festival, Cargo, Shoreditch, London, UK

20 July Wilton House, Horsham, UK

21 July Westival, Aldershot, UK

21 July Truck Festival Replacement Show, Brookes University, Oxford, UK

21 July Truck Festival Replacement Show, Port Mahon, Oxford, UK

25 July Revolution Fleet Street, Liverpool, UK

28 July Secret Garden Party, Cambridgeshire, UK

29 July Maker Festival, Cornwall, UK

2 August Soho Revue Bar, Soho, London, UK

3 August Y Not Festival, Matlock, UK

4 August Newton Stacey Festival, Winchester, UK

5 August Newton Stacey Festival, Winchester, UK

6 August The Purple Turtle, Camden, London, UK

7 August Lo Fidelity Disconnect, London, UK

8 August The Lazy Lizard, Weymouth, UK

9 August Ripcurl Boardmasters Festival, Newquay, UK

10 August The Studio, Durham, UK

11 August Beached Festival, Scarborough, UK

15 August Rocksound Party, Bloomsbury Bowling, Bloomsbury, London, UK

20 August The Twist, Colchester, UK

23 August The 12 Bar, Swindon, UK

24 August Reading Festival, Reading, UK

25 August Leeds Festival, Leeds, UK

29 August The Croft, Bristol, UK

6 September The Jericho Tavern, Oxford, UK

10 September Audio, Brighton, UK

11 September The Charlotte, Leicester, UK

12 September Cabaret Voltaire, Edinburgh, UK

13 September The Cathouse, Glasgow, UK

14 September The Cornerhouse, Middlesbrough, UK

15 September The Civic Hall Bar, Wolverhampton, UK

16 September The Ironworks, Inverness, UK

17 September The Tunnels, Aberdeen, UK

18 September Trillians, Newcastle upon Tyne, UK

19 September Clwb Ifor Bach, Cardiff, UK

20 September The Spitz, Spitalfields, London, UK

21 September The Cockpit, Leeds, UK

22 September The Social, Nottingham, UK

23 September The Barfly, Liverpool, UK

24 September Central Station, Wrexham, UK

25 September The Croft, Bristol, UK

26 September The Park, Peterborough, UK

28 September The Joiners Arms, Southampton, UK

2 October University of Bedford, Luton, UK

3 October Plug N Play, Reading, UK

4 October The Lower Deck, Dublin, Republic of Ireland

5 October Dicey Riley's, Strabane, UK

6 October Sandinos, Derry, UK

7 October The Black Box, Belfast, UK

8 October The Queen Charlotte, Norwich, UK

28 October The Fest, Gainesville, FL, USA

30 October House Show, St. Augustine, FL, USA

31 October Big Daddy's, Tallahassee, FL, USA

1 November Transitions Art Gallery, Tampa, FL, USA

2 November Newton Community Center, Sarasota, FL, USA

3 November Fleischmann Park Community Center, Naples, FL, USA

7 November The Crayola House, Harrisonburg, VA, USA

10 November Brett's Basement, UMASS Amherst, MA, USA

11 November SUNY, Binghamton, NY, USA

12 November Fontana's, New York, NY, USA

12 November Pete's Candy Store, Brooklyn, NY, USA

14 November Hotel Cafe, Los Angeles, CA, USA

15 November The Mint, Los Angeles, CA, USA

16 November SW Hill Country, Los Angeles, CA, USA

30 November 33 Portland Place, Marylebone, London, UK

6 December The Hideaway, Archway, London, UK

13 December The Luminaire, Kilburn, London, UK

20 December Pure Groove, Archway, London, UK

22 December Tony's House, Windsor, UK

28 December The Barfly, Camden, London, UK

31 December Brixton Academy, Brixton, London, UK

2008

9 January The Barfly, Camden, London, UK

12 January Equitruck, The Jericho Tavern, Oxford, UK

16 January The XFM New Music Awards, KOKO, Camden, London, UK

31 January The Boogaloo, Highgate, London, UK

15 February Safari Sam's, Los Angeles, CA, USA

16 February The Viper Room, West Hollywood, CA, USA

17 February Ted's House, San Francisco, CA, USA

18 February True Love Coffee, Sacramento, CA, USA

19 February Biko Garage, Isla Vista, CA, USA

20 February Acoustic Cordiale, Los Angeles, CA, USA

21 February Experi-Mental Cafe, Oxnard, CA, USA

22 February Muddy Waters Coffee House, Santa Barbara, CA, USA

23 February Water Canyon Coffee Co., Yucca Valley, CA, USA

24 February Pappy & Harriet's, Pioneertown, CA, USA

25 February The Bordello, Los Angeles, CA, USA

27 February Experi-Mental Cafe, Oxnard, CA, USA

1 March 2 Brydges Club, Charing Cross, London, UK

13 March Fontaine Palace, Liepāja, Latvia

14 March Sapnu Fabrika, Riga, Latvia

15 March FonoKlubs, Cēsis, Latvia

16 March Bar I Love You, Riga, Latvia

24 March Nambucca, Holloway, London, UK

26 March Oxford and Cherwell Valley College, Oxford, UK

27 March Rooz Studios, Hackney, London, UK

28 March The Bridge House, Copsale, UK

29 March Fopp Records, Bristol, UK

29 March The Joiners Arms, Southampton, UK

31 March The Brudenell Social Club, Leeds, UK

1 April Fibbers, York, UK

2 April The Cluny, Newcastle upon Tyne, UK

3 April The Corporation, Sheffield, UK

4 April The Sugarmill, Stoke-on-Trent, UK

5 April The Kasbah, Coventry, UK

6 April The Bar Academy, Birmingham, UK

7 April The Queen Charlotte, Norwich, UK

8 April The Zodiac, Oxford, UK

9 April Moles, Bath, UK

10 April Thekla, Bristol, UK

11 April Bodega Social, Nottingham, UK

12 April Old Redhouse, Workington, UK

13 April The Tunnels, Aberdeen, UK

14 April King Tut's, Glasgow, UK

15 April Joshua Brooks, Manchester, UK

16 April Crawdaddy, Dublin, Republic of Ireland

17 April The Speakeasy, QUBSU, Belfast, UK

18 April The Barfly, Liverpool, UK

20 April Clwb Ifor Bach, Cardiff, UK

21 April The Hanbury Ballroom, Brighton, UK

22 April The Barfly, Cambridge, UK

23 April 100 Club, Oxford Street, London, UK

24 April The Railway Inn, Winchester, UK

29 April Continental Hyatt House Hotel, Los Angeles, CA, USA

29 April House of Blues, Los Angeles, CA, USA

2 May The Viper Room, West Hollywood, CA, USA

5 May The Old Fire Station, Bournemouth, UK

5 May The iBar, Bournemouth, UK

6 May Students' Union 3Sixty, Reading, UK

7 May The Waterfront, Norwich, UK

8 May University of Hertfordshire Students' Union, Hatfield, UK

10 May The Foundry, Sheffield, UK

11 May 53 Degrees, Preston, UK

12 May Level 8, Strathclyde University, Glasgow, UK

13 May Stanley Theatre, Liverpool, UK

15 May University Union – Mine (outside), Leeds, UK

15 May University Union – Mine (inside), Leeds, UK

16 May The Asylum, Hull, UK

21 May 100 Club, Oxford Street, London, UK

22 May Badlands Records, Cheltenham, UK

22 May The Works, Kingston upon Thames, UK

24 May Dot to Dot Festival, Bristol, UK

25 May Underground Festival, The Jailhouse, Hereford, UK

31 May Pete's House, London, UK

3 June South Parade Pier, Southsea, Portsmouth, UK

4 June The White Rabbit, Plymouth, UK

6 June Inside Out, Darlington, UK

7 June Jam by the Lake, Van Mildert College, Durham, UK

8 June The Loft, Xscape, Castleford, UK

12 June Teenage Kicks, 93 Feet East, Brick Lane, London, UK

13 June Komedia, Brighton, UK

18 June Eton College, Windsor, UK

19 June London Calling SIN Club, Charing Cross, London, UK

20 June Nambucca, Holloway, London, UK

21 June Le Mécanisme Ondulatoire, Paris, France

22 June JH de Choke, Herselt, Belgium

24 June Le Manoir de la Cinquième, Mouscron, Belgium

25 June La Chimère, Lille, France

26 June Locaux Scouts, Ecaussinnes, Belgium

27 June The Field of Avalon, Glastonbury Festival, Glastonbury, UK

27 June The Left Field, Glastonbury Festival, Glastonbury, UK

29 June Boring by the Sea Festival, Weymouth, UK

30 June Valences, France

1 July Le Tapas, Nice, France

3 July Le Cri de la Mouette, Toulouse, France

4 July Bar de la Messageries, Marmande, France

6 July GuilFest, Guildford, UK

9 July Pure Groove, Smithfield, London, UK

11 July 2000trees Festival (Acoustic Stage), Withington, near Cheltenham, UK

11 July 2000trees Festival (Camp Reuben), Withington, near Cheltenham, UK

12 July Rise Records, Cheltenham, UK

12 July 2000trees Festival (Main Stage), Cheltenham, UK

20 July Truck Festival, Steventon, UK

24 July Trans Festival, The Waterfront, Belfast, UK

31 July Cambridge Folk Festival, Cambridge, UK

1 August The Arts Centre, Norwich, UK

2 August Y Not Festival, Pikehall, Derbyshire, UK

3 August The Lock Tavern, Camden, London, UK

4 August Sin City, Swansea, UK

6 August The Duchess, York, UK

7 August Central Station, Wrexham, UK

8 August The Leadmill, Sheffield, UK

16 August Minifest, Civic Hall, Trowbridge, UK

17 August Beautiful Days Festival, Escot Park, near Ottery St Mary, UK

21 August McCluskys, Kingston upon Thames, UK

22 August Reading Festival, Reading, UK

23 August Leeds Festival, Leeds, UK

24 August Regent's Park Open Air Theatre, London, UK

6 September Lexapalooza 3, Nambucca, London, UK

19 September Plush Lounge, Los Angeles, CA, USA

20 September The Echo, Los Angeles, CA, USA

21 September O'Connell's, San Diego, CA, USA

23 September Beauty Bar, Las Vegas, NV, USA

25 September Modified/Arts, Phoenix, AZ, USA

26 September Main Street Project, Anthony, NM, USA

27 September The Warhol, San Antonio, TX, USA

28 September Red 7, Austin, TX, USA

1 October The Mink, Houston, TX, USA

3 October Sluggo's, Pensacola, FL, USA

4 October Cave 9, Birmingham, AL, USA

7 October Bluebird, St. Louis, MO, USA

7 October The Creepy Crawl, St. Louis, MO, USA

8 October Skull Alley, Louisville, KY, USA

9 October Moria, Indianapolis, IN, USA

10 October Mac's Bar, Lansing, MI, USA

11 October Asbury Lanes, Asbury Park, NJ, USA

12 October The Space, Hamden, CT, USA

13 October Blender Theater, Manhattan, NY, USA

14 October The Black Cat, Washington DC, USA

21 October The Cockpit, Leeds, UK

22 October The Duchess, York, UK

23 October Oran Mor, Glasgow, UK

24 October Academy 3, Manchester, UK

25 October The Barfly, Birmingham, UK

26 October The Phoenix Arts Centre, Exeter, UK

27 October The Wedgewood Rooms, Portsmouth, UK

28 October The Anson Rooms, Bristol, UK

29 October Scala, London, UK

30 October The Tower Arts Centre, Winchester, UK

31 October The Rescue Rooms, Nottingham, UK

8 November The Joiners Arms, Southampton, UK

12 November Union Chapel, Islington, London, UK

18 November La Flèche d'Or, Paris, France

19 November The Paradiso, Amsterdam, Netherlands

20 November Effenaar, Eindhoven, Netherlands

21 November Schüür, Luzern, Switzerland

22 November Hirscheneck, Basel, Switzerland

23 November Grabenhalle, St Gallen, Switzerland

24 November Tiki's, Geneva, Switzerland

25 November The Flying Pig, Vienna, Austria

26 November Diagonal Loft Club, Forlì, Italy

27 November MADS, Rome, Italy

28 November Extra, Recanati, Italy

29 November Dolly Rockers Xmas Show, London, UK

3 December Hall for Cornwall, Truro, UK

4 December The Great Hall, Exeter, UK

5 December The Engine Shed, Lincoln, UK

5 December Quayside, Lincoln, UK

6 December The Academy, Manchester, UK

7 December UEA, Norwich, UK

9 December The Academy, Bristol, UK

10 December Town Hall, Middlesbrough, UK

11 December Octagon Centre, Sheffield, UK

12 December The Academy, Leeds, UK

13 December The Academy, Birmingham, UK

14 December The Guildhall, Southampton, UK

16 December The Academy, Oxford, UK

17 December The Ironworks, Inverness, UK

18 December ABC, Glasgow, UK

19 December Proud Galleries, Camden, London, UK

2009

11 January Midwinter Picnic, West Hill Hall, Brighton, UK

14 January The Astoria Farewell, Charing Cross, London, UK

15 January De Beurs, Groningen, Netherlands

17 January The Barfly, Liverpool, UK

18 January The Academy, Oxford, UK

19 January Cambridge Junction, Cambridge, UK

26 January Rise Records, Cheltenham, UK

27 January Fopp Records, Covent Garden, London, UK

28 January Banquet Records, Kingston upon Thames, London, UK

29 January Banquet Records, Kingston upon Thames, London, UK

3 February The Academy, Birmingham, UK

4 February The Academy, Manchester, UK

5 February The Academy, Bristol, UK

6 February Concorde 2, Brighton, UK

7 February The Wedgewood Rooms, Portsmouth, UK

8 February Shepherd's Bush Empire, Shepherd's Bush, London, UK

10 February Underground, Cologne, Germany

11 February Kato, Berlin, Germany

12 February KB, Malmö, Sweden

13 February Sticky Fingers, Gothenburg, Sweden

17 February Debaser, Stockholm, Sweden

18 February Lille Vega, Copenhagen, Denmark

19 February Knust, Hamburg, Germany

20 February Schlachthof, Wiesbaden, Germany

21 February 59:1, Munich, Germany

22 February Flex, Vienna, Austria

24 February Zoe Club, Milan, Italy

25 February Mascotte, Zurich, Switzerland

26 February Exhaus, Trier, Germany

27 February Botanique Orangerie, Brussels, Belgium

28 February Vera, Groningen, Netherlands

1 March Melkweg, Amsterdam, Netherlands

2 March The Waterfront, Norwich, UK

3 March Rock City, Nottingham, UK

4 March The Academy, Dublin, Republic of Ireland

5 March Masons, Derry, UK

6 March Auntie Annie's, Belfast, UK

7 March Pure Groove Records, London, UK

14 March 21 Portman Square, Marylebone, London, UK

19 March The Wave, Austin, TX, USA

19 March Latitude 30, Austin, TX, USA

19 March Plush, Austin, TX, USA

20 March Friends Bar, Austin, TX, USA

22 March The Warhol, San Antonio, TX, USA

24 March Chyro Arts, Phoenix, AZ, USA

25 March Hensley's, San Diego, CA, USA

26 March The Viper Room, West Hollywood, CA, USA

27 March The Blank Club, San Jose, CA, USA

28 March Thee Parkside, San Francisco, CA, USA

30 March Backspace, Portland, OR, USA

31 March Flying M Coffee Garage, Nampa, ID, USA

1 April SHO, Salt Lake City, UT, USA

1 April Bar Deluxe, Salt Lake City, UT, USA

2 April Marquis Theater, Denver, CO, USA

21 April Met Bar, Mayfair, London, UK

28 April The Wheatsheaf, Oxford, UK

29 April The Wheatsheaf, Oxford, UK

30 April The Cellar Bar, Oxford, UK

1 May The Cellar Bar, Oxford, UK

6 May The Flowerpot, London, UK

23 May Bar Matchless, Brooklyn, NY, USA

7 June Middlesbrough Music Live, Middlesbrough, UK

13 June Goldney Hall, Bristol, UK

19 June Abart Club, Zurich, Switzerland

20 June Hurricane Festival, Scheeßel, Germany

21 June Southside Festival, Neuhausen ob Eck, Germany

25 June The Flowerpot Roof, Camden, London, UK

25 June Evan's House, Holloway, London, UK

25 June James's House, Holloway, London, UK

25 June Sam's House, East Finchley, London, UK

25 June Gemma's House, East Finchley, London, UK

26 June Ash's House, Willesden, London, UK

26 June Lauren's House, Wembley, London, UK

26 June Kelly's House, Marylebone, London, UK

26 June Pete's House, Fulham, London, UK

26 June Ryan's House, Fulham, London, UK

26 June Banquet Records, Kingston upon Thames, London, UK

26 June Greg's House, Teddington, London, UK

26 June Del's House, Esher, UK

26 June George's House, Coulsdon, London, UK

26 June Paul's House, Bromley, London, UK

26 June Rich's House, Bromley, London, UK

26 June Tom's House, Bromley, London, UK

26 June Joe's House, Mottingham, London, UK

26 June Adam's House, Limehouse, London, UK

26 June *Rock Sound* magazine's offices, London, UK

26 June James's House, King's Cross, London, UK

26 June Xtaster's offices, Camden, London, UK

26 June Jenny's House, Camden, London, UK

26 June The Flowerpot, Camden, London, UK

27 June Pitkä Kuuma Kesä Festival, Helsinki, Finland

30 June CMAC, Canandaigua, NY, USA

1 July Mohawk Place, Buffalo, NY, USA

2 July Molson Amphitheatre, Toronto, Canada

5 July Le Divan Orange, Montreal, Canada

6 July Valentine's, Albany, NY, USA

7 July Starland Ballroom, Sayreville, NJ, USA

8 July Roseland Ballroom, New York, NY, USA

9 July DC's Tavern, Hoboken, NJ, USA

10 July Tsongas Center, Lowell, MA, USA

10 July Matt's House, Beverly, MA, USA

11 July Meadowbrook Arena, Gilford, NH, USA

12 July Titan House, Philadelphia, PA, USA

13 July Talking Head Club, Baltimore, MA, USA

14 July Boutique Amphitheatre, Charlotte, NC, USA

15 July House of Blues, Myrtle Beach, SC, USA

16 July Hard Rock Cafe, Orlando, FL, USA

17 July St. Augustine Amphitheatre, St. Augustine, FL, USA

18 July Pompano Beach Amphitheatre, Miami, FL, USA

23 July Town Hall, Cheltenham, UK
24 July Queen's Hotel, Weymouth, UK
25 July Camp Bestival, Lulworth, UK
26 July Truck Festival, Oxford, UK
31 July Y Not Festival, Pikehall, Derbyshire, UK
1 August Kendal Calling, Kendal, UK
13 August 93 Feet East, Shoreditch, London, UK
15 August Summer Sundae Festival, Leicester, UK
23 August Beautiful Days Festival, Escot Park, near Ottery St Mary, UK
27 August McClusky's, Kingston upon Thames, London, UK
28 August Cabaret Voltaire, Edinburgh, UK
29 August Leeds Festival, Leeds, UK
30 August Reading Festival, Reading, UK
4 September Ramones Museum, Berlin, Germany
5 September Jersey Live Festival, Jersey
13 September The Ogden Theater, Denver, CO, USA
15 September Amoeba Records, Hollywood, CA, USA
16 September House of Blues, San Diego, CA, USA
17 September The Fonda Theater, Los Angeles, CA, USA
17 September Austin's House, Los Angeles, CA, USA
18 September Chain Reaction, Anaheim, CA, USA
19 September Downtown Brewing Co., San Luis Obispo, CA, USA
20 September The Fillmore, San Francisco, CA, USA
22 September Berbati's Pan, Portland, OR, USA

23 September Showbox, Seattle, WA, USA
24 September Commodore Ballroom, Vancouver, Canada
26 September Edmonton Event Center, Edmonton, Canada
27 September MacEwan Ballroom, Calgary, Canada
27 September Black Lounge, Calgary, Canada
29 September Riddell Center, Regina, Canada
30 September The Yellow Dog Tavern, Winnipeg, Canada
1 October Garrick Center, Winnipeg, Canada
2 October The Aquarium, Fargo, ND, USA
3 October Cabooze, Minneapolis, MN, USA
4 October Turner Hall, Milwaukee, WI, USA
4 October Turner Hall car park, Milwaukee, WI, USA
5 October The Intersection, Grand Rapids, MI, USA
5 October The Tap House, Grand Rapids, MI, USA
6 October St. Andrew's Hall, Detroit, MI, USA
10 October Lexapalooza Lite, The Flowerpot, London, UK
13 October The Academy, Dublin, Republic of Ireland
14 October Stiff Kitten, Belfast, UK
15 October QMUnion, Glasgow, UK
16 October Academy 2, Manchester, UK
17 October University Basement, Newcastle upon Tyne, UK
18 October Rock City, Nottingham, UK
19 October Wulfrun Hall, Wolverhampton, UK

20 October The Academy, Oxford, UK

22 October Metropolitan University, Leeds, UK

23 October Cambridge Junction, Cambridge, UK

24 October Plymouth University, Plymouth, UK

25 October Oxjam, Coolings Bar, Exeter, UK

25 October Guitar Expo, Riverside Centre, Exeter, UK

25 October The Lemon Grove, Exeter, UK

26 October Rise Records, Bristol, UK

26 October The Anson Rooms, Bristol, UK

27 October Solus, Cardiff, UK

28 October Guildhall, Winchester, UK

29 October Outside Shepherd's Bush Empire, Shepherd's Bush, London, UK

29 October Shepherd's Bush Empire, Shepherd's Bush, London, UK

1 November Berbati's Pan, Portland, OR, USA

3 November Cooper's Ale Works, Nevada City, CA, USA

4 November The Blank Club, San Jose, CA, USA

5 November Blue Lamp, Sacramento, CA, USA

6 November Slim's, San Francisco, CA, USA

7 November El Rey Theater, Los Angeles, CA, USA

8 November The Casbah, San Diego, CA, USA

9 November The Beauty Bar, Las Vegas, NV, USA

10 November Chaser's, Scottsdale, AZ, USA

11 November Launchpad, Albuquerque, NM, USA

12 November Take 2, El Paso, TX, USA

13 November Red 7, Austin, TX, USA

13 November The Music Gym, Austin, TX, USA

14 November The Door Clubs, Dallas, TX, USA

15 November Juanita's Cantina, Little Rock, AR, USA

16 November Hi-Tone Cafe, Memphis, TN, USA

17 November One Eyed Jacks, New Orleans, LA, USA

18 November The Bottletree Cafe, Birmingham, AL, USA

19 November The Masquerade, Atlanta, GA, USA

20 November Common Grounds, Gainesville, FL, USA

21 November State Theater, St. Petersburg, FL, USA

22 November The Social, Orlando, FL, USA

28 November The Melkweg, Amsterdam, Netherlands

30 November AB Club, Brussels, Belgium

1 December Béi Chéz Heinz, Hannover, Germany

2 December Luxor, Cologne, Germany

4 December Parken, Gothenburg, Sweden

5 December Göta Källare, Stockholm, Sweden

7 December Tavastia, Helsinki, Finland

8 December The Academy, Manchester

9 December Loppen, Copenhagen, Denmark

10 December Molotow, Hamburg, Germany

11 December Magnet Club, Berlin, Germany

12 December 59:1, Munich, Germany

13 December Arena, Vienna, Austria

14 December PPC, Graz, Austria

16 December Hafenkneipe, Zurich, Switzerland

17 December Bleu Lézard, Lausanne, Switzerland

18 December La Péniche Alternat, Paris, France

19 December Union Chapel, Islington, London, UK

31 December The Spiegeltent, Gloucester, UK

2010

21 January The Hippodrome, Kingston upon Thames, London, UK

25 January Steve's House, Toronto, ON, Canada

26 January Horseshoe Tavern, Toronto, ON, Canada

27 January Gibson Showroom, Toronto, ON, Canada

27 January The Dakota Tavern, Toronto, ON, Canada

28 January Chez Baptiste Sur Masson, Montreal, QC, Canada

2 February Hotel Cafe, Los Angeles, CA, USA

3 February The Barn, Riverside, CA, USA

3 February Marty's House, Riverside, CA, USA

8 February Emo's, Austin, TX, USA

9 February House of Blues, Dallas, TX, USA

10 February House of Blues, Houston, TX, USA

12 February Minglewood Hall, Memphis, TN, USA

13 February The Tabernacle, Atlanta, GA, USA

14 February The Ritz Ybor, Tampa, FL, USA

15 February 1982 Bar, Gainesville, FL, USA

16 February House of Blues, Orlando, FL, USA

17 February House of Blues, Orlando, FL, USA

18 February Music Farm, Charleston, SC, USA

19 February Fillmore, Charlotte, NC, USA

20 February House of Blues, Myrtle Beach, SC, USA

21 February The Camel, Richmond, VA, USA

22 February The Norva, Norfolk, VA, USA

23 February Ram's Head Live!, Baltimore, MD, USA

24 February Asbury Lanes, Asbury Park, NJ, USA

25 February Webster Theater, Hartford, CT, USA

26 February Electric Factory, Philadelphia, PA, USA

27 February House of Blues, Boston, MA, USA

28 February Main Street Armory, Rochester, NY, USA

2 March Generation Records, New York, NY, USA

2 March The Hammerstein Ballroom, New York, NY, USA

3 March Dan's Basement, Pittsburgh, PA, USA

4 March LC Pavilion, Columbus, OH, USA

5 March House of Blues, Cleveland, OH, USA

7 March Mac's Bar, Lansing, MI, USA

8 March Egyptian Room, Indianapolis, IN, USA

9 March Bogart's, Cincinnati, OH, USA

10 March The Pageant, St. Louis, MO, USA

12 March Eagles Club, Milwaukee, WI, USA

13 March Aragon Ballroom, Chicago, IL, USA

15 March Northumbria University, Newcastle upon Tyne, UK

16 March The Picture House, Edinburgh, UK

17 March Academy 1, Manchester, UK

18 March Academy 1, Leeds, UK

19 March Academy 1, Bristol, UK

21 March Academy 1, Birmingham, UK

22 March UEA, Norwich, UK

23 March The Pyramids Centre, Portsmouth, UK

24 March The Roundhouse, Camden, London, UK

28 March Exil, Zurich, Switzerland

29 March Universum, Stuttgart, Germany

30 March Schlachthof, Wiesbaden, Germany

31 March Zakk, Dusseldorf, Germany

1 April Uebel & Gefährlich, Hamburg, Germany

3 April Lagerhaus, Bremen, Germany

4 April AB Club, Brussels, Belgium

5 April Effenaar, Eindhoven, Netherlands

6 April Tivoli, Utrecht, Netherlands

7 April Vera, Groningen, Netherlands

8 April La Péniche du Pianiste, Lille, France

9 April La Boule Noire, Paris, France

14 April Rickshaw Stop, San Francisco, CA, USA

15 April The Media Club, Vancouver, BC, Canada

17 April Coachella Festival, Indio, CA, USA

22 April The Zoo, Brisbane, Australia

23 April Annandale Hotel, Sydney, Australia

24 April Hermann's Bar, Sydney, Australia

25 April Cambridge Hotel, Newcastle, Australia

28 April Rosemount Hotel, Perth, Australia

29 April Enigma Bar, Adelaide, Australia

30 April Corner Hotel, Melbourne, Australia

1 May Brisbane Hotel, Hobart, Tasmania

2 May The Arthouse, Melbourne, Australia

4 May Kings Arms Tavern, Auckland, New Zealand

5 May Bar Bodega, Wellington, New Zealand

7 May Rockschool, Hong Kong

8 May I Du Tang, Shenzhen, China

9 May Hooley's Irish Pub, Guangzhou, China

12 May Vox, Wuhan, China

13 May Old Times Jazz Bar, Wuxi, China

14 May Yuyintang, Shanghai, China

15 May D-22, Beijing, China

19 May The Flowerpot, Camden, London, UK

23 May Wood Festival, Oxfordshire, UK

27 May Academy 2, Birmingham, UK

28 May Mandela Hall, Belfast, UK

29 May Academy 2, Dublin, Republic of Ireland

30 May Cyprus Avenue, Cork, Republic of Ireland

31 May Pine Lodge, Myrtleville, Republic of Ireland

1 June Doyles, Dublin, Republic of Ireland

4 June Sublime, Tel Aviv, Israel

6 June Syncopa Bar, Haifa, Israel

10 June Bonnaroo Festival, Manchester, TN, USA

12 June Bonnaroo Festival, Manchester, TN, USA

16 June Lancashire County Cricket Ground, Manchester, UK

18 June Hurricane Festival, Scheeßel, Germany

19 June Wembley Stadium, Wembley, London, UK

20 June Southside Festival, Neuhausen ob Eck, Germany

25 June Glastonbury Festival (Queen's Head), Glastonbury, UK

25 June Glastonbury Festival (Strummerville), Glastonbury, UK

26 June Glastonbury Festival (Left Field), Glastonbury, UK

26 June Glastonbury Festival (Left Field), Glastonbury, UK

5 July The Railway Inn, Winchester, UK

9 July Ruisrock Festival, Turku, Finland

11 July T in the Park Festival, Kinross, UK

14 July Komedia, Bath, UK

15 July Larmer Tree Festival, Wiltshire, UK

16 July 2000trees Festival, Withington, near Cheltenham, UK

17 July Latitude Festival, Suffolk, UK

19 July iTunes Festival, The Roundhouse, Camden, London, UK

23 July Calgary Folk Music Festival, Calgary, Canada

23 July Erin's House, Calgary, Canada

24 July Calgary Folk Music Festival, Calgary, Canada

25 July Calgary Folk Music Festival, Calgary, Canada

25 July Calgary Folk Music Festival, Calgary, Canada

31 July Lowertown Festival, St. Paul, MN, USA

1 August Osheaga Festival, Montreal, Canada

2 August The Webster Underground, Hartford, CT, USA

3 August Lost Horizon, Syracuse, NY, USA

4 August Brooklyn Bowl, New York, NY, USA

5 August The Stone Pony, Asbury Park, NJ, USA

6 August Mohawk Place, Buffalo, NY, USA

7 August The Magic Stick, Detroit, MI, USA

8 August Lollapalooza, Chicago, IL, USA

11 August Surfside 7, Fort Collins, CO, USA

13 August Ottawa Folk Festival, Ottawa, Canada

14 August Ottawa Folk Festival, Ottawa, Canada

14 August Ottawa Folk Festival, Ottawa, Canada

14 August Ottawa Folk Festival, Ottawa, Canada

15 August Ottawa Folk Festival, Ottawa, Canada

15 August Ottawa Folk Festival, Ottawa, Canada

20 August Highfield Festival, Germany

21 August Area 4 Festival, Lüdinghausen, Germany

22 August Musikfestwochen, Winterthur, Switzerland

25 August The Venue, Derby, UK

26 August Brewery Arts Centre, Kendal, UK

27 August Leeds Festival, Leeds, UK

28 August Reading Festival, Reading, UK

8 September The Troubadour, West Hollywood, CA, USA

9 September Berbati's Pan, Portland, OR, USA

10 September El Corazón, Seattle, WA, USA

11 September Middlewest Fest, DeKalb, IL, USA

25 September Reeperbahn Festival, Hamburg, Germany

26 September MuK, Gießen, Germany

28 September Exhaus, Trier, Germany

29 September Jubez, Karlsruhe, Germany

30 September Stattbahnhof, Schweinfurt, Germany

1 October Unikum, Erfurt, Germany

2 October Roter Salon, Berlin, Germany

3 October Meskalina, Poznań, Poland

10 October Austin City Limits Music Festival, Austin, TX, USA

12 October Low Spirits, Albuquerque, NM, USA

14 October The Saltair, Salt Lake City, UT, USA

14 October The Saltair car park, Salt Lake City, UT, USA

15 October The Fillmore, Denver, CO, USA

16 October Illegal Pete's, Denver, CO, USA

16 October The Fillmore, Denver, CO, USA

18 October Crosstown Station, Kansas City, MO, USA

19 October First Avenue, Minneapolis, MN, USA

20 October The Riviera Theater, Chicago, IL, USA

20 October Uptown Lounge, Chicago, IL, USA

21 October The Fillmore, Detroit, MI, USA

22 October Horseshoe Tavern, Toronto, ON, Canada

23 October The Kool Haus, Toronto, ON, Canada

24 October House of Blues, Cleveland, OH, USA

25 October Brillobox, Pittsburgh, PA, USA

26 October 9:30 Club, Washington DC, USA

28 October Northern Lights, Clifton Park, NY, USA

29 October The Electric Factory, Philadelphia, PA, USA

30 October House of Blues, Atlantic City, NJ, USA

31 October Eight Seconds, Gainesville, FL, USA

31 October Eight Seconds car park, Gainesville, FL, USA

31 October Holiday Inn, Gainesville, FL, USA

1 November House of Blues, Boston, MA, USA

2 November The State Theater, Portland, ME, USA

3 November Toad's Place, New Haven, CT, USA

4 November Roseland Ballroom, New York, NY, USA

5 November The Stone Pony, Asbury Park, NJ, USA

6 November Ram's Head Live!, Baltimore, MD, USA

7 November The Camel, Richmond, VA, USA

8 November The Orange Peel, Asheville, NC, USA

9 November The Valarium, Knoxville, TN, USA

10 November The Tabernacle, Atlanta, GA, USA

11 November Jack Rabbits, Jacksonville, FL, USA

12 November Jannus Landing, St Petersburg, FL, USA

13 November The Fillmore, Miami, FL, USA

14 November Park Ave CDs, Orlando, FL, USA

14 November House of Blues, Orlando, FL, USA

16 November House of Blues, New Orleans, LA, USA

18 November Stubb's BBQ, Austin, TX, USA

19 November House of Blues, Houston, TX, USA

20 November House of Blues, Dallas, TX, USA

22 November The Rialto Theater, Tucson, AZ, USA

23 November The Marquee Theater, Tempe, AZ, USA

23 November Yucca Tap Room, Tempe, AZ, USA

2 December ABC, Glasgow, UK

3 December 53 Degrees, Preston, UK

4 December The Plug, Sheffield, UK

5 December The Regal, Oxford, UK

6 December Corn Exchange, Cambridge, UK

7 December Guildhall, Southampton, UK

10 December The Academy, Leicester, UK

11 December The Academy, Liverpool, UK

12 December Brixton Academy, Brixton, London, UK

16 December Harry B James, Stockholm, Sweden

31 December Inside Out, Darlington, UK

2011

27 January R Bar, Gravesend, UK

4 February The Wheelbarrow, Camden, London, UK

12 February Lexapalooza, Old Queen's Head, Islington, London, UK

16 February The Lemon Tree, Aberdeen, UK

17 February Fibbers, York, UK

18 February The Borderline, Soho, London, UK

19 February The Bullingdon Arms, Oxford, UK

20 February The Lemon Grove, Exeter, UK

21 February The Old Fire Station, Bournemouth, UK

1 March Old Queen's Head, Islington, London, UK

4 March Trof, Manchester, UK

4 March Trof, Manchester, UK

5 March Santiago, Leeds, UK

2 April The White Rabbit, Plymouth, UK

4 April White Trash, Berlin, Germany

5 April White Trash, Berlin, Germany

6 April Blue Shell, Cologne, Germany

13 April The Arthouse, Melbourne, Australia

14 April Enigma, Adelaide, Australia

15 April The Annandale Hotel, Sydney, Australia

16 April Rosie's, Brisbane, Australia

17 April Amplifier, Perth, Australia

21 April Strummerville Spring Sessions, Shoreditch, London, UK
25 April Gallery Radiolaria, Toronto, ON, Canada
26 April El Mocambo, Toronto, ON, Canada
28 April Knitting Factory, Brooklyn, NY, USA
29 April The Red Palace, Washington DC, USA
30 April Bamboozle Festival, East Rutherford, NJ, USA
30 April Bamboozle Festival, East Rutherford, NJ, USA
2 May JBTV, Chicago, IL, USA
2 May Beat Kitchen, Chicago, IL, USA
4 May Bottom of the Hill, San Francisco, CA, USA
5 May Hotel Cafe, Los Angeles, CA, USA
5 May Hotel Cafe, Los Angeles, CA, USA
6 May Velvet Jones, Santa Barbara, CA, USA
9 May ARC, Stockton-on-Tees, UK
10 May The Doghouse, Dundee, UK
11 May PJ Molloys, Dunfermline, UK
12 May HMV, Brighton, UK
12 May Coalition, Brighton, UK
13 May The Rescue Rooms, Nottingham, UK
14 May The Library, Lancaster, UK
15 May Telford's Warehouse, Chester, UK
16 May Brudenell Social Club, Leeds, UK
18 May Night and Day Café, Manchester, UK
19 May Cathedral Crypt, Liverpool, UK
20 May The Sugarmill, Stoke, UK
22 May The Slade Rooms, Wolverhampton, UK
23 May Rise Records, Cheltenham, UK
23 May Guildhall, Gloucester, UK
24 May St George's, Bristol, UK
25 May Komedia, Bath, UK
26 May New Slang, The Hippodrome, Kingston upon Thames, London, UK
26 May New Slang, The Hippodrome, Kingston upon Thames, London, UK
27 May St Paul's Church, Cambridge, UK
28 May Playfest, Norfolk, UK
29 May The Wedgewood Rooms, Portsmouth, UK
30 May The Railway Inn, Winchester, UK
2 June Haus Auensee, Leipzig, Germany
3 June Meskalina, Poznań, Poland
4 June Rock im Park Festival, Germany
5 June Rock am Ring Festival, Germany
6 June The Barfly, Camden, London, UK
7 June Huxley's Neue Welt, Berlin, Germany
8 June Huxley's Neue Welt, Berlin, Germany
9 June Huxley's Neue Welt, Berlin, Germany
10 June Greenfields Festival, Interlaken, Switzerland
12 June Download Festival, Donington Park, UK
13 June Kerrang! Radio, Birmingham, UK
13 June Truck Store, Oxford, UK
18 June AuGartenFest, Graz, Austria
18 June Sub, Graz, Austria
19 June B72, Vienna, Austria
20 June Club Vaudeville, Lindau, Germany

22 June Paradiso, Amsterdam, Netherlands

23 June Docks, Hamburg, Germany

25 June Docks, Hamburg, Germany

26 June Docks, Hamburg, Germany

27 June Docks, Hamburg, Germany

29 June Vega, Copenhagen, Denmark

1 July Blissfields Festival, Winchester, UK

2 July Guernsey Live Festival, Guernsey

4 July Le Trianon, Paris, France

7 July The Playhouse, Whitley Bay, UK

9 July Fonofest, Cēsis, Latvia

22 July Port Eliot Festival, Cornwall, UK

29 July Cambridge Folk Festival, Cambridge, UK

30 July Oma's Teich Festival, Großfehen, Germany

31 July Kendal Calling, Kendal, UK

5 August Belladrum Festival, Inverness, UK

6 August The Academy, Newcastle upon Tyne, UK

7 August Mannifest, Isle of Man

9 August Terraneo Festival, Sibenik, Croatia

12 August Open Flair Festival, Eschwege, Germany

13 August Rocco del Schlacko Festival, Germany

14 August Taubertal Festival, Germany

15 August Festa di Radio Onda d'Urto, Brescia, Italy

20 August JK Zomaar, Itterbeek, Belgium

21 August Lowlands, Biddinghuizen, Netherlands

21 August Noorderzon Festival, Groningen, Netherlands

25 August The Roadmender, Northampton, UK

26 August Leeds Festival, Leeds, UK

26 August Leeds Festival, Leeds, UK

28 August Reading Festival, Reading, UK

28 August Reading Festival, Reading, UK

9 September Bestival, Isle of Wight, UK

13 September Set Theatre, Kilkenny, Republic of Ireland

14 September Cyprus Avenue, Cork, Republic of Ireland

15 September Roisin Dubh, Galway, Republic of Ireland

17 September Stiff Kitten, Belfast, UK

18 September Whelan's, Dublin, Republic of Ireland

20 September Heirloom Arts Theater, Danbury, CT, USA

21 September Bowery Ballroom, New York, NY, USA

22 September Mr Smalls, Millvale, PA, USA

23 September The Ottobar, Baltimore, MD, USA

24 September The Canal Club, Richmond, VA, USA

25 September New Brookland Tavern, West Columbia, SC, USA

27 September Park Ave CDs, Orlando, FL, USA

27 September The Social, Orlando, FL, USA

28 September The Double Down, Gainesville, FL, USA

29 September The Culture Room, Fort Lauderdale, FL, USA

30 September The Crowbar, Tampa, FL, USA

1 October The Masquerade, Atlanta, GA, USA

3 October Emo's, Austin, TX, USA

4 October The Loft, Dallas, TX, USA

5 October The Conservatory, Oklahoma City, OK, USA

6 October The Record Bar, Kansas City, MO, USA

7 October The Marquee Theater, Denver, CO, USA

10 October The Rhythm Room, Phoenix, AZ, USA

11 October The Glass House, Pomona, CA, USA

12 October Soma, San Diego, CA, USA

13 October The El Rey Theater, Los Angeles, CA, USA

14 October Slim's, San Francisco, CA, USA

15 October The Hawthorne Theater, Portland, OR, USA

16 October Neumos, Seattle, WA, USA

17 October The Biltmore Cabaret, Vancouver, BC, Canada

19 October Starlite Room, Edmonton, AB, Canada

20 October Republik, Calgary, AB, Canada

21 October The Exchange, Regina, SK, Canada

22 October WECC, Winnipeg, MB, Canada

23 October The Triple Rock, Minneapolis, MN, USA

25 October Turner Hall Ballroom, Milwaukee, WI, USA

26 October Bottom Lounge, Chicago, IL, USA

27 October The Magic Stick, Detroit, MI, USA

28 October The Phoenix Concert Theater, Toronto, ON, Canada

29 October The Corona Theater, Montreal, QC, Canada

30 October Mavericks, Ottawa, ON, Canada

31 October Le Cercle, Quebec City, QC, Canada

2 November The Middle East, Cambridge, MA, USA

3 November Generation Records, New York, NY, USA

3 November Bowery Ballroom, New York, NY, USA

4 November WXPN Live at Noon, Philadelphia, PA, USA

4 November Theater of Living Arts, Philadelphia, PA, USA

10 November AIM Awards, London, UK

15 November Melkweg, Amsterdam, Netherlands

16 November Faust, Hannover, Germany

17 November Sputnikhalle, Münster, Germany

18 November Crossing Border Festival, Den Haag, Netherlands

18 November Crossing Border Festival, Den Haag, Netherlands

19 November Crossing Border Festival, Antwerp, Belgium

22 November The Academy, Bournemouth, UK

23 November Newport Centre, Newport, UK

24 November The Academy, Birmingham, UK

25 November The Barrowlands, Glasgow, UK

26 November The Apollo, Manchester, UK

27 November Hammersmith Apollo, Hammersmith, London, UK

29 November E-Werk, Cologne, Germany

30 November Wagenhallen, Stuttgart, Germany

1 December Backstage Halle, Munich, Germany

2 December Postbahnhof, Berlin,
Germany

3 December Other Voices, Dingle,
Republic of Ireland

4 December Fabrik, Hamburg,
Germany

5 December Mau Club, Rostock,
Germany

7 December Divan du Monde, Paris,
France

8 December Schüür, Luzern,
Switzerland

9 December Ringlokschuppen,
Bielefeld, Germany

10 December Messepark, Trier,
Germany

11 December Schlachthof, Dresden,
Germany

13 December Meskalina, Poznań,
Poland

14 December Klub Powiększenie,
Warsaw, Poland

16 December Bronson, Ravenna,
Italy

17 December Abart, Zurich,
Switzerland

18 December WUK, Vienna, Austria

19 December PPC, Graz, Austria

20 December Karlstorbahnhof,
Heidelberg, Germany

2012

10 January *NME* offices, Southwark,
London, UK

27 January The Joint, Las Vegas, NV,
USA

28 January Orpheum Theater,
Flagstaff, AZ, USA

29 January Velvet Jones, Santa
Barbara, CA, USA

31 January Sunshine Theater,
Albuquerque, NM, USA

1 February The Rialto Theater,
Tucson, AZ, USA

2 February Tricky Falls, El Paso, TX,
USA

3 February The Marquee Theater,
Tempe, AZ, USA

4 February The Marquee Theater,
Tempe, AZ, USA

5 February SLO Downtown Brewery,
San Luis Obispo, CA, USA

7 February Blue Lamp, Sacramento,
CA, USA

8 February Thee Parkside, San
Francisco, CA, USA

9 February Civic Auditorium, Santa
Cruz, CA, USA

10 February Fox Theater, Oakland,
CA, USA

11 February Fox Theater, Oakland,
CA, USA

12 February John Henry's, Eugene,
OR, USA

13 February Senator Theater, Chico,
CA, USA

14 February Centre Plaza, Modesto,
CA, USA

15 February The Slidebar, Fullerton,
CA, USA

16 February The Majestic Ventura
Theater, Ventura, CA, USA

18 February The Fox Theater,
Pomona, CA, USA

21 February Off Broadway, St. Louis,
MO, USA

22 February Outland Live, Columbus,
OH, USA

23 February The Egyptian Room,
Indianapolis, IN, USA

24 February The Castle Theater,
Bloomington, IL, USA

25 February First Avenue,
Minneapolis, MN, USA

27 February House of Blues, Dallas,
TX, USA

28 February House of Blues,
Houston, TX, USA

29 February Emo's East, Austin, TX, USA

1 March House of Blues, New Orleans, LA, USA

3 March Pompano Beach Amphitheater, Pompano, FL, USA

4 March House of Blues, Orlando, FL, USA

5 March Ritz Ybor, Tampa, FL, USA

6 March The Tabernacle, Atlanta, GA, USA

7 March Marathon Music Works, Nashville, TN, USA

9 March House of Blues, Atlantic City, NJ, USA

10 March Mohegan Sun Arena, Uncasville, CT, USA

11 March The Paramount, Huntington, NY, USA

12 March Knitting Factory, Brooklyn, NY, USA

13 March Latitude 30, Austin, TX, USA

14 March Latitude 30, Austin, TX, USA

15 March House of Blues, Boston, MA, USA

16 March House of Blues, Boston, MA, USA

17 March Tsongas Center, Lowell, MA, USA

17 March Tsongas Center, Lowell, MA, USA

18 March Wonder Bar, Asbury Park, NJ, USA

30 March Muziekodroom, Hasselt, Belgium

31 March Bierhübeli, Bern, Switzerland

1 April Union Halle, Frankfurt, Germany

2 April Backstage Werk, Munich, Germany

3 April The Garage, Saarbrücken, Germany

4 April Rockhal, Esch-sur-Alzette, Luxembourg

5 April Paradiso, Amsterdam, Netherlands

13 April Wembley Arena, London, UK

18 April MacEwan Ballroom, Calgary, AB, Canada